Sherman's March and Vietnam

ALSO BY JAMES RESTON, JR.

To Defend, to Destroy, a novel, 1971

The Amnesty of John David Herndon, 1973

The Knock at Midnight, a novel, 1975

The Innocence of Joan Little, 1977

Sherman, the Peacemaker, a play, 1979

Our Father Who Art in Hell, 1981

Jonestown Express, a play, 1984

SHERMAN'S MARCH AND VIETNAM

JAMES RESTON, Jr.

MACMILLAN PUBLISHING COMPANY
NEW YORK

Macmillan Publishing Company
866 Third Avenue, New York, N.Y. 10022
Collier Macmillan Canada, Inc.

Library of Congress Cataloging in Publication Data

Reston, James, 1941-
  Sherman's march and Vietnam.

  Includes index.
    1. Sherman's March to the Sea.   2. Sherman's March
through the Carolinas.   3. Sherman, William T.
(William Tecumseh), 1820–1891.   4. United States—History
—Civil War, 1861–1865—Destruction and pillage.
5. Vietnamese Conflict, 1961–1975—Destruction and pillage.
I. Title.
E476.69.R48   1984   973.7'37   84-12264
ISBN 0-02-602300-8

Macmillan books are available at special discounts for bulk purchases for sales promotions, premiums, fund-raising, or educational use. Special editions or book excerpts can also be created to specification. For details, contact:

  Special Sales Director
  Macmillan Publishing Company
  866 Third Avenue
  New York, New York 10022

10   9   8   7   6   5   4   3   2   1

Printed in the United States of America

For
Alfreda Kaplan
with Affection and Thanks

Contents

CONTENTS

PART II

Present as Finale

Rules of Warfare

Any officer or soldier who shall quit his post or colors to plunder and pillage shall suffer death or other such punishment as shall be ordered by sentence of a general court martial.

ARTICLE I, Paragraph 52
American Articles of War, 1806

As the perpetrators of such outrageous deeds (as pillage and destruction of towns or ravaging or setting fires to houses) may attempt to palliate them, under the pretext of deservedly punishing the enemy, be it here observed that the natural and voluntary law of nations does not allow us to inflict such punishments.

H. W. Halleck, *International Law*, 1861

Particularly in the circumstances (of bombardments, assaults, and seiges), loss of life and damage to property must not be out of proportion to the military advantage to be gained. Once a fort or defended locality has surrendered, only such further damage is permitted as is demanded by the exigencies of war, such as the removal of fortifications, demolition of military buildings, and destruction of stores.

SECTION 4, Paragraph 41
Law of Land Warfare, 1956

It is especially forbidden to destroy or seize the enemy's property, unless such destruction or seizure be imperatively demanded by the necessities of war.

SECTION 5, Paragraph 393a
Law of Land Warfare, 1956

Any destruction by the Occupying Power of real or personal property belonging individually or collectively to private persons, or to the state or to other public authorities or to social or cooperative organizations, is prohibited, except where such destruction is rendered absolutely necessary by military operations.

SECTION 5, Paragraph 393b
Law of Land Warfare, 1956

YOU CANNOT AND MUST NOT: mistreat your prisoner, humiliate or degrade him, take any of his personal effects, which do not have significant military value, refuse him medical treatment if required and available. Always treat your prisoner humanely."

Card of instruction issued to all American troops in Vietnam

PART I
Past as Prelude

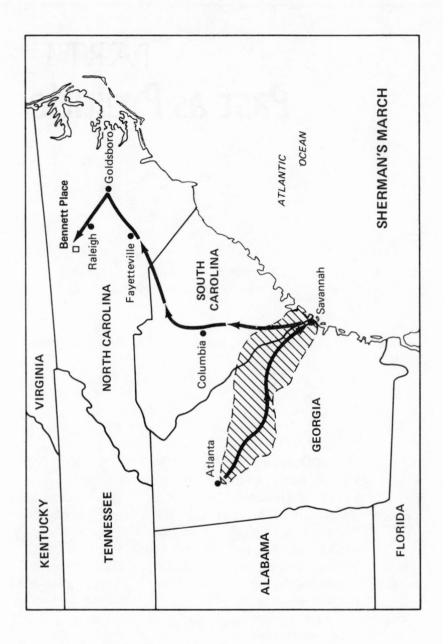

SHERMAN'S MARCH

Prologue

ON THE OUTSKIRTS of the aromatic tobacco town of Durham, North Carolina, some fifteen miles
from my home, there is a modest state historical site known
as Bennett Place. Generally, it is known to have something
to do with the Civil War, but most people are not sure. For
no great battle was fought over the land, and thus the tourist is deprived of that popular pastime of imagining immense armies clashing over rolling hills or through dense
undergrowth and trying to suppose what the scene must
have been like when a battle resulted in ten thousand casualties on each side in a single day. In that flight of the
mind lies an indisputable enduring excitement and accounts

for the high traffic through Civil War battlefields, maintained so immaculately by the National Park Service.

To take the trouble to visit Bennett Place risks deepening the disappointment. Under a trestle bridge for the Southern Railway, around a bend of an undistinguished byway, past a large metal farm implement shed, a vista opens to a wide pasture bordered by a low, well-pointed stone wall. Pressed up against the wall, near the traffic of the road, is a two-story log cabin, a reproduction of what stood on the spot in 1865, and several outbuildings. Inside the cabin, a simple fold-out desk is the only furnishing. Upon it rests a plain porcelain pitcher. In the back room, the spool bed, a genuine antique to be sure, is neatly made with a cotton quilt. Beyond the log buildings, looking somewhat out of place, but suggesting some significance beyond nineteenth-century yeoman farming, two marble Corinthian columns, north and south of one another, rise side by side and are joined by a slab bearing the word *Unity*.

To my mind, Bennett Place marks the most fascinating event of the American Civil War. It is the site of a peace, not a battle, a peace far more important than Appomattox. The characters who sat around the simple desk, who drank. together not water from the pitcher, but clear corn whiskey from the Union medical stores, are far more interesting than Grant and Lee. For Appomattox has little to teach us. It was a simple military surrender between two hostile armies. While it is fixed in the American mind as the end of the war, it actually disarmed only twenty-five thousand Confederates, leaving one hundred thousand Southern troops still in the field. Bennett Place, the site of the peace negotiations between Gen. William Tecumseh Sherman and Confederate General Joseph Johnston, on the other hand, became the neck of the hourglass between the two epic phases of that period, the war and the Reconstruction. There, the paramount issue of the next six years was

4

joined: whether the emphasis would be "to bind up the nation's wounds," to exercise "malice toward none, charity for all," or whether the emphasis would be on remaking the South without slavery and without a bloated aristocracy. Reconciliation and Reconstruction were antithetical. To bind up the nation's wounds might be to allow slavery to continue by another name. To salve the wounds of war alone might be to restore the status quo ante bellum. Similarly, to force a radical Reconstruction of the South might continue the de facto state of war indefinitely. What balance between these two apparently contradictory goods, then, was appropriate?

The issue of reconstruction after divisive war is modern. Ten years after the Vietnam peace, the post–Civil War experience is the only true parallel to the post-Vietnam period. The aftermath of one divisive war should guide another. One difference between the periods immediately presents itself. No circumstance, save perhaps the repatriation of war resisters from abroad, required sweeping action after the Vietnam war. No social class needed to be blamed for Vietnam, as the planter class in the South was blamed for the Southern rebellion. No set of men needed to be disenfranchised, barred from office, or impoverished, as were the high Confederate officials and the Southern planters after the Civil War. No allegiance to the Constitution needed to be sworn (although tens of thousands of young Americans were invited to sign such an oath), nor did an oath to uphold American values need to be administered. And yet, a generation of Americans suffered from Vietnam as surely as one suffered in the Civil War, but the Vietnam generation's travail went beyond the common tragedies and dislocation of war. Its experience was a moral suffering unique in American history. Its pain did not end with the conclusion of hostilities. It continues today. Wounds remain open, waiting to become scars. For ten

5

years after the Paris Peace Accords, amnesia became the tonic, the snake oil of our time. The rush to forget the whole unpleasant business, notwithstanding the fearful consequences that such denial has brought, was dizzying.

So, too, is the dominant figure at Bennett Place contemporary. Gen. William Tecumseh Sherman is considered by many to be the author of "total war," the first general of modern human history to carry the logic of war to is ultimate extreme, the first to scorch the earth, the first consciously to demoralize the hostile civilian population in order to subdue its hostile army, the first to wreck an economy in order to starve its soldiers. He was our first "merchant of terror," and the spiritual father, some contend, of our Vietnam concepts of "search and destroy," "pacification," "strategic hamlets," "free-fire zones." As such, he remains a cardboard figure of our history: a monstrous arch-villain to unreconstructed Southerners, an embarrassment to Northerners who wonder if "civilized war" died with him, whether without Sherman the atom bomb might not have been dropped or Vietnam entered.

The link from Sherman to modern warfare is metaphorical, of course. If he widened the license of war dramatically, his sins lay in the wanton destruction of property, rather than the wanton destruction of life. But where does barbarism begin? How does the process start? Once undertaken on a wide scale in one war, especially one that results in victory, does it not become accepted practice in the next war? And is the gulf between property and life so great? Does it not become easier to destroy the latter if the despoilment of the former has been widely practiced, especially if practiced without success?

Sherman remains one of the few figures of American history who can elicit an instant emotional response. To the American people at large, the clearest vision of him comes from Hollywood. No library of books will ever discard the image from *Gone With the Wind,* in which a Union straggler meanders up the road to Tara, enters the great empty mansion, rummages through Scarlett's jewel box, and then lurches—ugly, bristly, and presumably smelly—up the stairway toward her, before she shoots him between the eyes. It matters little that Sherman's armies were under strict orders about foraging or that stragglers, outside Sherman's official orders, were largely responsible for the abuses, large-scale as they were. Nor does it seem to matter that Sherman's tactics were approved and applauded by every major Union authority from Lincoln and Grant down, nor that Southern armies, when upon rare occasion they found themselves in an offensive posture, engaged in precisely the same behavior. If Sherman's actions constitute military crime, then the political crime of Lincoln stands behind it. No matter all of this. That image from *Gone With the Wind* will forever *be* Sherman. So, too, with Vietnam has Hollywood given us strong and lasting images of the American soldier. For the most part that image is of the psychotic killer and the broken empty man, haunted by grotesque memory of unbridled violence and of war crime within a war he never understood and now finds unspeakable. The veterans are perceived as the lost souls of the Lost Cause. Will that image of crazed ruthlessness from *Apocalypse Now* and *The Deer Hunter* and *Coming Home* forever *be* Vietnam? Or are these images mistaken, wholly or partially?

Some time ago I set out to explore this subtle equipoise between myth and reality. For there is a Sherman myth and a Sherman reality. How the Sherman myth came to be is a fascinating tale in itself. How Sherman sought to justify his actions, and how Southern patriots sought to excoriate them, points up a process of justification and excoriation that is now under way with Vietnam. How the Sherman myth lives in the modern South still has social consequences. For now, there is a Vietnam *mythology* in the making. We must be attentive. But it is in the Sherman *reality* that the profound and universal lessons about the ethics of war lie. Sherman's soldiers and Westmoreland's soldiers have important things in common.

Over the years I had visited Bennett Place a number of times. Beyond the plain buildings, the visitors' center was a shabby mobile home. Inside were the usual trinkets, a few weapons, a kepi, a tattered battle flag, the *Harper's Weekly* sketch of General Sherman and his opposite, Confederate Gen. Joseph Johnston, hard at work. But when I returned in the fall of 1982 the site had been transformed. In place of the mobile home now rose a new buff-colored permanent building with a high peaked roof and a commodious, but empty, display room. The room awaited the usually bland, official interpretation from the state capital.

The room's emptiness excited rather than disappointed me. For a brief moment, I longed to be a museum director. At Bennett Place so many possibilities presented themselves. It could be a monument to peace and national unity. It could explore the complex and fascinating psychology of a conqueror-villain, debunking the Sherman mythology without minimizing the horrors of his march, defining his crime without embroidering it, stressing his brilliance as a military tactician without shrinking from his contribution to a wider concept of "acceptable" behavior in warfare. It could dramatize what he was in 1865, what he did at Bennett Place, how he fell overnight from the heights of heroism not for his brutality but for his generosity there. In short, it could make the *peace* process exciting. And that might be instructive to the tourist. In Vietnam, the "peace process" lasted longer than the entire American Civil War.

As one raised in the North but who has spent his adult life in the South, I came to view a Southerner's attitude toward Sherman as a kind of litmus paper. Years ago I was inclined to dismiss this whole matter as an Old South hobgoblin, and anyone who took Sherman seriously as a throwback. But Vietnam, and my concern about its aftermath, changed that. There is a modern parable in his career and in the making of his historical reputation.

I began with a few questions. What is the Southern fixation with Sherman? Is his villainy the necessary converse of Robert E. Lee's heroism? Is the Lost Cause of the Confederacy made "noble" partly because Sherman was so ruthless, and if Ronald Reagan is to succeed in convincing the country that Vietnam is a "noble cause," who will be *his* Sherman? What is Sherman's true legacy, and were his footsteps present in Vietnam? How did he become so one-dimensional? Why does the name Sherman invoke such a strong reaction still in some Southern quarters? How could one general come to embody a modern concept of uncontrolled brutality? How could this very apotheosis of official violence come to the moment of total victory and nearly give away all that the Civil War was fought for?

So I set off to retrace Sherman's route and to fill, at least in my own head, that empty room at Bennett Place. But as I went, the questions and the modern connections multiplied.

West Point

WEST POINT seemed the right place to start listening for the echoes of General Sherman. There, young Sherman had studied Napoleon's "corps system," in which the emperor divided his vast army into corps and sent them across Europe along parallel lines, living off the land. He had studied the science of fortification and the tactics of guerilla warfare. The national irritation then was the Indian war in Florida. To defeat the Indians, he was taught, their supplies must first be destroyed.

But he also studied ethics, and, by all accounts, Sherman took to the subject when he was a cadet from 1836 to 1840. The textbooks in military ethics in those days were William

Paley's *Moral and Political Philosophy* and James Kent's *Commentaries on American Law*. Kent's view of human nature was bleak. Only through strong government could man hope to avoid the chaos of primitive fighting, but when the social compact broke down, when laws were disobeyed and war resulted, all morality dissolved. Conversely, Paley's view was utilitarian, but he counseled that certain practices, such as poison and assassination, must remain outside the limits of war between civilized nations. The first recourse by one side to these barbarities, Paley argued, would quickly be imitated by the other side, without giving advantage to either party. This would merely widen the license of war and aggravate its horrors and calamities. "The binding force of these rules," Paley wrote, "is the greater, because the regard that is paid to them must be universal or none. The breach of the rule can only be punished by the subversion of the rule itself: on which account, the whole mischief that ensures from the loss of those salutary restrictions is justly chargeable upon the first aggressor." Paley's view would become more apt to Cadet Sherman's future than he could have foreseen, just as it is apt today as the American programs in Vietnam of questionable ethical status, such as the Phoenix program which purportedly liquidated ten thousand Viet Cong political cadre or the Agent Orange program which poisoned vast sections of Vietnam's landscape, pass in review. Nevertheless, Sherman's instructor in ethics at West Point was not entirely pleased with Paley's thought, for he wrote that in its utilitarianism, it taught "the young men that they have no conscience, it diminishes their respect for truth, and perplexes, if it does not confound, the distinction between right and wrong."

I went to West Point to see the chaplain, Maj. John Brinsfield, who in June 1982 had published an article in the journal of the U.S. Army War College on the ethics of

General Sherman, and who teaches the only formal military ethics course of the three military academies. A short, stout officer greeted me, peering out owlishly from behind black glasses, but his uniform was adorned by three rows of military ribbons. His deportment was almost suffocatingly deferential at first, both to me and to the jog-toughened officers who hovered around us, looking somewhat more "professional." But soon enough, I concluded that his mien was his defense. For in the course of the day we spent together, Major Brinsfield emerged as something of an ethical mole within the stony ramparts of Thayer Hall, an advocate for a nuclear freeze, a soldier who believes there can be no such thing as "rules of conduct" in modern warfare, and to whom the modern battlefield is akin to the microwave oven. He spoke in the most disarming fashion about America *losing* the Vietnam war because its conduct on the battlefield was contrary to the values of American society, and therefore lost the support of the people. These are thoughts for which I believed the walls of Thayer Hall would have very big ears. But the major spoke them unperturbed and felt that so long as his research was solid, he was safe in embracing such ideas. It would not occur to me until later that perhaps Brinsfield's ideas were tolerated because they weren't taken seriously. Moral scruples were not on the minds of military scholars ten years after Vietnam. Rather, they were hallucinating about what American firepower might have done to win in Vietnam, had it not been so constrained by civilian meddlers.

Just as startling as his demeanor and his politics was Brinsfield's scholarly apology for General Sherman. For Major Brinsfield is a Georgian. His great-great-grandfather surrendered to General Sherman not once, but three times: at Vicksburg, at Missionary Ridge, and after Appomattox. His forbears had lived near Dalton, Georgia, directly in the path of Sherman's army as it pushed toward Atlanta. But his family folklore is the reverse of what one might expect. The retreating Confederate Army had taken all the family livestock (paying Confederate money for it, of course), and his ancestors were fed out of Sherman's stores. Ironically, this secured for succeeding Brinsfield generations a lasting gratitude.

"There's a very fine line ethically between soldiers taking your livestock and paying you worthless money for it, and just taking it," the major said wryly.

As a boy, Brinsfield had seen *Gone With the Wind* six times, and each time when the scene at Tara approached, where Scarlett shot the Union bummer between the eyes, he would brace tensely. For in 1948, "that was just about the grossest thing you could see at the movies."

After Yale Divinity School, he was ordained as a Methodist minister and for a time rode a "three-point circuit" between three small churches in north Georgia, again in the path of Sherman's march. Meanwhile, he worked on a Ph.D. in church history at Emory University. But partly because academic appointments were so hard to come by after he got his doctorate, he joined the army in 1974, and the West Point faculty in 1980, and thereupon instituted his course "The History of the Ethics of Warfare."

In modern times, formal instruction in military ethics at the U.S. Military Academy is only seven years old. The course was abandoned after the American Civil War in the astonishment over why so many fine officers had disavowed their oath, committing treason so blithely by joining the Southern Rebellion. (A better solution might have been to *double* the ethics load after 1865.) The degeneration of American military practice in Vietnam compelled no reëxamination of military ethics at the Academy. Rather, it was only after the 1976 cheating scandal at the Academy that ethics was reintroduced formally. This had been the recommendation of a commission headed by former astronaut Frank Borman, which investigated the scandal. (Later in

my day at West Point, the chairman of the history department said that ethical training was always implicit in the
"character building" of West Point education. But Major
Brinsfield would define ethical issues traditionally considered in the standard law course: the unacceptable weapons that cause "undue suffering" were not those that could
obliterate the human race, but hollow dumdum bullets
which expand upon impact, or plastic or glass land mines,
whose fragments cannot be detected by a medical X ray.
Such is the lag in the Geneva Conventions in dealing with
the contemporary state of the art.)

To Brinsfield, therefore, the West Point cadet in the nuclear age is presented with a double message. He is
schooled in an individual code of honor about cheating,
lying, and stealing . . . and the requirement to report these
offenses if he witnesses others committing them. Conversely, he is taught that as a commander he must use
whatever means are necessary to achieve a military goal
. . . including, if ordered by higher authority, the nuclear
arsenal.

The impossibility of this dilemma, that of the personally
self-righteous depopulator, is what drew Major Brinsfield
to the ethics of General Sherman, perhaps nostalgically.
While the casualties of the Civil War were staggering (close
to six hundred thousand), at least 90 percent of them were
soldiers. In nuclear war, over 90 percent of the casualties
would be civilian. Although Sherman's troops made war on
the Southern people, at least the cruelty was face to face.
And although Sherman had a concept of reprisal, its scale
had limits of possibility that were comprehensible to the
human mind. Sherman may have extended or expanded the
parameters of acceptable conduct in warfare. But his conduct, by Brinsfield's measure, must be judged against the
two historic standards of military engagment, enshrined in
the rules of land warfare. These two standards are "proportionality"—use no more force than is necessary to

15

achieve your objective—and "discrimination"—distinguish between combatants and innocents.

With Sherman's campaign, these standards were gradually, but relentlessly, destroyed. In his frustration in 1862, for example, Sherman would write that Article I, Paragraph 52, of the Articles of War, which made it a capital offense to despoil civilian property, had become "an old idea." Once these principles were destroyed, the course of American military warfare was altered irrevocably. To echo Paley, once a cardinal rule of land warfare is consistently breached by one side, it invites a like violation by all sides. The rule itself is thereby subverted, without any advantage to the first aggressor, and the calamities of acceptable warfare are made greater. Once proportionality and discrimination were subverted by Sherman, it is arguable that they made the severities of modern American warmaking at least conceptually possible, from the saturation bombing of World War II, to Hiroshima and Nagasaki, to the Christmas bombing of Hanoi and Haiphong in 1972.

In Sherman's approach to Southern guerilla acts against his troops, Major Brinsfield finds the intellectual roots of the American policy of "sustained reprisal" in Vietnam. That policy of tying American air strikes on North Vietnam to specific Viet Cong acts of terror in South Vietnam was proposed by McGeorge Bundy in 1965 and authorized by President Johnson after a Communist attack on the U.S. compound at Pleiku killed nine and injured seventy-six. Bundy's thinking was Sherman's, but Sherman's views of official revenge had evolved over three years of war.

"We may wish at the outset to relate our reprisals to acts of relatively high visibility such as the Pleiku incident," Bundy wrote to President Johnson on February 7, 1965. "Once a program of reprisals is clearly underway, it should not be necessary to connect each specific act against North Vietnam to a particular outrage in the South. . . . Such a generalized pattern of reprisal would remove much of the difficulty involved in finding precisely matching targets in response to specific atrocities.''

Here was a smooth glide from a matching scheme to a general system of retaliatory elephant blows. One wonders if a major air strike on a North Vietnamese city is "proportional" to a ground attack on an American military base in the first place. But Bundy was for scrapping quickly the matching scheme in favor of the general bombing later adopted, or a general pattern of terror, making the North Vietnamese people feel, in Sherman's words, "the hard hand of war.'' Enemy action became only the initial excuse for the grander scale of violence that Bundy intended from the outset. If Sherman had known the language of Vietnam, he might have written, as the Joint Chiefs did in a memorandum in 1964, that "the self-imposed restrictions now limit our efforts,'' and might convey to the Confederacy "signals of irresolution.''

The reaction to Bundy and Bundy's reprisal policy within the military is instructive. In his memoirs, Gen. William Westmoreland describes Bundy's shock at the smouldering ruins of Pleiku and then patronizes the civilian's longing to be in military command. "Once he [Bundy] smelled a little gunpowder, he developed a field marshal psychosis." And Westmoreland held out no hope that this specific and slowly graduated violence would have any military effect. The wild lashing-out simply relieved the frustration.

The decision made, I sensed among my colleagues a feeling of immense concern tempered by relief: by God, we had acted, and this was the turning point! Since it was a reprisal action, I failed to share their belief that it was so momentous. I also doubted that the bombing would have any effect on the North Vietnamese but I deemed it would at least help South Vietnamese morale.

The turning point, then, by his own admission, was merely philosophical.

Major Brinsfield's immediate superior on the West Point

history faculty was Col. Paul Miles, who had been General Westmoreland's aide for three years when Westmoreland was U.S. Army chief of staff, and who commanded the engineers who built the now-Soviet base at Cam Ranh Bay in Vietnam. By Brinsfield's account, Colonel Miles asked penetrating questions when Brinsfield first proposed his ethics course, about what kind of ethics the chaplain proposed to instill in the cadets. Would he be formalistic or utilitarian? Would he present a rigid set of rules ("Thou shalt not kill or allow to be killed, a prisoner of war" might be an example) . . . or flexible, "realistic" ethics that permitted an officer to tailor his standards to the expedience of the moment? If Major Brinsfield's reply to Colonel Miles was anything like his description of it to me, the colonel was smothered with warmth and noncommittal discretion.

West Point put on a real show of hospitality for me on my day back in the ranks. Col. Roy Flint, the chairman of the history department, was anxious to get his word on Sherman in, and so summoned me to his spacious quarters in Thayer Hall. There, beneath the prominent decoration of a map of Korea, Colonel Flint was more my picture of the professional soldier. Lean, tall, gray-haired, direct and terse in speech, he had been a battalion commander during the Tet offensive and had bridled throughout his tour under the "self-imposed" rules of engagement, by his account, whereby his troops could fire only if they had been fired upon. This was an overstatement of the case, for under the official rules of engagement in Vietnam, the American soldier was admonished simply "to use your firepower with care and discrimination, particularly in populated areas." This is open to wide interpretation, and was officially relaxed further during the Tet offensive.

Before we talked of Sherman, I wanted to know *our* rules of engagement. Was there an official West Point interpretation of history, a line which all West Point faculty members were expected to toe? Colonel Flint replied in the negative. His "mission was to provide a broad, balanced history education like any other academic institution, with one exception: all must take a course entitled "The History of Military Art." There would be no official line on Sherman.

He proceeded with the strategic picture. At the end, the Civil War was a struggle between two huge sumo wrestlers, leering at one another over the parapets of Richmond and Petersburg, while two other smaller, lightweight sprinters (*his* metaphors were mixed, not mine) vied for position in Georgia and the Carolinas. Sherman represented the mobile element of the Union army, the "arm of maneuver" (Lincoln had referred to Grant holding the bear by the toe, while Sherman took off the hide), and was positioning his army south of the Appalachian Mountains and below the army of his adversary, wily old Joe Johnston.

In policy and execution, Sherman was not to be distinguished from Grant. Indeed, in Colonel Flint's opinion, Sherman was simply a reflection of Grant, and so if ethics was the issue, Sherman stands with the rest of the top of Union leadership, not in the special place that popular folklore has prescribed for him. The two generals were an inseparable team by the end game of the conflict. It was a friendship of opposites. Sherman was quick-witted, beautifully read, a quoter of Shakespeare; Grant, when he began his own memoirs after the war, was found to have no books whatever on military history in his library. Together they had endured the second guesses after Shiloh, the victories at Vicksburg and Chattanooga, the Mississippi campaign, which would become the inspiration for Sherman's March to the Sea. In Mississippi, not Georgia, it was Grant, not Sherman, who began the liberal foraging upon the countryside to support his army far from its base of supply.

I was not anxious to get drawn into the details of grand

strategy with Colonel Flint, for that is consigned for me to the bin of pure history. Rather, it is the question of terror as part of the "military art" that I find modern. Sherman, after all, was supposed to be our first "merchant of terror." Colonel Flint did not disappoint me. The "genius of Sherman," he remarked, was to realize that the military defeat of the opposing army was not his only mission. Rather, his mission was punitive and psychological and must be felt by the civilians behind the troops. By taking a "reasonably carefully controlled army"—*reasonably* seemed the operative word—through the South, Sherman *reintroduced* terror to the art of war.

Neither was terror a new idea with Sherman, Colonel Flint argued. From the Vandals and the Goths to the Thirty Years' War, war was total, in the prenuclear sense. Limited war came only as a revulsion against the Thirty Years' War, and war became total again in the nineteenth century at the hands of Napoleon, not Sherman. It was Napoleon, through his corps system, who dispersed his armies along parallel routes and had his mass armies live off the land, as they marched through Europe. Grant adopted the Napoleonic strategy in Mississippi, and Sherman widened it in Georgia. So the strategy was new only in that Grant and Sherman Americanized it.

Grant had not given Sherman a set plan for his Georgia campaign, but had only defined the broad objectives of penetrating the enemy's innermost recesses and damaging his "war resources." He left it to Sherman to accomplish these objectives in his own way. To Colonel Flint, Sherman's March to the Sea was "a creative approach" to Grant's order. "Sherman knew his army was not big enough to occupy the entire South, and, therefore, he applied a selective scorched earth policy seeking to gain the reputation (as a terrorist) and spread that word through the South. His loose control over his army created the very element of terror he desired."

For a Vietnam veteran and an educator of our future officer corps, this was a considerable statement, and I wondered what lesson I was being asked to draw, especially if I had been a future commander sitting in his class in the military art.

"Sherman could have exercised tight control. If it's your desire to stop a certain practice, there are ways of accomplishing that," Colonel Flint continued. "You just court-martial a few troops, and it stops." Several times in Vietnam, Colonel Flint had threatened to do that very thing when his soldiers got out of hand, "but it didn't have to get that far. Sherman just wasn't all that interested." It only went that far, it seems, with William Calley.

Soon we repaired to lunch with five other officers on the history faculty. All had had experience in Vietnam, and all professed confusion about my parallel between Sherman's excesses and the excesses of American troops in Vietnam. If terror was the issue, they wanted to talk about the Viet Cong, as if the barbarities of the Viet Cong justified everyone else's. Quickly, we moved into the realm of "utilitarian ethics" that Major Brinsfield had defined as one side of the equation. "Terror doesn't work," said one officer with some passion (he teaches a course in the ethics of revolutionary war). But later he confessed that it worked very well for the Viet Cong against the Americans and the Algerians against the French. Perhaps it is only the American brand of terror that does not work.

Of the officers present at the table, I was particularly interested in Lt. Col. Walter S. Dillard. His praise of General Sherman had been delivered in a soft Southern tone, and yet he was so definite in his assertion that formal rebellion dissolves all rules of military conduct. Later, I cornered him in his office. He is a South Carolinian, and, yes, he had been raised on the Southern "mythology" of the Civil War: Lee, the marble man, the stars marking Sherman's direct hits on the State Capitol in Columbia, the icons of the Confederacy like Wade Hampton, Stonewall Jackson, and all of that. But he said, somewhat wistfully, he had not lost his admiration for Lee until he had held command at high level in Vietnam. (With an infantry battalion, he was held in support during the U.S. and South Vietnamese Army operation against Ben Suc; that painful effort to conquer, to pacify, relocate, and reëducate "hostile civilians" was expertly chronicled by Jonathan Schell in his book *The Village of Ben Suc*.)

"You have to understand that in late 1864, Sherman was a frustrated man," Dillard asserted. "The end of the war was in sight, but he couldn't quite see how he was going to accomplish it. After I came back from Vietnam and was doing graduate work at the University of Washington—that was 1967, not a great time to be in uniform on a college campus—I began to understand better what it took to win the Civil War."

His admiration for Sherman's victory had supplanted all else. As to the matter of troops running amok, Dillard knew the problem. He had watched his troops move through rubber plantations, smashing the bottles that hung from the trees to catch the rubber extract. Why do that? he would ask them. "So the V. C. won't get it," invariably came the reply.

"Responsibility never stops in any army, but at what level can you find someone who is actively responsible, who actually can stop it? Sherman couldn't be everywhere. Sometimes an atmosphere is created that you don't intend. Things happen not by policy or design or orders, they just happen, and it's hard to get control."

The proportion of atrocity in Sherman's army and in Westmoreland's, Lieutenant Colonel Dillard supposed, was about the same.

Northwest Georgia | 2

THE CAMPAIGN against Atlanta began on May 5, 1864, when Sherman moved out of Chattanooga toward Johnston's well-entrenched positions along the ridges of Rocky Face and Buzzard's Roost, above Dalton, Georgia. It would be a campaign far different in character from Sherman's March to the Sea and through South Carolina, for Gen. Joseph Johnston was the best strategist in the Confederate Army, and while he commanded an army half the size of Sherman's, he had the advantage of difficult home soil and well-constructed fortifications. Later, Sherman would argue that Johnston's geographical advantages in northwest Georgia equalized the discrepancy in their troop strength (Sherman had forty thousand more soldiers), to which Johnston responded: "I would gladly have given all the mountains, ravines, rivers, and woods of Georgia for such a supply of artillery and ammunition proportionally, as he had."

My retracing of Sherman's route began at Tunnel Hill, the site of the first contact between the armies. The November day was windy and clear, temperatures in the thirties, and the trees along the slopes of the Chattooga Mountains were still ripe with color. I had with me Dr. Philip Secrist, a historian who had studied the Atlanta campaign for twenty-five years and had written on the battle at Resaca and the siege of Atlanta. During 1976 he was the chairman of the Atlanta Civil War Roundtable (one of two hundred such roundtables in America), which meets once a month and takes an annual pilgrimage; its members are scholars and "semischolars," whose approach to the war, Secrist admits, is balmily romantic.

Always, there seems to be a personal reason why Civil War buffs are made. Mine is Bennett Place. Secrist's is ancestry. His great-grandfather was a soldier in the Eighteenth Virginia Regiment, captured at Spotsylvania and imprisoned in Elmira, New York, for the last year of the war. Now Secrist, a solemn, heavy-set scholar, lives near Kennesaw Mountain, where the Confederate trenches of the Greater Kennesaw Line run through his backyard. Some years ago, he bought the old Manning plantation house out on the Sandtowne Road and had it moved ten miles onto his present property. The house had been used as a Union hospital, as Sherman's troops skirmished with Johnston's around Kennesaw Mountain. Secrist points proudly to a few Yankee bloodstains in the floor boards. In the corner is the familiar glass case, chock-a-block with buckles and Minié balls and uniform buttons, which he has found while traipsing the battlefields.

So Secrist would be my first exposure to the well-stocked

breed known as the Civil War buff. Indeed, he is the best of the breed, for he combines the scholar with the relic hunter, the genealogist with the teacher. He has walked every battlefield in the Shenandoah Valley campaign in which his forbears fought.

As we made our way slowly south, starting with the tunnel at Tunnel Hill which Sherman, to his surprise and delight, still found intact, through the battlefields of Resaca and New Hope Church, ending our day at the awful place of Kennesaw Mountain, Dr. Secrist spun out the details. He pointed out trenches and graveyards, strategic gaps and flooded streams, and he piled up his anecdotes. If one tours like Sherman, rather than speeding down Interstate 75, which paralleled us, the names are irresistible: Pickett's Mill, Dug Gap, Lost Mountain, Trickum, Allatoona Pass, Gilgale Church, Big Shanty, Nickajack Gap, Gravelley Plateau, Sweat Mountain, Little Pumpkin Vine Creek, Rough and Ready, Blackjack Mountain, Stop and Swap, and Cassville . . . Cassville, Secrist says with shuddering emphasis, the first town in Georgia that Sherman burned, the seat of ante-bellum culture in north Georgia. The town was never rebuilt. Today it is marked by a simple flagstone shaft and an overgrown WPA resting place, whose brass plaque has been stolen and never replaced.

To tour this leg of Sherman's campaign is the particular pleasure of the military strategist, for there was no question yet of the Yankee vandals making war upon the people, no refrain about Sherman "burning, pillaging, and raping" across Georgia. The route to Atlanta was determined by three things: the railroad, the terrain, and Johnston's actions. Only at Resaca, and at Kennesaw Mountain, and, finally, in the three battles for Atlanta itself, which Sherman did not initiate, is the conflict full-scale. The rest of the action is maneuver, usually Johnston fortifying the high ridges and Sherman bypassing them to the west.

"He's all hell at flanking," one of Sherman's admiring

soldiers said of him. "He'd flank God Almighty out of Heaven, and the Devil into Hell."

It is Dr. Secrist's theory that Sherman hoped to catch Johnston's army immediately around Resaca, and end it all then and there. That very nearly happened, but Sherman's forward element under McPherson was too slow and cautious as it moved through Snake Creek Gap and did not cut the rail line above Resaca before Johnston slipped down it.

For those interested in strategy, the trip from Tunnel Hill to Atlanta—and for that matter across the whole of Sherman's path through Georgia—can be rich. For the state of Georgia in the last twenty years has developed a superb system of roadside markers which trace in detail the movements of troops, down to the regimental level. This system was my first indication of the implicit recognition by Georgia that its mythology about Sherman had far outstripped historical reality. Nowhere in these relatively new roadside signs did I find the old tiresome chauvinism about the righteousness of the Southern cause. In many instances, later in the campaign after the capture of Atlanta, where there is documentation of outrageous pilferage and burning by Federal troops, the signs use flat, matter-of-fact description or ignore the atrocities entirely.

This is not to say that north of Atlanta, Sherman folklore is dead, however. The next day, for example, I paid a visit not far from the ruins of Cassville to Norton and Henry Tumlin. Now in their seventies, these brothers have an ancestor named "Colonel" Lewis Tumlin, who owned a vast cotton plantation along the Etowah River of some eight thousand acres. Weighing more than three hundred pounds and owning several hundred slaves, the colonel's rank was probably honorary, because there is no record of formal military duty in the Georgia archives. He may have been the head of the local militia, for the Tumlin brothers have a vague notion that the colonel hanged an Indian squaw in the Cassville town square for supposedly attacking a white woman, and he must have done so in official capacity. Norton Tumlin, a portly retired farmer whose wife is a rural mail carrier, told me this by the grand staircase of Colonel Tumlin's plantation house, where he lives. At the foot of the stairs hangs a huge portrait of the colonel himself, looking distinctly flush, and up the stairs hung pictures of succeeding Tumlin generations in ever smaller frames. As one climbed the stairs, Mr. Tumlin remarked wryly, the Tumlins descended the social scale. I didn't walk to the top to inspect the size of his own frame.

I had looked up the Tumlins because Sherman had visited the Tumlin estate on two occasions. The first time had been as a young soldier, in 1844, when he was on a legal mission from Charleston. Then he had stayed with Colonel Tumlin, purportedly to visit the imposing Indian Mounds dating back to the year 1000, situated on the Tumlin estate. The visit had meant that Sherman, as a young soldier, had traversed the very route over which, twenty years later, he would lead a vast army. When Sherman came the second time, in 1864, as he wrote in his *Memoirs*, "Colonel Tumlin was not home."

But more important for the folklorist, the 1844 visit involves a Sherman romance. Not far from the Tumlin estate, in a grand house called Etowah Heights, there lived a Southern beauty named Cecilia Stovall; so beautiful, the Bartow County garden club pamphlet informs us, that "her superior personal charms rendered her a queen in the social and military affairs of her time. In her veins coursed the bluest blood of several generations of Southern aristocracy."

The fair Cecilia had a brother who was a cadet at West Point at the same time as Sherman and had upon occasion visited her brother, where, so it goes, Cecilia and Sherman

27

danced the night away. Apparently, in 1844, Sherman had not come to the Etowah River Valley so much to contemplate Colonel Tumlin's Indian Mounds—with full respect to Sherman's archaeological interests—as to court Cecilia. So deep was his affection that he offered marriage, but she turned him down, writing (the letter is supposed to exist somewhere): "Your eyes are so cold and cruel. How you would crush an enemy! I pity the man who ever becomes your foe." But Sherman, young and crestfallen, protested: "I would ever shield and protect you."

In 1864 Sherman returned, maneuvering around Johnston between Stilesboro and Dallas, when he came upon one of the six lovely mansions in the valley and there found a black servant in a fright, as, according to the Garden Club, "soldiers greedily possessed themselves of valuables before applying the torch." Sherman inquired about the house and the servant blurted out that it belonged to Miss Cecilia.

"His face softened as memories of the past flashed through his mind," continues the narrative.

" 'Where is your mistress?' " he asked.

" 'Bless de Lawd, sah, when misses hear tell dat de Yankees wuz comin' an' de Marster gone to war an' dat dey gwine kill an' burn, she called ter me an' say, Joe, we is all gwine 'way to be safe frum de enemy. Pray to de soldiers to spare our home an' God bless you, Joe. She went with de chil'lin 'round her, Lawd only knows whar, sah.' "

Promptly Sherman posted a guard around the house and penned a note to Miss Cecilia, before he rode off to plunder elsewhere.

My dear Madam: You once said that you pitied the man who would ever become my foe. My answer was that I would ever shield and protect you. That I have done. Forgive all else. I am but a soldier.

W. T. Sherman

So it is that nearly every ante-bellum building still standing along the route is there only by the grace of Sherman. Sherman *spared it,* usually from some personal quirk of his restless and unpredictable personality. I saw so many pre-1864 mansions right across the breadth of Sherman's path and heard so often the story of this or that house spared only because of a prior Sherman amour, that young Sherman emerges as one of the great ladies' men of all military history.

Dr. Secrist and I made our way south along the railroad: Dalton, Resaca, Calhoun, Kingston, Adairsville . . . delightful, bypassed hamlets with sparkling old houses and movie-set main streets. By the time we reached Kingston there were two Sherman campaigns to contemplate: the push on Atlanta between May and July 1864, and the aftermath of Atlanta's capture. Before Atlanta fell, Johnston had been replaced by the brazen failure, John Bell Hood, who never won a battle as a supreme commander and frittered away the effectiveness of his fighting force. Hood had the use of only one arm and had only one leg (the other he lost at Chickamauga); he had to be strapped on his horse and was probably dazed by laudanum to deaden his pain. (Anyhow, Southerners would like to think so.) Hood tried to lure Sherman out of Atlanta, back over the very territory in Alabama and Tennessee and north Georgia that he had already conquered. Sherman went back as far as Kingston (after relieving a siege at Allatoona Pass and inspiring the air "Hold the Fort, for I Am Coming," a song which still exists in many Christian hymnals). At Kingston, he rested for several days at the Hargis Tavern, now a classic Texaco station worthy of Billy Carter. There, Sherman decided he had had enough of backtracking and concocted the March to the Sea.

This twilight phase, after the capture of Atlanta and before the burning east of Savannah, interests me particularly, for the Vietnam parallel emerges strikingly. The invader was now the conqueror, and the frustrations of occupation had begun to surface. Sherman, like Westmoreland, now had the vastly superior force. He could move his troops anywhere he wished, but he could not get the enemy to engage him in open combat. Instead, guerrillas harassed his lines at every point and then receded into the woodwork. He could not find them, and he could not count how many there were. To use Westmoreland's language, it was like fighting roaches.

Sherman's tenuous line of supply to Nashville (some hundred eighty miles along the railroad) was bedeviled by ambushes. On October 29, 1864, his annoyance took the form of the only Sherman order directing indiscriminate burning and killing. It was sent to Brigadier General Watkins, his commander at Calhoun, and it was Sherman's rudimentary but forthright version of what Westmoreland called his "hamlet evaluation system."

Cannot you send over about Fairmont and Adairsville, burn ten or twelve houses of known secessionists, kill a few at random, and let them know it will be repeated every time a train is fired on from Resaca to Kingston.

His perception deepened that all Southern people, not just the soldiers, were his enemy. He took other actions at pacification. He ordered the evacuation of all civilian homes within a mile of the railroad. Closer to Atlanta, at Roswell and Sweetwater, where clothing mills turned out Confederate cloth, he issued this order:

I repeat my orders that you arrest all people, male and female, connected with these factories, no matter what the clamor, and let them foot it, under guard to Marietta, whence I will send them by [railroad] to the North. . . . The poor women will make a howl. Let them take along their children and clothing providing they have the means of hauling or you can spare them.

Over four hundred mill workers, mainly women, were loaded into railroad cars and transported to Indiana, where they were put to work in Union textile mills. Few ever returned. But at this stage, Sherman's actions remained surgical. The mills at Roswell and Sweetwater were destroyed. As he prepared to move east on his "great raid," he ordered the railroad ripped up and legitimate targets destroyed. In the course of this destruction, fires sometimes raged out of control. Sherman still tried to control them. At Marietta, for example, the courthouse caught on fire and the flames were put out three times by the Union troops before they gave up. The commander came upon the scene and had this conversation with his aide, Maj. Henry Hitchcock as the major himself later recounted it.

"Twill burn down, Sir," Hitchcock said.

"Yes, can't be stopped."

"Was it your intention?"

"Can't save it. I've seen more of this sort of thing than you."

"Certainly, sir."

They rode on, passing a clutch of troops.

"There are men who do this," Sherman said. "Set as many guards as you please, and they will slip in and set fire. The Court House was put out—no use. I dare say the whole town will burn, at least the business part of it. I never ordered the burning of any dwelling—didn't order this, but it can't be helped. I say Jeff Davis burnt them."

"[I was] anxious that you not be blamed for what you did not order," Hitchcock persisted.

"Well, I suppose I'll have to bear it," Sherman replied.

This is hardly the "lust for destruction" that is ascribed to Sherman—not now, not yet. Rather, it is a resignation to destruction as an inevitable outgrowth of warfare. But does lust begin with acquiescence? First, acceptance, resignation, acquiescence . . . then condoning, shifting of

31

blame, trivializing . . . then recasting as valid revenge, certified rage bred of frustration . . . finally, enjoyment: is that how the license of war broadens? In Vietnam, only the safety of one's buddy and oneself had come to matter.

At Roswell, the mill down by the Chattahoochee River was burned, but in a century that fact has been embroidered into the certainty that the whole town, high on the bluff above the river, was burned and Union troops went on a wild, drunken spree. But the lovely mansions of Roswell do a brisk tourist business today. One is Bulloch Hall, where Mittie Bulloch was married to Theodore Roosevelt, Sr., a marriage which produced a son, Theodore, Jr. (who went on to a great calling). Another is Barrington Hall. In 1923, a reporter from the *Atlanta Journal* came to Roswell to write about Mittie Bulloch and her grand recollections of the Civil War and its dreaded aftermath. In her article for the newspaper, the reporter described Barrington Hall as follows:

The tall white columns, glimpsed through the dark green of cedar foliage, the wide veranda encircling the house, the stately silence engendered by the century old oaks evoke Thomas Nelson Page's "Ole Virginia." The atmosphere of dignity, peace, and courtesy that was the soul of the Old South breathes from this old mansion, as it stands at the end of a long walk, bordered by old-fashioned flowers.

The reporter's by-line was Peggy Mitchell, and she went on, using Mittie Bulloch and Barrington Hall as prototypes to write a novel of considerable popularity about mansions and carrots and the gritty resilience of these flouncy Southern belles in times of adversity.

Thus, the romantic defense of "a way of life" is left in this area to literature . . . and Dent Myers. Dr. Secrist and I would cap off our journey South with a visit to "General" Myers in his junk shop in Kennesaw.

The town of Kennesaw was known to Sherman as Big Shanty, but it dawned on the village bigwigs a few years back that the old name was undignified, and it was changed. Kennesaw had been prominent in the news recently, when the mayor, the city councilman, and the police chief thought up the brainy idea of requiring all its town residents to own a gun and "adequate ammunition for personal safety." Kennesaw's ordinance was meant to be the Rebel comeuppance to Morton Grove, Ohio, which weeks before had passed an ordinance banning all its residents from owning firearms. The gimmick to promote the name of Kennesaw worked, and Dent Myers, the self-proclaimed Wild Man, got his picture in *Newsweek,* slouching against the doorway of his shop, Civil War Surplus and Herb Shop, packing a pistol on his hip.

Sitting behind a foggy glass cabinet filled with genuine Yankee and Confederate guns and belt buckles and whatnot, gold chains and baubles of various description jangling about his neck, a leather band around his head to keep his randy curls in place, a .357 Magnum on one hip and a .44 Colt on the other, Dent looked quite self-satisfied. Ever since he portrayed Stonewall Jackson in a promotional film for the commonwealth of Virginia, a part he beat out *many* professionals for, they say he's never been the same. Strange but significant coincidences began to occur. In grooming for his starring role, his photographic likeness was superimposed upon Jackson's, and he was found to be the spitting image of his hero; the only difference in the faces was Jackson's higher hairline. Dent discovered that Jackson, like him, was an Aquarius, and a psychic from Rossville, Georgia, who had advised such personages as Doris Day and Eddie Albert, made it official: Dent Myers was the reincarnation of Stonewall Jackson. The evidence piled up. He had ridden a horse only once in his life and was terrified of the animals. But in battle uniform, as the cameras began to roll, mounted upon the reincarnation of Old Sorrel, he instantaneously became "the best rider in the world," especially when four hundred muskets went off and the horse ran away with him. He realized it was "a flashback."

"It all came back to me! This was it!" he exclaimed.

And then, every year on the anniversary of Gettysburg, his old wounds in his leg and arm get sore. I decided not to point out that Stonewall Jackson had been killed at Chancellorsville two months before Gettysburg.

This would not be the first time I would hear about such mystical reëmbodiments. An Atlanta relic collector would tell me of trading Civil War artifacts with a Brooklyn Jew, with whom he had dealt for many years, when the Brooklyn man confessed, in a confidential whisper, the reward of their long association—that he was really J. E. B. Stuart! Slowly, reverently, he opened his shirt to reveal a Confederate undershirt and pulled up his trousers to display Stuart's boots. The Atlanta collector started to kid his dealer, thought better of it, and beat a hasty retreat.

I was not about to make jokes about Dent's prior life— not to his face anyway. Before he opened his shop, he had worked twenty-seven years for Lockheed in their "bummer" plant, a Southernism for "bomber"—not to be confused with Sherman's iron brigade of bummers. His Civil War shop plays court to hundreds of relic hunters in north Georgia, who, Geiger counter and trowel in hand, pursue this hobby which Dent describes as "healthy and educational, especially about such subjects as poison ivy, snakes, and yellow jackets, and instructive about your ancestry . . . but don't call it *roots!*" Decorated with a number of photographs of him in uniform and full beard, his shop abounds with cannon balls, uniforms, kepi, and overpriced books. The Nazi flags, machetes, modern fatigues should not confuse: they are remnants of a defunct partnership.

"I have no feeling for any war since *the* war. The others are so impersonal. *The* war was the last war between gentlemen . . . and Yankees."

Those who have dealt with the Wild Man over the years find behind his bravura madcap performance both substance and even a code of honor. He may not always volunteer whether an article is an original or a reproduction, but he'll tell you if you ask. And he keeps his best customers, some of whom are as far away as Belgium, well informed if something special comes into his hands. An example might be a battle map of Atlanta, printed by a field cartographer on a handkerchief, that could be quickly tucked into a pocket if something unexpected turned up. Twice, Dent has been a technical adviser to Hollywood: on the disappointing *Ordeal of Dr. Samuel Mudd,* when the producers painted Fort Pulaski outside Savannah to make it look older,—its weathering from 1847 did not look old enough on film—and in the preliminary planning for the television adaptation of Bruce Catton's *The Blue and the Gray*.

General Myers derives his rank from his command of the Georgia Division, an organization of six hundred, dedicated to the reënactment of Civil War battles. His "division" consists of eleven units of infantry, four sections of artillery, and a pride of cavalry. This too turns out to be a considerable enterprise. The biggest "battle" where Dent commanded troops was at Antietam, "in 18 . . . I mean 1963," when five thousand participated and fifteen thousand watched. The units drill hard before a show—Dent uses the old "straw-foot/hay-foot" method of teaching his men to march—and his soldiers can get quite sensitive about their uniforms. The serious Johnny Rebs are intent to destroy the misconception that ragtag Confederates put any old thing on their backs toward the end of the war. The very worst thing you can say to a "reënacter" is that his uniform is "farby"—implying that the soldier picked up a set of J. C. Penney grays. (Nobody quite knows where the term "farby" came from, but one theory is that it is a shortening of the phrase "far be it from me.")

But being authentic can have its perils too. If this was supposed to be "living history," soldiers were heard to complain, then the reënactments were too "sterile." Troops experienced the "Sergeant Rock Syndrome," feeling themselves to be invincible on the battlefield. Nobody got hurt. So the local butcher was visited for a few raw bones to throw around, and a "hospital" was decorated authentically with bandages soaked in gelid stage blood. But that spoiled the fun of the mothers and children who attended the outing, and the practice had to be discontinued. Living history had become livid history. (This problem was echoed in 1971 in a Vietnam reënactment. Then a restaging of a search-and-destroy mission as part of "Operation Dewey Canyon III" took place on the U.S. Capitol steps, and it too ran into the theatrical peril of authenticity. At that entertainment, soldiers bore toy M-16 rifles and vigorously pulled the hair of a girl who in a conical hat was being "interrogated" as a possible V. C. captain, before she ran away and was "wasted" near the statue of John Marshall, splattering stage blood over marble. Congressional secretaries were horrified and turned away in disgust. The theater had lost its audience.)

And wearing woolens at a weekend reënactment in July can get a mite uncomfortable. Several summers ago at Ringgold, Georgia, first it rained and then it rounded off at ninety-eight degrees. Confederates and a few Yankees began to wonder if living history was really worth it and retreated to the motel for a shower and a case of beer. Later, one of General Myers's staff officers told me, it made you understand what it must have really been like for those soldiers. Nonetheless, everyone was quite dejected to learn of the entry in a Union soldier's diary (*Soldiering*, by Rice Bull) that he bathed at Cassville on May 17 and didn't have a chance to take his uniform off again until after the Battle of Atlanta on July 22. Therein seemed to lie an insight into why Sherman's march of sixty thousand such randy troops through Georgia was so horrid.

For the reënactment at Ringgold, the Georgia Division mustered about 150 Confederates, but only 35 Yankees, a common difficulty for the group, since Ringgold was a skirmish before the Battle of Chickamauga, won by a vastly superior force of Sherman's Federals.

"I just can't understand why people don't want to be one of *them*," said the loveable Dent—I mean General—Myers.

So sentimentalizing a Lost Cause can have its embarrassments, the chief of which is coming very close to being ridiculous, and the William Westmoreland of a hundred years from now runs the risk of being represented by the reincarnation of a Dent Myers.

Atlanta  3

I CONFESS I gathered a handful of my old college chums around a television in Atlanta to watch the CBS production *The Blue and the Gray* with a naughty motive. I had in mind Sherman's analysis of the social classes of the South one hundred thirty years ago. First, there were the planters, the "ruling class," who were "bitter as gall" at their losses but who understood "the logic of events." Time was required, Sherman surmised, for this ruling class to adjust to the vast revolution the war had brought, but their help in Reconstruction would be essential. (By contrast, the change that the Vietnam defeat brought in the way Americans perceive themselves is denied and suppressed and ignored by the leaders who produced that defeat.)

Then there were the small farmers, merchants, and laborers, who, he said—Dent Myers notwithstanding—never had any interest in a Southern Confederacy but who followed the lead of the planters, and who swerved "to and fro according to events they [did] not comprehend or attempt to shape." "The Southern politicians who understand this class," wrote Sherman as he pondered Reconstruction, "consult their prejudices, while they make their orders and enforce them. We [the Union conquerors] should do the same."

Then came the "Union men of the South." Forget them, Sherman advised. They were afraid of their own shadow.

Finally, there were the young bloods. This class of bucks, Sherman felt, would be the bane of Reconstruction.

Sons of planters, lawyers about town, good billiard players and sportsmen, men who never did work and never will. War suits them, and the rascals are brave, fine riders, bold to rashness and dangerous subjects in every sense. They care not a sou for niggers, land or anything. They hate Yankees per se and don't bother their brains about the past, present, or future. As long as they have good horses, plenty of forage and an open country, they are happy. . . . They are the most dangerous set of men that this war has turned loose upon the world.

Among this class of "the very devils," Sherman counted generals Stonewall Jackson, Bedford Forrest (who would become the Grand Wizard of the Ku Klux Klan in 1866), J. E. B. Stuart, and Joseph Wheeler, the raiders, cavalrymen, and guerillas who had tormented his lines. Later Sherman would add John Wilkes Booth to the group.

My pals are about ten years too old now to be considered the "young bloods" of the New South. Generally speaking, they are useful citizens, but there are a few harmless lawyers-about-town, billiard players, and sportsmen among them. We gathered around the television under framed Confederate money, but I knew the decoration was playfulness, and I suspected it had been brought down from the attic for my benefit.

I wanted to see how involved they would be in the production, for I recalled a bit of rebel yahooing in their youth, especially when we Yankees were trying to desegregate their movie theaters and restaurants. Once, twenty years ago, they had made a point of taking me to Aunt Fanny's Cabin, a restaurant in Cobb County, where to this day the young black waiter comes out to your table with a blackboard, bearing the night's fare, collared around his neck, and reads off the specials in a tone straight out of the slave quarters. My shock then had been profound—which, of course, was the point of the visit—and occasioned peals of laughter from my hosts.

Compelling them now to watch *The Blue and the Gray* was my affectionate revenge.

Out of middle-aged manners to me, they sat through the endless three hours, their eyes occasionally flickering toward the screen, as yet another famous actor as John Brown or Ulysses Grant or Abraham Lincoln made a cameo appearance. (The producers had not found a place for Sherman in their "epic.") My friends grew impatient for the first battle scene to take place, so that the movie might have some life. Most of the conversation, even during the love scenes, had to do with how to get tickets to the A. C. C. basketball tournament, which was to be held in Atlanta's Omni in the coming season.

Perhaps this is not scientific proof that they are one generation too late for Civil War emotions, and I could not blame them for their lack of interest in the leaden production. Few were moved by it in any way. The United Daughters of the Confederacy urged its membership of twenty-seven thousand to complain to CBS that the Johnny Rebs had once again been portrayed in the national media as barefoot and cross-eyed, but CBS ended up with fewer than ten critical letters along these lines, a minuscule outpouring. By contrast, the network got ten thousand letters about an abortion documentary.

Sherman had said that the Union could do only one of two things with this class of young bloods after the war: either kill them or employ them. After the war, he wished to "throw upon the South the care of this class of men, who will soon be as obnoxious to their industrial classes as to us." As I looked at my friends that night, still full of fun and tricks, at heart forty-year-old sophomores all, as I enjoyed our reunion in the comfort of their Buckhead homes and ogled their Jaguars and Lincoln Continentals all in a row outside, I thought that the modern generation of young bloods had been employed very well in the New South!

In Atlanta, good humor, rather than rancor, is the current attitude toward Sherman. In recent times, bumper stickers like "General Sherman! Where are you now that we need you?" or "Sherman: the original Urban Renewer" could occasionally be seen on cars around town. Several years ago, a restaurant called Seven Steers offered a breakfast of eggs and grits and "Shermanized toast" . . . "burned to a crisp," but the establishment went out of business. The wags have it that General McPherson, Sherman's beloved commander of the Army of the Tennessee, wasn't killed in the vicinity, which is now a very rough neighborhood—he was mugged; that Maj. Gen. W. H. T. Walker, a Confederate division commander, was really dispatched trying to dart across I-20; that Confederate forces were really driven back from the ridges of Peachtree Creek, now the fanciest address in town, by Yanks shouting "Keep off the Greens!"

Even Beverly Dubose, one of the best-heeled residents

of Peachtree, who is a descendant of the unrepentant senator from Georgia, Robert Toombs, and who renamed his
ridge above the Chattahoochee, Rebel Ridge, and whose
Confederate cannon on his expansive lawn encourages a
visitor to straighten his tie, likes to tell humanizing stories
about Sherman. You remember the one, don't you, about
Sherman and the press? Before the Battle of Peachtree
Creek, Sherman was informed of the death of one of those
scoundrels and spies, and he replied, "Well, now we'll
have news from Hell to breakfast."

Sherman's contempt for the press would be echoed by
Westmoreland; both saw the press as gossips and sensa-
tion-seekers, who knew only to look for the negative. In
the *opéra bouffe* of Saigon, as Westmoreland called it,
"newspapermen-crusaders" confused reporting with influ-
encing foreign policy and thrilled to parading their cross to
the world. The breed irritated the commander mightily:
"Finding fault was one way to achieve the sensational,"
Westmoreland wrote bitterly in his memoirs, "and finding
fault with an Oriental regime with little background in
Western democracy was easy. . . . the young iconoclasts
were folk heroes whose record demonstrated that the more
criticism and the more negativism, the greater the possibilities of recognition and reward."

In Atlanta, this brassy Gate City of the New South, the
proof of the Phoenix risen from the ashes which graces the
Seal of Georgia, it has finally sunk in that Sherman is
overrated. That the city in 1864 was a clapboard town of
ten thousand, two-thirds of whose civilian population had
"refugeed" away and whose remainder had been fairly
warned by the Federal general advancing against formidable fortifications and a host of valuable military targets behind them, is finally accepted. The lurid fires through which
Scarlett O'Hara and Rhett Butler perilously made their way
on film are now understood, even in popular folklore, to

have been set mainly by the withdrawing, outflanked, out-generaled troops of the pitiful Confederate commander, John Bell Hood.

The Civil War, at long last, has become pure history to Atlanta, rather than a *cause célèbre*. Amid the knarl of expressways, the glass towers, the overhead tramways, the three battlefields within the city limits are hard to find and hard to remember. Even the Eternal Flame of the Confederacy has had to fight for respect in modern Atlanta. A gas lantern on the spot where one of Sherman's cannon balls fell, it was lit with great fanfare at the world première of *Gone with the Wind* on December 15, 1939, by the United Daughters of the Confederacy. But when the Atlanta subway was under construction several years ago, the Eternal Flame had to be moved across the street, and it is now situated on a downtown block, dominated by retail clothing businesses which sell ready-to-wear suits on the reasonably priced side.

The Atlanta campaign, from Tunnel Hill to the breast-works of the city, is memorialized by the national monument at Kennesaw Mountain. The three battles for Atlanta itself (the Battle of Peachtree Creek, July 20, 1864; the Battle of Atlanta, July 22; and the Battle of Ezra Church, July 28) find their curious commemoration in the grotesque extravaganza known as Cyclorama. Located now in a be-columned marble building patterned in design, if not in spirit, upon the Petit Trianon at Versailles, Cyclorama is a realistic, three-dimensional painting and diorama, some 400 feet in circumference and 50 feet in height. It purports to recreate in exact detail the slaughter of July 22, when over five thousand soldiers died. In its newly renovated configuration, which cost $11 million, one sits on a steeply banked platform which rotates slowly on the principle of rotating restaurants, while the music, sound effects, light, and narration are supposed to make you feel (if that's what

you really want) "part of the conflict." The pamphlet pre-
pares you to be thrilled, awestruck, and stirred by what
you see. It is a war lover's Mecca, a romantic representa-
tion of a human abattoir.

The entertainment was created in 1886, not by Southerners but by German and Polish artists from Milwaukee, and
this fit a pattern. The heroic cycloramas at Gettysburg and
Missionary Ridge were painted in Berlin and Brussels re-
spectively. Atlanta's monument began not as a testament
to the glories of the Lost Cause at all, for it is distinctly
Yankee in its bias, but to promote the presidential fortunes
of the Union general John A. Logan. Logan was one of the
political generals whose breed Sherman regarded with contempt as "volunteers." Nonetheless, the commander
found Logan's stewardship on July 22 "indefatigable" and
gave him much of the credit for the Union victory. Logan
returned to Congress after the war, became one of the floor
managers of Andrew Johnson's impeachment, and, in 1884,
after Sherman declared to his presidential boosters, "I will
not accept if nominated, and I will not serve if elected,"
Logan was the unsuccessful Republican candidate for vice-
president.

In the Cyclorama, Logan insisted upon being painted
three times the size of any other figure (Sherman is a minuscule, distant figure on a faraway hill), and Logan leads a
fiery charge upon a galloping steed. On this cumbersome
vehicle of political advertisement, the general hoped to ride
into the presidency in 1888, but, unfortunately, the hero
died in 1886.

Thereafter, the epic painting became something of a tour-
ing roadshow (next to the fat lady and the talking duck?),
traveling around America and narrated by veterans of the
battle. Somehow, it sustained its reputation as being accurate history, despite its quirks. Above the carnage there
appears to be a vulture, but, no, it is the mascot of a Wis-

consin regiment, an eagle named Old Abe which in battles, so the narration announces, "would take to the air with defiant screams." The only problem is that the Wisconsin regiment in question did not fight in the Battle of Atlanta, and the bird was painted in by the Milwaukee artists as a gesture of gratitude to their commissioners. And the only recognizable face in the mass of humanity is that of Clark Gable. During a restoration of the painting in the 1930s, the Atlanta conservator, Wilbur Kurtz, heard that Gable would be coming to the Cyclorama to soak up élan before the filming of *Gone with the Wind*. Kurtz promptly painted Gable's face on a figure, albeit a dead Yankee, and hoped by this brazen flattery to the star to secure the job of scenic designer for the film. The ploy worked, and Kurtz was hired.

Over the years the Cyclorama was somehow transformed into a Confederate shrine. But this took some doing. During its face lift in the 1930s, the section of the painting which portrayed Confederate prisoners being conducted to the rear was done over. Their uniforms were repainted blue, and the narrator told receptive Southern audiences that these were Yankee deserters fleeing the coop. As late as the 1930s, an elegant, diminutive Confederate veteran of the battle, leaning on a cane and doffing a sprightly straw hat, provided the color commentary.

But the great actor, Victor Jory, had as much to do with the shrine's graying as anybody. Among his many screen roles as the evil-eyed heavy, Jory had been the harsh overseer of Tara who returns after the war, carpetbag in hand, his tacky wife on his arm, to take over the plantation from Scarlett. One wonders if the soaring tones and stirring language of Jory's narration for the Cyclorama might not have had in it an air of atonement.

In any event, Jory's narration was masterful. Its range of emotion was extraordinary. Its pacing was brilliant. His reading of Ecclesiastes, Chapter 3—a time to rend, and a time to sew, a time to keep silence and a time to speak, a time to love and a time to hate, a time of peace and a time of war—savored each sentiment, so that you could *hear* and feel it. His concluding passage could only be carried off by a great actor: "In the hot forge of blazing battlefields like this, the steel of this nation was forged. Here were principles established. Here were bounds of unity tested and strengthened. Here from this battle and from others like it emerged . . . the United States of America."

But it was Jory's passage about the futile (and foolhardy) charge of three Confederate divisions against overwhelming odds that came to be so cherished by latter-day Confederates like the Sons and the United Daughters of the Confederacy. Jory infused his lines with an almost unbearable excitement.

Against that fiery summit, three Confederate divisions hurl their thunderbolts from two different directions. The fate of their charge is the fate of Atlanta. The fate of the South. The gate city is depending upon them, and to this end, they continue to charge, boys against lead and steel. . . . Attack, attack, again, again, again. Fight, fight, . . . until you die. And die they do by the thousands. In the face of the superior strength and arms of the Union forces. Under their banner of pure white stars and royal blue bars, on a field of blood red, these lads become fighting men. But their individual courage can not overcome the overwhelming odds.

Here, youth as the universal victim of war finds its ultimate celebration, and for the damp-eyed throngs that pass through at the cost of two dollars no connections seem to be made between the youth of the Atlanta battles and the youth of Vietnam, and of Lebanon and El Salvador and Grenada and . . . and. . . .

In 1982, during its retouching, this hideous monstrosity

was given a new, toned-down narration. "Dixie," "The Battle Hymn of the Republic," and "Marching through Georgia" were thought to be too chauvinistic and were replaced with such obscure melodies as "Goober Peas," "Gay and Happy," and "Farewell Forever to the Star-Spangled Banner." The effect of this immense effort comes out in the wash. It is unclear what one is supposed to think about the marvel. The sad fife-and-drum music undercuts revulsion at the carnage. The absence of the real rallying songs dampens the fun of the old competition. The down-played narration removes chauvinism. The civic pride in the achievement of two black mayors in its restoration cuts across the monumental indifference within their black con-stituencies toward Civil War lore. The slow death produced by the rudimentary engines of war in that day has nothing to tell us in the nuclear age.

◈ ◈ ◈

In Sherman's first actions as emperor of Atlanta, the tug within him between punishment and generosity was evi-dent. He was visited by a resident of Madison, Georgia, who seemed to appreciate what might be ahead for his town and others in central Georgia, and so offered to act as an emissary to the governor of Georgia, Joseph Brown, to see if Sherman's ministrations might be avoided. Through this intermediary, Sherman put a proposition to Brown: if the governor would withdraw the Georgia militia from the Con-federate Army and pursue a policy of "separate State ac-tion," Sherman promised to "spare the state," to confine his troops to the main roads, and pay greenbacks for all the corn and food his army required.

The offer was, characteristically, more psychological than military. To Abraham Lincoln, Sherman wrote: "It would be a magnificent stroke of policy if we could, without surrendering principle or a foot of ground, arouse the latent enmity of Georgia against Davis." Georgians, Sherman

47

felt, were generally lukewarm toward the Confederate cause and resentful at the resistance in Richmond toward sending more troops south for the defense of their state. While Sherman's proposition was making its way to Governor Brown, Jefferson Davis himself had slipped into Georgia. His purpose was to mollify criticism of his obsession with the Virginia theater of war. At Macon, he argued that if only half the Confederate deserters returned to their posts, Sherman would be crushed. For the Yankee invader, he predicted the fate of Napoleon at Moscow. So far from his line of supply, Sherman would soon face the choice of starvation or retreat. The Rebel cossacks would harass and eventually destroy the enemy, and Davis encouraged his Macon audience to visualize Sherman skulking out of Georgia, like Napoleon out of Moscow, with only a bodyguard.

A day later, at Palmetto Station, south of Atlanta, Davis proceeded to divulge the entire battle strategy of the Confederate command. To his Army of Tennessee, he tried to cheer the troops by telling them their feet would soon tread their native Tennessee soil. This not only telegraphed the Confederate military strategy to Sherman but made clear to him that with such a movement westward by the remnant of Hood's army, the way to the sea was wide open.

With Davis in Georgia bombastically taunting Sherman and criticizing Southern politicians like Governor Brown for cowering before the invaders, Sherman's proposition for an independent Georgia course was soon overtaken by events. Governor Brown did succeed for a short time in removing the Georgia militia from Hood's army, but his legislature voted to continue the fight.

Sherman had tried generosity, and he had been rejected. His response to the rejection was rage and opened up still wider his determination to punish the Rebels severely. This, at least, is the theory of Maj. John Brinsfield at West Point, who even finds a psychohistorian's diagnosis for

Sherman's condition: "institutional child syndrome," the oscillation between gentle conduct and uncontrolled rage. Whatever clinical validity such a designation may have, the idea of a commander subject to childish temper tantrums at the head of sixty-two thousand lathered-up troops, is a distressing notion—for that and all time.

Meanwhile, Sherman had delivered a highly charged order to the remaining citizens of Atlanta. They must evacuate the city entirely, turning it into a ghostly military depot. They were free to go either north or south, "depending on their inclinations." Profiteers and sutlers from the Northern side would be permitted no closer than Chattanooga. Sherman wanted to eliminate profiteering and to avoid endless solicitations from women, but, as usual, he also had a psychological purpose. He expected howls at his evacuation order, but "I know that the people of the South would read in this measure two conclusions: one, that we were in earnest; and the other, if they were sincere in their common and popular clamor 'to die to the last ditch,' that the opportunity would soon come." Pitiful wagon trains of refugees clogged the muddy roads out of the city, a spectacle modern man has come to associate with Indochina, Central America, and the Middle East.

From this unusual, if not unprecedented, order a spirited correspondence arose between Sherman and Hood over the ethics of their respective conduct of warfare. Hood acknowledged that he had no alternative but to cooperate in receiving whatever civilian refugees from Atlanta now preferred Southern rather than Northern protection. But with Victorian indignation and grand orotund phraseology, he protested, in the name of God and of humanity, against this unprecedented measure which "transcends in studied and ingenious cruelty, all acts ever before brought to my attention in the dark history of war."

In Sherman, Hood had chosen the wrong literary, as well

as military, adversary, for Sherman on the page as on the battlefield overwhelmed him with twice the firepower and twice the skill. Sherman pleaded with Hood not to appeal to a just God "in such a sacrilegious manner," for it had been Hood and his colleagues "who in the midst of peace and prosperity plunged the nation into war—dark and cruel war—who dared and badgered us to battle, insulted our flag, seized our arsenals and forts, . . ." and on and on went the litany of Southern sins. As to the unprecedented nature of his action, Sherman claimed that Hood and his predecessor, Joseph Johnston, had done the very same thing in evacuating the town of Dalton, Georgia, and he, Sherman, saw no reason why Atlanta should be an exception. (On this, Sherman stood on weak ground, for the scale of his Atlanta action far exceeded any rebel evacuation. To be sure, only three thousand civilians out of a prewar population of ten thousand remained in the beleaguered city, but that was a sizeable population in the nineteenth century, especially to be under siege for six weeks.)

Sherman then charged Hood with deliberately placing Atlanta's line of embattlements so close to the town that every cannon ball which overshot its mark crashed into the dwellings of women and children. Hood wailed at this two days later, writing that Sherman's artillery had continuously overshot his "modest field works" by miles for weeks and weeks. "I have too good an opinion . . . of the skill of your artillerists to credit the insinuation that they for several weeks unintentionally fired too high . . . and slaughtered women and children by accident or want of skill," Hood wrote.

In this correspondence, Sherman had become a twentieth-century man at work in the nineteenth century, displaying a ruthlessness, a cold-bloodedness, a calculation that the modern world has come to admire openly in its warriors. In the nineteenth century, these qualities had to be admired secretly. Nobility, heroism, and decency in war were in the process of being ruined, and Sherman was coming to represent, by the old rules of warfare, an official dishonor that is now accepted as standard. But once rules become old, they cease to exist. Once political authority condones or promotes their breach, soldiers need not worry. To violate old-fashioned rules ceases to be dishonorable.

Sherman had devised a terrible way to make war, but it was working. He was pursuing abhorrent new measures that he deemed necessary to the military objective. If war is hell, what gradations can hell have? If his little skirmish at Pickett's Mill outside Atlanta was a "hell-hole," how much worse can a nuclear microwave oven be? This is Sherman's legacy: not so much his practice of "total war" as his intellectual justification for it, his lack of remorse at it, his readiness to distort the record for psychological advantage. By denying any ethical gradations of warfare, he moved the argument into the abyss. Similar justifications, without remorse or reëvaluation, are now put forward for American practices in Vietnam, and the rules of warfare that existed before that war have similarly ceased to exist.

"You cannot qualify war in harsher terms than I will," Sherman wrote Hood in this correspondence that was later widely published both in Northern and Southern newspapers. "War is cruelty, and you can not qualify it, and those who brought war in our country deserve all the curses and maledictions a people can pour on."

But it was a war of aggression, Hood replied. "You came into our country with your army, avowedly for the purpose of subjugating free white men, women and children. You make negroes your allies, and desire to place over us an inferior race which we have raised from barbarism to its present condition, which is the highest ever attained by that race in any country, in all time."

Sherman disputed that. "We have no negro allies in this army; not a single negro left Chattanooga with this army or is with us now." As to Hood's claim that Sherman was obligated to give Atlanta notice before he began shelling it, Sherman went on, "I was not bound by the laws of war to give notice of the shelling of Atlanta, a fortified town with magazines, arsenals, foundries, and public stores; you were bound to take notice. See the books."

For one who at that moment was rewriting the books, this was a curious way for Sherman to conclude their debate. Both men were writing not so much to one another as to history. Hood was writing to distract attention from his disastrous failures on the battlefield; Sherman was writing to justify the manner of his victories. (In his memoirs, Westmoreland would have the triple problem of justifying both his battlefield failures and the atrocities of his soldiers, while maintaining in old-fashioned language that he was an honorable soldier and man.) Later, both Sherman and Hood would include the entire correspondence in their respective memoirs. But here, too, Hood was hopelessly outmatched. The Sherman memoirs were greeted upon their publication in 1875 as a work of literature, Mark Twain declared Sherman to be a master of narrative, and in the twentieth century the memoirs were proclaimed by Edmund Wilson to be "the finest example of military memoirs in American letters." Hood's memoirs were a dry, bleak little foray, defensive and incomplete. (He did not even mention his disaster at Kolb's Farm in the Battle of Kennesaw, where in an afternoon he lost a thousand men.) Ironically, Hood in the early 1880s, being somewhat long in the tooth, solicited Sherman's help in getting his own book published, and Sherman acceded to the plea, presumably realizing that he would once again be cast as the barbarian.

If Hood's memoirs were dry, they were no more so than

the rest of the military writing by Confederate commanders. Joseph Johnston's narrative is a dismal affair, and Lee did not finish his memoirs. Perhaps there is a dynamic here: victors write about war better than losers.

In the end, Sherman's lasting dread image in the South was not created by his battlefield adversaries but by Jefferson Davis. In 1881, Davis published his massive apologia, *The Rise and Fall of the Confederate Government,* and just how damaging it was to Sherman is pointed up by the Southern attitude toward its conqueror before the book's publication. In 1879, Sherman's memoirs had been in print for four years, and had been very well received. Southerners had settled into the belief that Sherman had been a harsh, but skillful, commander who had done a tough job that, by his lights, needed to be done, and that, once victorious, he had been a constant voice for generosity toward the South. He also shared their contemptuous attitude toward the Negro and was critical of Reconstruction.

At that time papers all over the South were urging Sherman to run for president against Grant, who was then being pushed for a third term. In the same year, 1879, as general in chief of the United States Army, Sherman deemed the time to be right for a mission of reconciliation over the path of his march. He began in Chattanooga, where he was met at the station by a warm, friendly crowd and later toasted at a "hop" in his honor. The papers there shouted his praise, contrasting him favorably with Grant, who was considered the sponsor of Reconstruction. With this auspicious beginning, it was on to Atlanta, where again he was greeted by a large and friendly crowd. But Sherman gallows humor, which endures to this day, began at that moment. When it was suggested that Sherman be given the freedom of the city, someone complained, "He made too free with it when he was here last." Someone else suggested that Sherman should be greeted by a parade of widows in mourning

53

clothes, clutching kindling wood. As Sherman's trains appeared outside Atlanta's station, the cry went up, "Ring the fire bells! The town will be gone in forty minutes!"

But the general danced his way through a three-day visit, hobnobbing with such dignitaries as the Civil War governor of Georgia, Joseph Brown, in whose Milledgeville mansion Sherman had stayed, uninvited, fourteen years before. In his public pronouncements, Sherman praised Atlanta's energy in rebuilding and spoke of its bright future. In one frank statement that put his listeners off center, he chided the city for being hostile to carpetbaggers. Outside blood had made other Southern cities great and could help Atlanta similarly, he proclaimed. After the civil rights revolution of the 1960s, the New South has finally come to accept this maxim.

Sherman proceeded by train to Macon, where he dined elegantly on the town, and then continued to Savannah. Southern papers began to refer to his "pleasure trip through the South." From Savannah, he turned South, visiting St. Augustine and New Orleans, where he shared a theater box with John Bell Hood and presumably discussed literary matters.

But on his return trip, somewhere between Vicksburg and Jackson, a former Confederate officer approached Sherman with the news that Jefferson Davis was in the next car. Wouldn't Sherman like to meet him? Sherman demurred. While he held no malice toward Davis, he would not pay court. The ex-Confederate officer understood. Davis, he said, "clung too long to his prejudices." Little did they appreciate the extravagance of Davis's prejudice. Two years later, in his book, Davis called Sherman's evacuation of Atlanta the most barbaric act "since Alva's atrocious cruelties to the non-combatant population of the Low Countries in the sixteenth century." Davis charged the burning of Columbia, South Carolina, directly to Sherman (a claim, as we shall see, which is very difficult to prove), placing it in league with "the barbarous excesses of Wallenstein's army in the Thirty Years' War." Perhaps it is just as well that Sherman and Davis did not get together for a chat on the train to Jackson.

Not long after the publication of the Davis book, Sherman again visited Atlanta to attend an international cotton exposition. This time, the reception was frigid, to be frozen for a hundred years. One newspaper went to the length of reprinting the Alva reference for Sherman's breakfast reading, and the *Atlanta Constitution* editorialized that only politeness was due Sherman. In a passage that could be read several ways, the paper wrote: "No one need . . . fear that Atlantans will do anything to disgrace the name of the state, lower the dignity of its people, or sacrifice the least particle of respect due its history or traditions."

Marching through Georgia

ICANNOT claim to have left Atlanta, one
hundred eighteen years and one day later, with quite Sherman's exhilaration. For Sherman, it was a bright, bitterly
cold November 16, and his description of the mood, as the
smouldering city was lost behind a screen of trees, is perversely lyrical. The band struck up "John Brown's Body"
and from there the men took up "Glory, Glory Hallelujah,"
sung with more spirit and harmony, by Sherman's lights,
than he had ever heard it rendered. One wants to imagine
what it would be like for 62,204 men to take up a lusty air
in quarter-tone, and to suppose Stone Mountain as a lush,
fertile knoll turned to a cold, bald rock by the Yankee din.

"The day was extremely beautiful," Sherman waxed. "Clear sunlight, with bracing air, and an unusual feeling of exhilaration seemed to pervade all minds—a feeling of something to come, vague and undefined, still full of venture and intense interest." In retrospect, his eloquence seems understated.

He sensed in his troops a "devil-may-care" attitude on that day, which Southern patriots no doubt ascribe to the vision of silver goblets and family jewels dancing in their heads, but which the general interpreted in strictly military terms: they were headed for Richmond to relieve Grant by way of Augusta and Charlotte. As usual, Sherman was busy promoting this fallacy to confuse the enemy. He split his army into two wings, the left wing pointing toward Augusta, the right wing toward Macon, and he had no intention of storming either place. For obvious strategic reasons, he needed to make contact with the sea-based navy, which through most of the war had effectively blockaded Southern ports and had held Beaufort and Hilton Head, South Carolina, since 1862.

Sherman's orders to the army had been issued a week before departure. They were to "forage liberally" on the countryside, and such foraging was theoretically restricted to regular, well-commanded "parties." The orders specifically forbade trespass in dwellings and discouraged the troops from using "abusive or threatening" language. The command directed soldiers to leave families who were plucked with a "reasonable portion" for sustenance afterwards. The most important thing, Sherman wrote in his orders, was that "men during marches and in camps, keep their places and do not scatter about as stragglers or foragers."

For the record, there was in Vietnam a similar set of official orders which were supposed to govern the conduct of American soldiers in the field. Each soldier got an hour of instruction in the laws of warfare during his eight weeks of basic training. Upon landing in Vietnam, he was required to carry MACV (Military Assistance Command, Vietnam) cards at all times, entitled "The Enemy in Your Hands," "Code of Conduct," and "Geneva Convention." In the soldier's instruction, "grave breaches" of the rules of war were defined as willful killing, torture or inhuman treatment, willfully causing great suffering or serious injury to body and health, unlawful deportation or transfer or unlawful confinement of a protected person, taking hostages or extensive destruction or appropriation of property, "not justified by military necessity and carried out unlawfully and wantonly." *Not justified by military necessity* was, as always, the slippery aspect of these violations, for the precept has wide latitude, especially when the essential mission is to punish rebellion. Nonetheless, every violation of the laws of war was specifically deemed to be a war crime.

General Westmoreland was also on record personally with a number of statements that stressed the necessity for humane treatment of civilians. On August 28, 1966, for example, he told a commander's briefing: "It is extremely important that we do all we can to use our fire with discrimination and avoid noncombatant battle casualties. This is a very sensitive subject, both locally and among our own press corps. Unfortunately, we've had a rash of incidents caused by everything from mechanical failure to human error. . . ." He made no mention of human cruelty or wanton pillage or violence bred of frustration. "The percentage of incidents has been minuscule," Westmoreland continued. "Nonetheless, every civilian killed is a calamity, and we must cut the percentage to the minimum possible." But this enjoinder was being proclaimed during the same period that Westmoreland was devising his concept of "free-fire zones," and no one seemed ready to point up the bald contradiction.

Sherman too was given to this same conflict of signals within official orders, or between the official order and the unofficial practice. Put differently, the dilemma from the foot soldier's viewpoint was between the order to be restrained and humane on the one hand, and to unleash the full measure of punishing firepower on the other. In Memphis, in 1862, for example, Sherman was appalled by his soldiers' pilferage. "Stealing, robbery and pillage has become so common in this army that it is a disgrace to any civilized people," he wrote in an order in July 1862. "This demoralizing and disgraceful practice of pillage must cease, else the country will rise on us and justly shoot us down like dogs and wild beasts." But a month later, he was writing to Salmon Chase, then the secretary of the treasury, "Most unfortunately, the war in which we are now engaged has been complicated with the belief that all on the other side are *not* enemies. It would have been better if, at the outset, this mistake had not been made. . . . Not only are all in the South unfriendly, but all who can procure arms now bear them as organized regiments or as guerrillas. There is not a garrison in Tennessee where a man can go beyond the sight of the flag staff without being shot or captured." In the South, as in Vietnam, every man, woman, and child had become the enemy.

It was not until the My Lai massacre that the whole matter of "civilized" warfare under the laws of war was put under official review. A commission, headed by Lt. Gen. W. R. Peers, devoted a chapter to the laws of war in its report and concluded that humane treatment of civilians was not receiving adequate emphasis. If an order violated a rule of land warfare, the Peers Commission stated, executing that order was a war crime. Therefore, it would be an illegal order. But of disobeying an illegal order, the Peers Commission concluded:

It is apparent that directives and training are inadequate concerning an individual's responsibilities concerning illegal orders. There is a dearth of written information concerning this subject. There is but little discussion of illegal orders in Army regulations or training manuals and even less at subordinate levels. What little discussion is included in any publication is cumbersome and indecisive and presented in such a manner that it takes a legal officer to interpret it. Indeed, the average officer or enlisted man would have difficulty comprehending it.

Further, the directions are deficient in explaining that a soldier is a reasoning human being who is expected to exercise judgment in obeying the orders of a superior. An individual is not expected to blindly obey all orders.

For all this good analysis, the Peers Commission undermined its own argument by stating that a soldier disobeys an order "at his own peril," and thereby risks being charged with insubordination and court-martialed, and that this is proper. Within these cross-currents do atrocities breed. And so did they begin, slowly but gradually, in Sherman's March to the Sea.

Through the first phase of the march, these orders stayed in force (to borrow the phrase of West Point's Colonel Flint) with *reasonable* order and discipline. Knowing what would come later, and how Southern history would eventually vilify the march, Sherman's comment on the "charm" of foraging upon the Southern landscape sounds droll today: "Although this foraging was attended with great danger and hard work, there seemed to be a charm about it that attracted soldiers, and it was a privilege to be detailed on such a party." To the end, he maintained that theft of jewelry was exceptional, and instances of rape and murder nonexistent. He admitted hearing stories of plunder, but not of rape and murder—but how hard was he listening?

With some emphasis, he related an incident near Covington, Georgia, of passing a soldier dangling a ham from his musket, pressing a jug of molasses under his arm, and dribbling honey down his chin from a honeycomb on his hand. Upon noticing the commander, the soldier mumbled the order about foraging liberally, but it was not enough to avoid a dressing-down. One senses that such reproaches were just as incidental as the instances of rape and murder, and it should be remembered that Robert E. Lee fell into a rage at Sharpsburg near Antietam at seeing a soldier with a stolen pig—and had the soldier shot as an example.

The army was spread across a wide front of fifty miles, rather than in a single column along one path, and there was good reason for this. By dispersing an army of sixty-two thousand in that fashion, everyone, except those who are getting picked clean, gets a decent meal. Along a single file, the old saw has it, the first soldier gets the eggs, the second soldier gets the chickens, but what about everyone who comes after? One modern military historian has reduced foraging to a mathematical equation and compared Sherman's problem of starvation to Napoleon's. His conclusion is that in the lean, sparsely populated piney woods of Georgia, Sherman needed to scour an area eight times as large as Napoleon's in Europe to sustain a comparable number of troops.

I struck out for Gray, Georgia, on a dismal, rainy day, for I had an appointment to teach history in the Jones County High School. A year ago I had come to Gray with a professional basketball player of my acquaintance, who would give me a tour of the sites, including the house where Sherman slept, and the orchards where, as a boy from the Baptist Bottom, he picked peaches at ten cents a bucket. At a current salary of over $400,000 a year with the Seattle Supersonics, Al Wood is doing his part to redress a historical imbalance. But now, at his alma mater, in Mrs. Stevens's history class, weightier matters were at issue.

The broadcast of *The Blue and the Gray* that week, I thought, would be a sufficient handle for a lively discussion. Mrs. Stevens, a cheery, well-nourished lady, had dutifully passed out to her class a handout provided by the CBS affiliate in Macon from the CBS Television Reading Program. The handout was part of a nationwide program by CBS, whose purpose was "to utilize children's enthusiasm for television to help improve their reading skills, and to increase their motivation for further reading, learning, and creative thinking." This seemed to be a noble public service, and I expected the supplement to contain extensive passages from Bruce Catton or Carl Sandburg, if not *Lee's Lieutenants*. Instead, it turned out to be page upon page of the television script for the program, as if to suggest that the television generation would learn the love of reading by concentrating on television scripts.

My brief tenure as an eleventh-grade teacher, I'm embarrassed to report, was not memorable. Perched upon a stool near Mrs. Stevens, I probed for knowledge and sentimentality about the Lost Cause. Of knowledge, there was none, save the certainty that Sherman had burned down all the homes and killed all the people; and sentimentality was lodged, for the white students, in the ubiquitous decals and front-end license plates with the Stars and Bars, which graced their souped-up cars and pickup trucks—in case any Yankee might show up. The display advertised their "pride in the South" or vaguely suggested a rebellious and fun-loving spirit. The Stars and Bars, one student announced, was, after all, a very pretty flag. I replied that it also symbolized the most overt treason of our history and bedrock racism to many. (In the summer of 1979, North Carolina leftists disrupted a Ku Klux Klan screening of D. W. Griffith's *The Birth of a Nation,* and in the process ripped and burned the Klan's Confederate flag. Afterwards, the Klan leader held up the tattered battleflag for television cameras and promised revenge. Four months later, at an anti-Klan demonstration in Greensboro, North Carolina, five leftists were murdered by the same Klansmen.) My association of racism with Confederate symbols was greeted first with blank stares and then I was asked for confirmation of the obvious—that I was a Yankee.

Georgia history is still taught in most public schools from Bernice McCullar's book, *This Is Your Georgia*. In it, the rumors of Sherman's insanity are underscored, while Joseph Johnston is described as capable, cautious, thoughtful, kind, and humorous. Grant is labeled a strange, silent man, married to a near-midget, whereas John Bell Hood was sad-eyed and tall, even as he stood on one leg. Both characterizations were provided, the book states, because "personalities illuminate history."

But the visit to Jones County was not a total bust. There, I came upon the only historical site on my entire journey that *did* illuminate the Sherman campaign. It is the Jarrell Plantation—mailing address, Juliette, Georgia, which is surely the most melodious name for a town in all America —and it is operated by the state of Georgia as a working farm of the nineteenth century. So faithful to historical accuracy is the place that its supervisor comes very close to believing that he is the reincarnation of the nineteenth-century Georgia poet, Sidney Lanier. Jarrell Plantation is a place where arcane Southern verities, and a few Northern ones as well, are debunked. The plantation house is "plantation plain," a solid, clapboard dwelling with low ceilings, exposed heart-pine beams, and a certain forbidding Faulknerian darkness beneath the huge oaks that press in upon it. It is not a place for hoop skirts, but work clothes, strong muscles, and the ingenuity to make life rich in a low-tech age.

In 1864, John Fitz Jarrell was the fifty-five-year-old master of the estate. No aristocrat, he had carved out his place in the piney woods with unromantic, resourceful hard labor. On his 300 acres, by the 1860 census, he had 42 slaves, 10 milch cows, 3 horses, 8 mules, 30 cattle, 140 swine, 5 oxen, and other assorted animals and birds, most of which are represented on the lawn as you walk onto the site. All in all, the totality made a pretty fair haul for a foraging party. John Fitz was his own skilled craftsman: farmer, mason, blacksmith, tanner, cobbler, weaver, distiller (of fresh water from salt), ginner, carpenter, furniture maker, hunter, fisherman, bridge builder, and Baptist preacher. (His sermons were as strong as his bridges, they say.) Too old to serve himself, he had eleven members of his immediate family who fought, and indicative of the terror as severe as the battlefield, had lost his wife and daughter to typhoid fever in 1863. In short, John Fitz had much to fear as the western sky was aglow from the flames of Atlanta, eighty miles away, and these fears became well-grounded as Sherman's men undertook their six-day "rampage" in Jones County.

How terrifying Sherman's visit must have been, as his men discharged their *official, authorized* military business, is poignantly displayed here. John Fitz had buried his family gold and had driven his livestock down into a canebrake far from the house as the black pine smoke from neighboring farms foretold the approach of the Federals. Having just cured the winter pork after the first frost, he buried the meat deep beneath cane mashings in the barn.

With ruthless efficiency, the official foragers went about their business. The two-story cotton gin and large barn were burned, along with three hundred bushels of wheat. Buckets of cane syrup, then the staple of the diet, were poured out on the ground. John Fitz would later find only one worthless horse down in the canebrake. Jarrell's slaves rushed to the Yankee troops as saviors, but the hand of deliverance was harsh. One slave, named Prince Clark, informed his liberators that the cured meat was beneath the mashings, but the Yankees, unused to the exotic plant, took shovels to the layers, became frustrated at the job when the first layer uncovered no prize, and concluded that Prince was lying. So, they strung him up by his thumbs, with his toes just reaching a nail, and left him to be cut down by his master.

One wonders, therefore, how terrifying it must have been for a Vietnamese peasant, living in an area designated as "V. C.-controlled," when Americans came through on a routine sweeping operation that involved no "wanton violence." If one is to take General Westmoreland's memoirs seriously, a sweep of U.S. Marines could provide "the festive air" of a country fair, as a village was cordoned off and entertainers brought in to amuse the villagers while their identity cards were checked and their homes searched. Attempts to sanitize and then perfume military exactions have become an American pastime.

Left to interpret the "living history" at the Jarrell Plantation is the supervisor, Marty Willett. Thirty-three years old, with a thick beard and wonderfully sparkling eyes, Willett possesses a degree of poignant, mystical nostalgia that makes the site glitter. For audiences that range from senior Daughters of the Confederacy to junior Boy Scouts, Willett plies the skills of John Fitz Jarrell with cheerful enthusiasm and endless anecdote. As a bona fide soldier of the General James Longstreet camp of the Sons of Confederate Veterans, and a private in Dent Myers's Georgia Division, he stages an annual Confederate commemoration in the plantation, in which he portrays John Fitz.

But, as he put it, his job can be "precarious and uncomfortable" when it comes to relating history accurately, especially about Sherman. Diplomatically, he will try to caution a camp of Confederate reënacters that their outing is no excuse to be "redneck and racist," that their purpose is to ennoble rather than defile the Confederate flag, but this can be a quarrelsome message. Generally, his rebels have trouble swallowing any interpretation other than that the Yankee march was "marauding to the sea."

Willett's curious nostalgia becomes the more strange for the fact that he was once a cadet at the Air Force Academy and resigned from the Academy during the downslide of the Vietnam War. He had come to the conclusion that Richard Nixon and Spiro Agnew were crooked and wanted no part of their enterprise. In his application for conscientious objector status, he described himself religiously as a "hybrid Pantheist deist" and no doubt that designation hastened him into alternative service. He thinks of himself as "aggressively pacifist."

Once again, distaste for the modern idiom of warfare was transformed into sentimentality for the Lost Cause and the grand virtues that supposedly died with it. His modern pacifism and his cavalier longings come together in his love for the romantic Georgia poet, Sidney Lanier. For deep emotional reasons, Lanier's thoughts of how Trade killed Chivalry, how Trade hatched John Brown, and "broke the saintly heart of Robert E. Lee" make a strong connection in Willett, as well as the florid passages in Lanier's novel, *Tiger Lilies,* that speak of war as the hardy "sin flower" which has so many fanciers. In April 1982, to his great pleasure, Marty was asked by the United Daughters of the Confederacy to deliver the commemorative address at the Confederate Cemetery in Macon. He chose to repeat, with his own emphasis, Lanier's address on the same site in 1870. Amid the silence of the Jarrell Plantation, and with grand theatrical gestures, he delivered a few lines for me: "I know not a deeper question in the Southern life than how we shall bear out our load of wrong and insult and injury with calmness and tranquil dignity that becomes men and women who would be great. . . ."

Macon is a delightfully well-preserved historical town, and it is so because Sherman threatened and then bypassed it. There, I had dinner at a Greek Revival house-cum-restaurant on College Street called Beall's 1860. I dined beneath a *Harper's Weekly* etching of Sherman's triumphant march through Savannah.

In the morning, I toured the Hay House, reputedly the finest example of Italian Renaissance architecture in the South, whose catchy pamphlet uses the headline: "Sherman Missed It—Don't You!" Indeed, Sherman missed everything in Macon, except the Cannonball House, which fell victim to a single cannon shot in July 1864, when Stoneman was retreating from his abortive attempt to liberate Andersonville. The ball came to rest at the feet of Mrs. Asa Holt, the wife of Judge Holt.

Today, the Cannonball House is a Confederate Museum, maintained by the Sidney Lanier Chapter of the United Daughters of the Confederacy. I was greeted at the door by a sceptical little lady, who gave me a profoundly sympathetic look when I announced that I had come all the way from New York. Nevertheless, I got a courteous tour of the place, including the slave quarters in the back. There, amid the lace pinafore laid out on the bed, the spinning wheel, the farthingale, the now familiar ragged battleflag and rumpled gray uniform, I found the old plaque which once graced the front of the Sidney Lanier House in Macon. The hotel, which burned down some years ago, was where Jefferson Davis had been brought after his capture in Irwinville, Georgia, in May 1865.

Historians generally believe that had Davis not been so roughly treated after the war—jailed at Fort Monroe, his ankles manacled, a lantern kept burning in his cell day and night—and threatened with trial as a war criminal for several years, he would never have been immortalized. Sherman himself would later be charged with trying to engineer

Davis's escape, after vague prompting by Lincoln (see Chapter 7), and with bruised indignation, wrote to his wife: "The clamor over Davis was all bosh anyway. Any young man with a musket was more dangerous than Davis. When he was caught, he was old, infirm, a fugitive hunted by his own people." But Northerners went overboard in their effort to discredit Davis. The false rumor was broadcast far and wide that Davis was dressed in woman's clothing when he was caught—a greater assault on Southern manliness cannot be imagined—and the *New York Herald* made the most of it. Davis's last free act, wrote the paper, was "to unsex himself and deceive the world."

The plaque, resting haphazardly against the slave wall, showed both the degree of Davis's glorification and the grand hyperbole with which historical plaques used to inform tourists. Beneath the garlanded letters, C.S.A., the information that Davis had been held prisoner in the hotel after his capture, and then:

His noble words have now been realized:
"When times shall have softened passion and prejudice,
When reason shall have stripped the mask of misrepresentation,
Then Justice, holding evenly her scales, will require
much of past censure and praise to change places."

Perhaps it is these sentiments that Ronald Reagan longs to apply to the modern Lost Cause, when he declares Vietnam to be a "noble cause," but it is unlikely that his noble words, seductive as they are to some, will ever appear on a bronze historical marker. For there was no reconstruction after Vietnam, no harsh exactions for any leader who might be charged with dragooning the country into a hopeless situation. Therefore, no leader has been "martyred" by the enthusiasts for the "cause" of anticommunism, and then later glorified, as Jefferson Davis was martyred and then glorified in the Civil War's aftermath. To some extent, time has softened passion and prejudice. But for ten years after Vietnam, about the length of the Reconstruction after the Civil War, the country denied its memory, as if it had sedated itself with Hood's laudanum.

After I dutifully examined the mended column and the dented parlor floor which marked the path of the famous cannon ball, I started to leave for Milledgeville, but not before my guide pulled reverently from a drawer the yellowed onionskin that chronicled the various indignities heaped upon Judge Holt by the "Satan-inspired enlisted men" of Sherman's army. Before I read the document, my guide cautioned me that it made "ugly reading." It seems the unlucky judge fled Macon to his Jefferson County plantation ahead of Sherman, and, ironically, would have been perfectly safe had he stayed at home. But in Jefferson County, the Yankees stormed onto his land and demanded to know the whereabouts of the Confederate repository of gold in Macon, figuring that a man of the judge's stature would be apprised of the secret. (Much Confederate gold had been sent from Richmond to Macon toward the end of the war.) When the judge denied any knowledge of it, he was hanged *three times,* the affidavit relates, but he miraculously recovered after he was cut down by "the poorer class of people in the piney woods."

Rain poured as I drove from Macon to Milledgeville, a distance of thirty-five miles, spanning the breadth of Sherman's swath. The commanding general had ridden with the left wing of his army through Social Circle, Covington, and Madison, making his feint at Augusta. He left the command of the slower right wing to the devoutly religious, one-armed O. O. Howard. Howard was probably the only racial progressive of the top Union staff. Later, he would head the Freedmen's Bureau and found Howard University. But he was also an early and consistent voice of alarm over the depredations of Federal troops. East of Macon, at Pitt's

Mill, near Gordon, Georgia, Howard officially reported abuses to Sherman on November 23, 1864:

I regret to say that quite a number of private dwellings which the inhabitants have left, have been destroyed by fire, but without official sanction; also many instances of the most inexcusable and wanton acts, such as the breaking open of trunks, taking of silver plate, etc. I have taken measures to prevent it, and I believe they will be effectual. . . . Having soldiers in the command who have been bitten by bloodhounds, permission has been given to kill them.

This last sentence was not Howard's literary flourish. The day earlier, Howard had issued this general order:

It having come to the knowledge of the major general commanding that the crime of arson and robbery have become frequent throughout this army, notwithstanding positive orders both from these and superior headquarters having been repeatedly issued, and with a view to the prompt punishment of offense of this kind, it is hereby ordered: that hereafter any officer or man of this command discovered in pillaging a house or burning a building without proper authority will, upon sufficient proof thereof, be shot.

But there were no executions. Even into South Carolina, when the abuses became far worse, Howard carried on the crusade. He wrote to Sherman of the "banditti" in the army, "thieves and robbers" who should be dealt with severely and summarily. But when a thieving soldier was arrested, he was freed by armed companions who threatened the guard.

Several weeks before I arrived in Milledgeville, an old myth was stoked. To his many ladies fair across the breadth of Georgia who were given credit for saving so many mansions was added the myth of his charitable masonry. If mansions were not "spared" because of a youthful amour, some Rebel had flashed the magical Mason's sign. Shortly before I came to Middle Georgia, this latter myth received another pumping up on local television. The latest antebellum mansions supposedly spared by the Masonic tie were the lovely Greek Revival homes of Madison, Georgia, set amid cedars and magnolias, and distinguished by their fluted Doric columns. The myth surrounds Milledgeville. To the east, it lives in the country history of Washington County. By that account, Federal troops were fired upon, and Sherman ordered the town of Sandersville razed in retaliation.

"Then old Brother Anthony, the Methodist minister, went to him in the name of the women and children, declaring that those who did the atrocious [firing] were not even Georgians, much less inhabitants of Sandersville and Washington County. The stern commander was not moved. Brother Anthony pleaded in the name of Christ, but General Sherman was not a Christian. He did not care if delicate women and little children perished in the cold. Finally, Brother Anthony tried a masonic sign. That had its effect. The town was saved and a guard stationed in every house—after everything of value and of comfort had been destroyed."

Before this trip, Milledgeville was known to me only as the home of Flannery O'Connor. I knew her wonderfully droll story, "A Late Encounter with the Enemy," about the one-hundred-four-year-old Confederate "general" who passes away while witnessing his granddaughter's graduation, resplendent in his gray uniform. In the story, the general was probably a foot soldier in the War Between the States . . . he couldn't remember. Actually, he couldn't remember the war at all. Nor could he remember the Spanish-American War, in which he had lost a son. . . . He couldn't remember the son. People were always asking him "a dreary black procession of questions about the past," but he had no use for history. "To his mind, history was con-

71

nected with processions, and life with parades, and he liked parades."

The story was actually inspired by a slightly more bizarre real event in August 1951 in Milledgeville. Then, a one-hundred-six-year-old "general" (referred to as the "Kissing General") witnessed the graduation at Georgia State College for Women, not of his granddaughter but of his wife, aged sixty-four. The wife had been working on her B.S. degree for thirty years, and the occasion was filled with good fun. The general had been put up in the old Governor's Mansion, now the home of the college president, and the next morning it was pointed out that Sherman had slept in the same room.

"I just wish he'd been there last night," the general remarked. "He would have sure had a hot reception."

In some ways, the clipping in the *Macon Telegraph,* which no doubt caught Flannery O'Connor's eye, had a better ending than hers—with its characteristic dark Catholic vision of death.

"The last time we saw the General, walking across the campus, toward a big barbeque dinner," the clipping read, "he was still living up to his motto: I never let a pretty girl go by without a kiss."

Naturally, one cannot always count on the accuracy of the reporting on this subject in Middle Georgia. In 1937, for example, the *Milledgeville Times* wrote that the issuance of a three-cent commemorative stamp portraying Sherman's face caused a considerable stir in the town, where Sherman "burned many homes." The lone surviving Confederate veteran in Milledgeville was predictably solicited for his reaction and pronounced Sherman not only an unfit subject for such a stamp but for history books as well. The newspaper also reported a *national* debate over the appropriateness of such commemoration, but the sting was mitigated somewhat in Milledgeville by the simultaneous issue of a Robert E. Lee stamp, worth four cents.

In Milledgeville, I sought out the dean of Civil War historians, Dr. James C. Bonner, a charming gentleman of seventy-nine years, who had written extensively on the March to the Sea and who, by his own admission, had spent much of his career defending General Sherman. Now retired from Georgia College, Dr. Bonner is the very soul of Deep South courtesy; it is probably his courtly mien that has led many of his countrymen to overlook his assault on Sherman mythology.

On the evening we spent together, Dr. Bonner was mildly incensed by the television report on the "sparing" of the Madison mansions. Many killed and many houses burned in Milledgeville? Fact: only two houses were destroyed, one belonging to Judge Iverson Harris, who had urged planters to burn everything upon which the Federal Army might subsist, the other destroyed after a feisty Irish gardener had fired upon the approaching troops. In the ensuing skirmish, the ill-starred foreigner became the only known fatality. Even the cotton warehouses went untouched in Milledgeville, probably because they were owned by Northerners and Irishmen. The penitentiary did burn, but Dr. Bonner lays the deed to inmates who were trying to cover their escape. Actually, Sherman would have been justified in burning the place, since it was manufacturing Joe Brown pikes (the Civil War spear). The female inmate who was responsible for the arson was later caught plying an ancient trade among the Federal invaders.

Many raped? In all Dr. Bonner's research he found only one documented case of rape, the pitiful case of a woman who went mad afterwards. Clearly, rape is not the sort of thing that would be documented in those times. When the crime obtained, its victims were overwhelmingly black, and its incidence was exaggerated by Southern writers. A South Carolina novelist of the time, William Gilmore Simms, for example, represented the prevailing view: "Regiments in successive relays, subjected scores of these poor wretches [black women] to the torture of their embraces, and—but we dare not further pursue the subject. There are some horrors which the historian dare not pursue—which the painter dare not delineate. They both drop the curtain over crimes which humanity bleeds to contemplate.''

Why has the embroidery upon the Sherman severities, as awful as the reality was, remained so vivid?

"Perhaps it's because people have a sentimental attachment to that romantic vision as they think it existed," Dr. Bonner replied, "and it contrasts with the drab reality of the present—something they may be ashamed of to some extent.''

In this, Sherman has become the scapegoat.

But Bonner laments the loss of the old symbols. If the Confederate flag has become a symbol of racism to blacks, their interpretation is inaccurate, he feels.

"The flag is the symbol of a gallant army, fighting for what it believed in, right or wrong. It was adored by many people and has a highly sentimental place in their thinking.''

"Dixie," too, is nearly gone. Composed in New York by a Yankee named Daniel Decatur Emmett, who was one of America's first and greatest blackfaced minstrels, the tune was called by Abraham Lincoln one of the best he ever heard, and the president asked the band to play it when he heard the news of Lee's surrender to Grant at Appomattox. But because today it causes blacks "unhappiness," it was dropped from the repertoire of college bands at the University of Georgia and Georgia Tech in the early 1970s. In 1975, students at the University of Georgia launched a noisy campaign to have the band leader fired for dropping "Dixie," but the president of the university said he would no more force a band leader to play a certain song than he would force a history professor to assign a certain book. The issue, said the president, was academic freedom. And in April 1983, the last pocket of Confederate symbolism was whipped out. At the University of Mississippi, the Stars and Bars had for decades been the school flag, "Dixie" the fight song, and "Colonel Rebel" the mascot. But after a noisy and well-publicized confrontation with black students, university officials wistfully furled the flag and took Emmett's air away from the university band.

"Music is music, not politics," Dr. Bonner said sadly. "I'm sorry to see it go."

◊ ◊ ◊

As I traveled through Middle Georgia, I searched small county libraries for the literature of Sherman's march. As they were experienced by white planters, particularly women, the horrors dominate the books. The diaries of women seethe with passion about their ordeal, as they extol the virtues of the lost civilization. Along with Jefferson Davis's, these feminine narratives are the wellspring of the Sherman bitterness as well as the most florid treatment of the Lost Cause as noble cause. Nevertheless, the image of the isolated, helpless, heroic victim is not all-encompassing. In Macon, toward the end of the war, for example, when sheeting sold at five dollars a yard and corn meal at three to five dollars a bushel, women, very different from Southern womanhood of lore, took to the streets. The *Macon Telegraph* described how a mob of "Amazons," hundreds of wives and widows of soldiers, dressed in tattered shawls and men's coats, armed with fishing poles, brooms, and "woman's only weapon, her tongue," administered tongue-lashings to the "extortioners" and browbeat them into giving over the bare necessities of life.

If the horrors dominate, then touching stories of slave loyalty to their white masters run a close second . . . but loyalty is usually associated with the recovery of valuable property. In the history of Washington County, Georgia, we learn of the slave who begged the invaders to spare his

mistress's "pianer," and then, "with the help of other negroes who loved their white folks," hid the instrument,
covered with quilts and blankets, in the swamp until their
masters returned. In the history of Jefferson County, one
reads that until the "uncivil war" came along, never in all
of human enterprise had such tender feeling existed between the races.

The feeling between slaves and their owners was like the depen-
dent trust and love of children, combined with the protecting care
for their white folks. The white family was responsible for the
food and clothing and medical attention of the slaves; religious
services were conducted by themselves, sometimes by white
ministers. The slaves, in turn, gave love and service to their
white folks. This was demonstrated after Sherman's march to the
sea, when but for these faithful servitors, many a child . . . at the
"big house" would have suffered more; for negroes have an
uncanny way of finding things to eat, and they shared it all liberally with their mistress and her children, leaving their own family
to get what was left.

In a book of reminiscences about Burke County called *A
Lost Acadia,* the tale of Jacob Walker is related. Now,
Jacob had been entrusted with the family silver as the Federal troops approached, and he hid it in an unused well at
his plantation, Ivanhoe. Entering Ivanhoe was none other
than Judson Kilpatrick, the dreaded bantam general, who
commanded Sherman's five thousand cavalrymen, and who
is said to have been such a hard rider that he wore out over
two thousand horses on the March to the Sea; to him many
of the worst abuses against Southern civilians were attributed. According to *A Lost Acadia,* "Kilpatrick, having
possibly in his baggage wagon still space for a few more
sets of family treasure, took occasion in a private interview
with Jacob to inquire where the family silver could be
found." But faithful Jacob, "believing that even the law of
absolute truthfulness had its limitations in war times," said
it had all gone to Augusta with Massa. Poor Jacob hap-

pened that day to be wearing gold shirt studs which had been given to him by his young master (who "on the bloody slope of Malvern Hill . . . went down to death gallantly bearing the regimental colours"), and "the gleam and glitter that shone from the negro's brawny breast" was noticed. "While the raiders were earnest advocates of 'free silver' . . . they were in no way adverse to the 'double standard' when the occasion offered." But sly Jacob convinced the officer that the studs were brass, and the disappointed officer turned away, not "wishing to go off the gold standard."

At the Macon chapter of the Georgia Historical Society, I acquired for six dollars the handsome leatherbound volume containing the legend of *Eneas Africanus*, which is privately printed upon toothed, pastel paper and continues to have a brisk sale. Eneas, a "fast-vanishing type . . . dear to the hearts of Southerners young and old" also was entrusted with the family silver, particularly a silver Bride's Cup, but he was dispatched with a bag of Confederate money onto the open road in a rickety wagon pulled by a flea-bitten mare called Lady Chain, before Kilpatrick could arrive. Eneas was destined to wander the South for seven years, from Mississippi to North Carolina, in search of his master. He finally made his way back to Louisville, Georgia, in 1872, somewhat the richer, wearing a silk hat and a flapping linen duster, and he found his master, the major. The reunion was warm. So grateful was the major to get back his silver Bride's Cup that he let Eneas keep the bagful of Confederate money. In the portrait, says the author, in the frontispiece, are Southerners who are "so kind of heart, tolerant, and appreciative of the humor and pathos of the Negro's life. Eneas would have been arrested in any country other than the South. In the South he could have traveled his life out as a guest of his white folks. Is the story true? Everyone says it is."

These touching stories are the underpinning of the noble

cause, and in their number and diversity and stamina, they show how far Ronald Reagan will have to go to convince many that Vietnam was a noble cause. As with Vietnam longings, the Civil War romances are difficult to square with the more professional accounts, such as Dr. Bonner's, of jubilant throngs of freedmen in Milledgeville. By the time Sherman's army reached the state capital, thousands of liberated slaves followed in its train. This was a matter of great concern to Sherman, for military and moral reasons. He had emphasized speed and mobility, and he could ill afford to concern himself with the feeding of so many "useless mouths." Moreover, in a point which Dr. Bonner put delicately in his work, but more bluntly to me, Sherman was deeply concerned with the effect on his troops of so many black women within reach.

In a spectacle that was often repeated, Sherman addressed a large crowd of merry blacks from the second story of the Humphries House in Milledgeville. He pleaded with them to stay on the plantations, rather than slow his army. But here, too, history intersects with folklore, and it is difficult to ascertain where truth lies. "Finish the story!" a staunch South Carolina patriot urged me later. "He told them: 'Stay on the plantations . . . for they will soon be yours!' "

It is difficult for me to imagine Sherman saying such a thing, unless he was again plying psychological warfare. For the central irony of his position as the great liberator lies in his profound racism. To explain, I must go back in time to his life before the Civil War. Sherman had three extended stays in the South (Florida, 1841; Charleston, 1842 to 1846; and Louisiana, 1859 to 1860). His two years in Louisiana were among his happiest years, and it is said that he had picked out a magnolia tree under which he hoped to be buried. He had assumed the superintendency of the Louisiana Military Seminary of Learning and Military Academy, which would later become Louisiana State University. A marker to Sherman's presidency is still on the L. S. U. campus.

During his Louisiana period, Sherman had endeavored to stay aloof from the slavery question, but his views were naturally a matter of intense interest. His brother, John Sherman, was then a candidate for Speaker of the U.S. House of Representatives and was perceived in the South as the abolition candidate pitted against a Virginia rival. Once at a dinner in the governor's mansion the question of slavery arose, and this time Sherman could not hide. He denied being an abolitionist and denied that his brother was one. The severest criticism he could muster against the institution of slavery was that the legal condition of slaves should be brought "more near the status of human beings under all Christian and civilized governments." Domestic slaves, he complimented his audience, "were probably better treated than any slaves on earth," but field hands had a far harsher lot, depending upon the temperament of their overseers.

Sherman's solution? He would forbid the separation of slave families, and he would repeal the injunction against teaching slaves to read and write, for that, he told his eager listeners, only reduced their value as property. His mildly reformist remarks received the polite applause of the guests.

Sherman's allegiance to the Union, therefore, had nothing to do with the "dreadfully excited" question of slavery. Rather, he feared that the Southern drift toward secession presaged anarchy, proving the European commentators right in suggesting that the American Constitution was a mere "rope of sand which would break at the first pressure." His actual decision to leave the South was prompted in January 1861, when rebels marched on the Federal arsenal in Baton Rouge, compelled its surrender without a fight, and then distributed the arms to state arsenals. Among those arsenals was Sherman's seminary, which had been designated a central arsenal upon its founding. When over two thousand muskets arrived, packed in boxes with their *U.S.* markings scratched out, Sherman considered himself a receiver of stolen goods, and he resigned.

Sherman, thus, departed the South as a jilted and disappointed lover. Ambivalence was his strongest emotion. The South's grace and softness engaged his affections; at the same time he bridled at its seediness, at the fatuousness and pretense of its upper class. This affection and this ire were crucial to his actions during the war, I think, for love/hate can become a far more devastating mixture than hate alone. Sherman was leaving on a high, even noble, point of principle—that secession was anarchy—and this made him all the more dangerous to the South. But it had nothing to do with slavery.

Just how torn he was is demonstrated by the letters he wrote at the time of his resignation and a few days before Louisiana seceded from the Union. To the governor of Louisiana, Thomas O. Moore, he wrote that "as long as a fragment of [the Constitution] survives," he preferred to maintain an allegiance to the Union. In a private note to the governor, which he attached to his official resignation, he closed with the words: "I entertain the kindest feelings towards all and would leave the State with much regret; only in great events, we must choose, one way or the other."

Two days before secession was proclaimed by the legislature, Moore responded: "You can not regret more than I do the necessity which deprives us of your services, and you will bear with you the respect, confidence, and admiration of all who have been associated with you."

And a week after secession, still in Alexandria, Louisiana, and dutifully transferring public property to authorities that were now in official rebellion, Sherman wrote to Braxton Bragg, who was soon to become a Confederate general: "Now that I can not be compromised by political events, I will so shape my course as best to serve the institution which has a strong hold on my affections and respect."

Throughout his *Memoirs,* Sherman's view of the blacks as an amusing, poignant subrace shows through. He took particular delight in relating ethnic jokes. He chortled at the Negro's "simple" character and was amused by how they flocked to him shouting praises of "de Lawd and Abrum Lincom." Near Cheraw, South Carolina, for example, map in hand, Sherman encountered a slave on the road and asked directions. As he relates it in his *Memoirs,* the conversation went this way:

" 'Him lead to Cheraw, master.' "

" 'Is it a good road, and how far?' "

" 'A very good road, and eight or ten miles.' "

" 'Any guerillas?' "

" 'Oh no, master, dey is gone two days ago; you could have played cards on their coat tails, dey was in sich a hurry!' "

"I was on my Lexington horse, who was very handsome and restive, so I made signal to my staff to follow, as I proposed to go without escort. . . . General Barry took up the questions about the road and asked the same Negro what he was doing there. He answered:

" 'Dey say Massa Sherman will be along soon.' "

" 'Why,' said General Barry, 'that was General Sherman you were talking to.' "

"The poor negro, almost in the attitude of prayer, exclaimed, 'De great God! Just look at his horse!' "

"He ran up and trotted by my side for a mile or so and gave me all the information he possessed, but he seemed to admire the horse more than the rider."

With a slight adjustment of the knob, I can imagine Sherman appreciating the tale of Jacob Walker or the "humor and pathos" of Eneas Africanus. The idea of freedmen presiding over the great plantations of Georgia would not have pleased him, and his sour solution for the blacks would soon become apparent in Savannah. In any event freedmen rarely respected his request to stay at home. Even after the "massacre at Ebenezer Creek," they were not discouraged. Then, at the broad and swift stream east of Milledgeville, Union troops pulled up their pontoon bridges immediately after the last soldier crossed at nighttime, leaving thousands of sleeping freedmen on the bank behind. When they awoke to find themselves slaves again, amid pursuing Confederate cavalrymen, many panicked and tried to swim the swollen stream, drowning. "Others may have been cruelly killed by (the Confederates)," Sherman wrote in his memoirs, "but this is mere supposition. . . . General Jeff. C. Davis (the Union commander at the scene) was strictly a soldier, and doubtless hated to have his wagons and columns encumbered by these poor negroes, for whom we all felt sympathy." Savannah would become a refuge for more than fifty thousand blacks when Sherman liberated the city.

❖ ❖ ❖

From Milledgeville, I struck out for Louisville, following the route of Sherman's left wing. I passed through Washington County, which proudly claimed to have raised more military companies for the Confederacy than any county in Georgia, and through Sandersville, whose courthouse Sherman had surgically taken out after Wheeler's retreating cavalrymen fired from it upon his approaching columns. Not fifty yards beyond the new courthouse, the inevitable row of ante-bellum mansions begin, most in a somewhat timeworn woebegone condition, proving the maxim that neglect and moisture and termites devastated the Acadian dream far more than Sherman ever could.

Traveling east, the country opens up from the piney woods into long vistas across well-tended fields. Giant seventeen-hundred-pound roll bales dot the landscape, enlarging the scale, as if this were the land of some superspecies. By my attention to the herds of cattle, the peach and pecan orchards, the buff fields of protein-rich soybeans drying in the November wind, I could tell I had begun to look covetously at the countryside the way Sherman's men did.

The racial landscape seems to change as well. With the first Spanish moss and the first narcotic chinaberry trees outside Louisville, here in the heart of the old Cotton Belt, the solitary shanty in the midst of a vast, friable plowland becomes a common sight. It is as if Steinbeck's and Sherman's grapes of wrath have come together on this terrain.

I was heading into the region of Cudjoe Fry's Insurrection of 1870. In years past, it has been cited and disputed as the sole exception to the theory that slaves were generally amenable to their condition of servitude in the Old South. The slaves never took advantage of innumerable opportunities to revolt against their masters once the Civil War was underway, so the theory runs, and had it not been for the Union liberators they would have happily continued in slavery.

If one consults the treatment of the Cudjoe Rebellion by E. M. Coulter in the *Georgia Historical Quarterly,* it can be deduced that Cudjoe Fry was a "wily, clever scoundrel" who aroused the illiterate "black mobs" of Jefferson County (in 1870 outnumbering whites two to one) to a frenzy over the jailing of a man who had shot a stray mule. When the whites went to church ten miles out of Louisville one Sunday morning, "General" Fry marched into town with sixty armed followers, freed the mule shooter, and then "drunk with victory" and "damning the white man promiscuously," cavorted about for a time before "melting" back into the countryside. So much for the Insurrection. Fry was arrested eventually by Federal troops (much to the delight of E. M. Coulter), tried, and sentenced to twenty years. Coulter's conclusions sounds much like the Southern defense of segregation in the 1960s:

[The Cudjoe Fry Story] is a tribute to the self-control of the white population so clearly shown under provocations that could hardly have been more intense. Every element was present for a bloody race conflict which might well have gone beyond the limits of what could be called a riot and might have developed into a savage war of extermination. It showed a discipline and a highly developed regard for law and order under government. And it should not be forgotten that the people turned to Federal soldiers for protection, who only a half dozen years previously burned and ravaged their way through Georgia, through Jefferson County, and even through Louisville, left by them in ashes as they departed. . . . The Stars and Stripes looked beautiful again, and the Federal soldiers could now be trusted as protectors.

In historic Louisville, I had come to see the Old Slave Market, built in 1758, which marks the center of town, for this is the only memorial I know in the South which celebrates not the virtues, but the chief vice of the Lost Cause. In fairness, it is a structure eminently worth saving: an open-air, shingled pavilion, about thirty feet square, crowned with a cupola of interesting design, which houses a bell. But somehow, as the manicured centerpiece of a rural farming county of the Deep South, it grates. Local residents try as best they can to explain it away. I caught Jim Horton, the editor of the *News and Farmer*, who had dropped into the office in his deer-hunting togs on his way out to his shelter. To the whites of the county, he said, the monument is "history"; to the blacks it represents "what they came from." That seemed to take the bite out of it. But such explanations are not swallowed by all. In 1971, after the suspicious hanging of a young black in the county jail, Hosea Williams of the Southern Christian Leadership Conference came in to protest and held his demonstrations around the Old Slave Market. During several nights of tension, someone threw kerosene-soaked rags into the structure, trying to burn it down. Sheriff Zollie Compton had to post guards around it for a few days, while, as the *News and Farmer* reported it, "mobs of blacks", ruled the streets, provoking a "near riot." It was as if Cudjoe Fry had returned.

In the Jefferson County Court House, I sought out Sheriff Compton to inquire into his efforts at historic preservation. He turned out to be a fine specimen of a well-known American type, probably as fast vanishing as Eneas Africanus, a lot closer to real life, and just as much maligned. Slouching his plentiful frame in a high-back, claw-foot chair, he leaned over regularly and let fly into the spittoon next to the wall. The maneuver was handled with such precision that one felt like cheering. He tried hard to remember the year of "the disturbance" and received varying guesses from several deputies who sat around. Finally, he pulled from his desk a fistful of yellowed Polaroid photographs, showing a few blurry figures bearing rudimentary signs of protest, and there on the back was the very date. The line "we don't have any trouble with 'em now" rolled off his lips the way it has no doubt for the last twenty years, and I had to admire his lack of self-consciousness. From a call he took from an assistant coach at Georgia Tech, the riot that concerned him now was the upcoming one at the Georgia–Georgia Tech football game that weekend, and he was beginning to think he might just pass the game up, for the first time in many years. It was getting too rough up there, and those "Georgia hoodlums" wanted to kill every opponent.

"I'm afraid I'll get into another fight," he confided, "and I'm getting too old for that."

As for the Old Slave Market, he wasn't exactly sure when the town had changed its name to The Market House, but it probably was in the year after "the trouble." The town manager of Louisville would later confirm this, and argue to me that "Market House" was more appropriate than "Old Slave Market" anyway, because in the old days vegetables and earthenware and shelves were also sold along with slaves at the facility.

Savannah 5

IN WALKING the lovely squares of this city, one soon realizes that Savannah's historical fixations are with the colonial period rather than the Civil War, and this comes as a refreshing break from the seemingly endless parade of Confederate statues, foisted upon the Southern towns by the United Daughters of the Confederacy in the early twentieth century. General Oglethorpe suddenly commands the scene. There are, to be sure, the well-preserved Civil War sites: Fort Pulaski, Fort McAllister, and Fort Jackson outside of town; the Oglethorpe Club, where Sherman had his headquarters, and the Green House, where he stayed downtown; and the lesser-known places for the aficionados: the Confederate breastworks at the Savannah Golf Club, and the overgrown earthworks at Causten's Bluff, which is now a dump, a lover's lane, and a treasured spot for dirt bikers, who find the steep sandy grades of the fortifications a challenge.

Once again, the relevance of history is not easily encased in glass or cast in bronze. By reaching the sea, Sherman had accomplished his strategic objective of making contact with the navy, which for most of the war had effectively blockaded the Southern coast. (Savannah had remained in Southern hands, protected by what Sherman called a perfect chain of five forts.) Militarily, Sherman considered his march a mere shift of base, ensuring resupply from ocean frigates, and he assigned a fraction of importance to it when he later compared it to the forthcoming campaign through South Carolina. He presented Savannah as his Christmas present to President Lincoln and would consolidate his gains for a month, as he planned his next climactic move.

Here, military and civilian problems united in revealing ways. Sherman was visited by Secretary of War Edwin Stanton, a fellow Ohioan, whose complexity exceeded even Sherman's, and whose agenda, it soon became clear, was to explore Sherman's political ambitions and racial attitudes. Sherman had been warned privately by the Union chief of staff, H. W. Halleck, of rumors circulating in Washington of the commander's supposed "criminal dislike" for "the inevitable Sambo," an impression based largely on the episode at Ebenezer Creek, where Sherman's troops had left so many freedmen stranded without a bridge. Halleck urged Sherman to concentrate anew on opening avenues of escape for the slaves, suggesting that the rice fields and cotton plantations around Savannah might make an appropriate refuge for the ex-slaves.

In Sherman's racial views, Stanton sensed a political weakness, for suddenly racial bigotry was out of step with

Republican politics. The talk of the general as a possible presidential candidate troubled the war secretary, and here was an area where Stanton could impute disloyalty to Sherman over the direction of administration policy. Savannah became the opening gambit in Stanton's strategy to undercut Sherman over the Negro question, but to Sherman their discussion was perfectly appropriate as one of many areas where civilian and military preoccupations were inseparable.

Their conversation lasted many hours. Sherman proposed that the sea islands south of Charleston, as well as the abandoned rice fields along the St. John's River in Florida, be made into reservations for blacks, where no white man would be permitted to reside. Stanton seemed to egg him on. The secretary requested Sherman to commit his apartheid plan to paper. Rather than sense a trap, contemptuous as he was of politicians generally, Sherman considered the request a compliment. With the plan on paper, Stanton still interposed no objection, and Sherman took the silence as approval, publishing the plan in an official order. By his order, he sought to solve his greatest social worry: that the Lincoln administration intended not only to free the slaves, but to enfranchise them, thus, without preparation or qualification, transforming them into "political capital."

What war museum can grapple with such ironies?

In 1859, Sherman had said: "I would not if I could abolish or modify slavery."

As a young soldier in South Carolina, he had written: "As far as I can judge, [Negroes] feel very lightly indeed the chains of their bondage we read of. . . . I am no advocate of slavery as a means of wealth or national advancement, but I know that the idea of oppression and tyranny that some people consider the necessary accompaniment of slavery is a delusion of their own brain."

89

In 1860, he wrote that the black "must amalgamate or be destroyed. Two such races cannot live in harmony, save as master and slave."

And in his attitude toward Indians, his racism and his notion of "counterinsurgency" were joined. As a young soldier in the mangrove swamps of Florida (rather than Vietnam), during the rebellion of the Seminoles, he described a process that could easily be advanced a century to the mangrove swamps of Indochina.

An army supposed to be strong enough is sent, seeks, and encounters the enemy at a place selected by the latter, gets a few hundred killed. The Indians retreat, scatter, and are safe. This may be repeated ad infinitum. The best officer is selected to direct the affairs of the army—comes to Florida, exposes himself, does all he can, gets abused by all, and is glad to get out of the scrape. Treaties, truces, and armistices have been and are still being tried, with what success is notorious.

Eventually, that counterinsurgency problem was solved by the genocide of the Seminoles.

More than thirty years later, after the Civil War, the attention of the nation turned to the pacification of the American West. Sherman viewed the Indians as aborigines and indicated what his attitude toward official revenge for Indian resistance would be. "If I were in command, I would act with vindictive earnestness against the Sioux, even to the extermination of men, women, and children." By 1870, he was in command of the West. After a siege of an Indian village in April of that year resulted in the death of 173 Piegans, 53 of which were women and children, and the death of only one American soldier, and the *New York Times* was decrying it as a massacre, Sherman dismissed it as an incident of war. "Did we cease to throw shells into Vicksburg or Atlanta because women and children were there?" he asked rhetorically. And after a Modoc chief rose up at a peace parley in April 1873 and killed Gen. E. R. S. Canby (who had captured Mobile, Alabama, at the very end of the Civil War as Sherman was negotiating at the Bennett Place), Sherman ordered an attack on the Modocs "so strong and persistent that their fate may be commensurate with their crime. You will be fully justified in their utter extermination."

Throughout his command in the West, Sherman encouraged the wanton slaughter of buffalo by professional hunters. He believed that if the bison were killed off, the pacification of the Plains Indians would quickly follow. It was the Sherman seed for the Agent Orange and Agent Blue programs of food deprivation in Vietnam.

His Savannah plan, therefore, simply mirrored an inflexible bigotry that had not altered through his campaign which freed the slaves.

In the well-preserved Civil War forts around Savannah, several things catch the eye. At Fort Jackson, I found the first and only acknowledgment of the presence of blacks in the war. It was a display of the uniforms worn by the First South Carolina Volunteers, a black unit enlisted in the Federal Army in Hilton Head in April 1862. And at Fort McAllister, I found one display of weaponry relevant to the modern state of the art. During the War of Rebellion, as it is known in the official records, the rudimentary "land torpedo," sometimes called "infernal machines," now called land mines, received considerable development, particularly by the Confederate Army which was so often in a defensive posture.

On the outskirts of Savannah, one incident happened which will echo for any Vietnam infantryman. Sherman came upon soldiers gathered around a "handsome" officer lying by the road with his foot blown off. The officer had stepped on a mine planted in the road, and the ugly sight threw Sherman into a raging storm. There being no resistance at the time, and no warning having been given beforehand, Sherman considered the act an atrocity—not war, but murder. Promptly he ordered Confederate prisoners brought forward, provided them with picks and shovels, and had them walk the road. The spectacle that followed amused Sherman, as the Rebels first begged to be excused and then stepped gingerly down the road.

But, as always in war, Sherman's outrage was selective about the distinction between war and murder, for he, too, had been planting mines in underbrush along the railroad as he tore it up, to discourage the Confederates from relaying the track. When the enemy used mines, it was criminal; when he used them, it was hellish warfare. Whatever justifications he might later devise, Sherman's ethics textbook at West Point did not ring in his head: once a rule of war is breached by one side, it invites breach by all, resulting in the subversion of the rule itself and making war that much more horrible. What ethical difference might exist between the Savannah episode and Sherman's policy is hard to discern, unless it be that the maiming of a "handsome officer" was somewhat different to him than the killing of a slave in a Confederate pioneer corps.

In the gulf between official orders and unofficial encouragement to "punish" rebellion, ethical standards for "civilized warfare" were relentlessly withering away. This was Sherman's major contribution to total war, not the hardships he visited upon the families of Georgia. If war is made synonymous with hell, what point is there in standards of civilized behavior? Ethics in hell? The very notion is absurd. It is the philosophy of Sherman, and his selective outrage, rather than the locust desolation he visited upon the land, especially South Carolina, that leads conceptually straight to Dresden, Hiroshima, and Vietnam. By the time he captured Savannah, the standards of proportional response and discriminating protection of civilians had nearly ceased to exist. He had encountered virtually no resistance, and yet he had laid to waste a thirty-mile swath. When a rash Confederate ventured a shot on his trains from a courthouse, the courthouse was burned. When a lady burned her corncrib, she lost her house. The "proportionality" of that retaliation is roughly the same, if geometrically less, as hostile fire from a jungle rifle being greeted by a B-52 strike.

As for discrimination, Sherman expressly set out to make Georgia howl. But neither states nor soldiers howl; civilians do, particularly women. It took someone who knew the South and Southern pieties well to understand just how effective making war on women could be. The problem with historical writing about the end of the Civil War is that its language is grandiosely and deliberately imprecise. Sherman would break "the will of the South" to fight, but his technique was to demoralize the women back home, and let that have its effect on the soldiers at the front. Similarly, the American goal in Vietnam was to break the will of the Viet Cong insurgency, and General Westmoreland was ready to try any technique of "unconventional warfare" that might have a prayer of discouraging the rebels. To this end, a battalion was devised known as SOG, Study and Observation Group, but also known as "the joint unconventional warfare task force." To its historical credit go the provocative maneuvers of the U.S. Navy destroyers *Maddox* and *C. Turner Joy* which resulted in the Gulf of Tonkin episode in 1964, and small unit operations in Laos, which were consistently covered up and disclaimed to the American people. Of the SOG operations, General Westmoreland wrote in his memoirs: "Few associated with [SOG] held any real hope for a conclusive result . . . [but] in a war that as much as any in history pitted will against will, it was worth a try."

The *idea* of discrimination was dead by the time Sherman

reached Savannah. His official order to the troops not to enter dwellings or commit trespass was hollow, unfortified by consistent action to back it up. Article I, Paragraph 52, of the *Articles of War,* at the time, made it a capital crime for a soldier to leave his post to pillage, but to Sherman this had long since become an old idea. In a letter twenty years after the war, his lack of remorse glares:

The Rebels wanted us to detach a division here, a brigade there, to protect their families and property while they were fighting. . . . This is a one-sided game of war, and many of us . . . kind-hearted, just and manly . . . ceased to quarrel with our own men about such minor things and went in to subdue the enemy, leaving minor depredations to be charged up to the account of rebels who had forced us into war, and who deserved all they got and *worse.*

What influence Sherman's techniques might have had on succeeding generations of American soldiers is hard to define, but here was a precedent for trivializing, and thereby sanctioning plunder. Sherman stood for the practice of fobbing off this behavior on the enemy as a tool of psychological warfare.

If the idea of discrimination was dead at Savannah, all pretense of protecting private property did not dissolve entirely until Sherman moved north into South Carolina. Across Georgia, the burning was generally confined to military objectives, and was, certainly by the standards of Hanoi or Beirut, surgical. The myth notwithstanding, the instances of rape and wanton killing were virtually nonexistent. What in popular idiom is known as Sherman's looting applies primarily to the official foraging, which was fully justified even under the Victorian standards of warfare, and was an absolute necessity in preventing the "Moscow" disaster which Jefferson Davis predicted. (Later, Sherman would quote the Duke of Wellington's maxim that an army moves not upon its legs, but upon its belly.) But if over a period of five weeks an army is authorized to appropriate everything it can eat, and signaled that its mission is largely psychological, a mob spirit develops. If the soldier is told to requisition the widow's pigs and burn her cotton gin, how much more of an outrage can it be to take her silver goblet? And if he and his buddies steal many goblets over time and hear no rebuke, the effect is obvious. Georgia howled as the last standards dissolved, but South Carolina would shriek.

"The truth is," Sherman wrote his superior from Savannah, "the whole army is burning with an insatiable desire to wreak vengeance upon South Carolina. I almost tremble at her fate, but feel that she deserves all that seems in store for her."

While Sherman pondered these awesome thoughts, he luxuriated in the finest mansion in Savannah, the home of Charles Green, an English cotton merchant. Green had offered his house to the Union general ostensibly to spare a native the embarrassment and humiliation of harboring their conqueror, but he may also have had in mind saving his cotton bales from appropriation. The ploy did not work.

The house on Bull Street is today the parish house of St. John's Episcopal Church. It was built in the 1850s for $93,000 and purchased by the church in the 1950s for about $40,000, undoubtedly a record of some sort, before downtown Savannah began its remarkable restoration and became fashionable. At one point in my tour of the Green house, the guide leveled me with a profound stare and remarked, "Sherman did no damage to the house while he stayed here."

The pastor of St. John's is the ebullient Rev. John Ralston, who for some years taught Shakespeare at the University of the South and edited the *Sewannee Review*.

When he came to St. John's and took up residence in the rectory (Sherman's horse stable), he ingratiated himself with his new congregation by boasting that his first act was to play "Dixie" so loud on the organ that Sherman would forever be exorcised from the church. The crowd-pleasing boast would soon give the Reverend's humility and sense of irony a test. In July 1981, in a large church wedding, Reverend Ralston married a lovely Savannah woman, Helen Harris, to a mild-mannered Atlanta investment banker, with a soft, adopted Southern accent. The mother of the bride was the head of the local chapter of the United Daughters of the Confederacy. The groom's name was William Tecumseh Sherman IV. SHERMAN RETURNS blazed the headline across the society page of one Savannah paper. LATEST SHERMAN MARCH ENDS AT ALTAR read another. The Atlanta paper put a picture in its "People" column not of young Bill Sherman, but of craggy old General Sherman, as it took note of the droll Savannah event. Bill Sherman, it turns out, has learned far more from his in-laws about his ancestry (some would call it a real earful—all good-natured, of course), than he ever did from his own family.

On a bright Sunday morning I drove down to Fort McAllister, not so much to look at its well-preserved Confederate earthworks (which Sherman's troops overran in handsome fashion after a fifteen-minute assault), as to meet its supervisor, Roger Durham. Along the way I stopped at the Savannah Golf Club, which stoutly claims to be the cradle of golf in America, with records dating back to 1794. Its interest both for the historian and the golfer derives from the Confederate breastworks and gun emplacements which form its hazards and bunkers, lending the course a difficulty beyond a drive-and-pitch course that might normally be expected here in "the marshes of Chatham." The curiosity of the fortifications is also said to have given rise to the phrase "Civil War golfer": out in 61 and back in 65. That was one story on this trip I was prepared to accept as gospel truth.

At the course, the chipper Mr. Kayton Smith, an honorary member and unofficial historian of the club, piled me in an electric cart, handed me his treasured dog-eared photographs of the course in 1930, and drove me out to old No. 8. Once a blind shot off the tee, the driver faced a twenty-foot mound dead ahead and often found himself at its sandy base flailing away with a mashie-niblick far from the green. From there, it was on to the hole which used to be a challenging par five dog-leg around Hardee's cannoneers, but lamentably that mound had been removed, and finally to old No. 1, where you drove off a thirty-foot emplacement, making it "mighty hard to make a bad first drive."

At Fort McAllister, I was looking forward to meeting Roger Durham, for among the younger clique of Civil War "interpreters," Roger has quite a reputation. At thirty-five, he ran several historical installations before he came to McAllister four years ago. As a safety officer and artillery commander in Dent Myers's Georgia Division, he is an energetic reënacter and was preparing to restage the assault on the fort when I went to see him. With ambitions to be a writer, he labors away in his spare time on a novel about a blockade runner whose escapades during THE WAR provide the stuff, he says, of tragicomedy.

From there, his story grew strange. A native of Illinois, with distant lineage to Abraham Lincoln on the Hanks side, he attended college in Wisconsin. He is a Vietnam veteran whose tour was at Dong Ba Thin, a small helicopter base near Cam Ranh Bay.

What was going on here? Why would a Vietnam veteran want to throw himself so enthusiastically into the interpretation of the Civil War, or lose himself in literary pipe-dreams and bygones, or a Yankee take on, so often, the trappings of the Lost Cause?

I was met by a bespectacled, bearded man erect in his bearing, starched in his khaki uniform, clipped and precise in his speech. Soon enough, we were walking the giant earthen fortifications, looking out across the swift-moving Great Ogeechee, trying to imagine the approaching Union ironclad commanded by John Worden who, the year before (March 1862), had fought the CSS *Merrimack* from his *Monitor* off Hampton Roads, Virginia. We cast our eyes across the sturdy marsh grass swamps to Cheve's Rice Mill a mile away, where Sherman had watched the crushing assault through a telescope. As it was a bright Sunday morning, Durham did not tell me the story of John B. Gallie, who lost his head to a union cannon ball on February 1, 1863, and still walks the fort with his head in his hands at night. Halloween was three weeks past.

In his cluttered office, the themes I had heard before reverberated: the precarious business of interpreting the Civil War, and particularly Sherman, for a Southern audience, the constant association of Confederate symbols with racism, the quaint quality of displaying in a nuclear age cannon balls that might tear away an eight-foot-wide divot from an earthwork, the near impossibility of interesting the black visitor in the details of his ancestral liberation. Sherman and slavery were two subjects you can get into an argument over in the blink of an eye.

"Some people don't want to be confused with facts," Durham remarked. "Sometimes it's better to leave them with their illusions. Better to keep your mouth shut than to try to change opinions."

It was not long before I realized that Roger Durham's embrace of the Civil War lay in all the lofty romance of soldiering that he had never felt in Vietnam. It was not the cause of the Confederacy or the Union, but the grand sacrifice and even nobility of the individual soldier that both moved and confused him. In all his Vietnam experience, he confessed, he had met only one American soldier who had the same "belief structure" as the Civil War soldier. With that soldier, Roger had logged many hours on night duty in the tower at Dong Ba Thin, discussing military strategy, not of Vietnam, but of Gettysburg and Verdun. So it was that Durham derived profound pleasure from putting himself in "their place" rather than his own.

His own experience seemed so banal by comparison. He had seriously contemplated exile in Canada, and his decision to join or disconnect had come down to how he felt on the morning he was supposed to report for duty. With an air of self-deprecation he recalled watching a Tab Hunter war movie and finding in it the critical tilt toward stepping across the line the next morning at the local armory. Once in the service, the war had always been a punishment rather than an honor. "Goof off, and I'll send you to Vietnam" is a line that still rings in his head. Once in Vietnam, the officers and the NCOs were the proverbial enemies, not the Viet Cong. The soldier fought for his own survival, not a cause. The prevailing attitude was: do your time, look forward to your R & R, keep your head down, stay out of trouble, get out alive.

How different, how exciting was his vision of the Civil War soldier by contrast.

"In three days, a civil war battle could involve as many casualties as it took ten years to accomplish in Vietnam. In an inferno like Gettysburg, there in the midst of that carnage, knowing the odds were against you, they stood in the front lines, and nobody shirked their duty. Nothing was important but that moment. There was no future, only right now. They got behind one another, felt somehow, they might survive. Tomorrow? They would deal with that tomorrow. And after a battle, they picked up their rifle and moved down the road to the next battle. If it had been me, I'd have said, no, not me, I've done enough. . . . So I find that kind of devotion . . . mystifying.''

His was as romantic a vision of the Civil War soldier as was the experience of the Vietnam soldier discounted. Perhaps romance of the past must always be coupled with contempt for the present. That the romantic impulse for war never occurs to the participants is close to the point Sherman was making in his ''war is hell'' speech in 1880. He was talking not to the ladies, but to his former soldiers.

''The war is away back in the past, and *you* can tell what books can not. When *you* talk, you come down to the practical realities just as they happened. . . . There is many a boy here today who looks on war as all glory, but, boys, it is all hell.''

Was the experience of the Civil War soldier really so different from the Vietnam soldier? Did a profound belief in the cause really keep them all in the ranks?

Sherman himself describes an episode early in the war, parts of which could just as easily have happened in Vietnam. The incident took place in the wake of the Bull Run disaster in July 1861, at which Sherman commanded a brigade with distinction. He had been appalled at the laxity of the Union troops upon the road to the battle, straying continuously as they did to pick blackberries and wade in the streams. A great many of the early recruits had signed up only for a three-month tour, and they suddenly began remembering the exact letter of their contract. In the general chaos after Bull Run, discipline was the overriding concern. The whole military enterprise seemed on the verge of collapse.

One morning, after Sherman had reviewed and dismissed his regiment, near Washington, he found himself near a drawbridge, and there he noticed an officer in a group of ragtag troops.

''Colonel, I am going to New York today. What can I do

for you?'' the captain shouted out to Sherman, as if sending Sherman a box of his beloved cheroots might be appreciated.

"How can you go to New York?'' Sherman snapped. "I do not remember signing a leave for you.''

"No, sir, I do not want a leave. I engaged to serve three months, and have already served more than that time. If the government does not intend to pay me, I can not afford to lose the money. I am a lawyer and have neglected business long enough.''

The blast that greeted this must have started slow and risen to a crescendo. "Captain, this question of your term of service has been submitted to the rightful authority, and the decision published in orders. You are a soldier and must submit to orders till you are properly discharged. If you attempt to leave without orders, it will be mutiny, and I will shoot you like a dog!'' Reaching under his overcoat as if going for his pistol, he shouted, "Go back into the fort now, instantly, and don't dare leave without my consent.''

The captain and the men around him scattered.

Later that day, Lincoln appeared in the vicinity in a carriage, accompanied by Secretary of State William Seward. "We heard you had got over the big scare,'' Lincoln called out to Sherman, "and we thought we would come over and see the boys.''

Sherman wanted no more "hurrahing, no more humbug,'' and he respectfully urged the President to speak to the men in a manner that would induce "cool, thoughtful, hardfighting soldiers.'' Farther on, the troops gathered and Lincoln delivered a somber message, much to Sherman's pleasure. At one point the cheering started, and Lincoln checked it.

"Don't cheer, boys. I confess I rather like it myself, but Colonel Sherman here says it's not military, and I guess we'd better defer to his opinion.''

At another stop, Lincoln spoke again and concluded his

speech with the invitation that any soldier could appeal to him personally if he felt himself wronged. From the crowd, the very captain from New York whom Sherman had earlier upbraided, elbowed his way forward.

"Mr. President," he called out, "I have cause for a grievance. This morning I went to speak to Colonel Sherman, and he threatened to shoot me!"

"Threatened to shoot you?" the President repeated, surprised and stalling.

"Yes, sir, he threatened to shoot me."

Lincoln looked at the captain and then at the colonel. Stooping his frame toward the captain, he said, in what Sherman later described as a "stage whisper," loud enough to be heard by all, "Well, if I were you, and he threatened to shoot, I would not trust him . . . for I believe he would do it!"

The captain disappeared amid the cackles of the troops.

It is said that over 60 percent of the American soldiers who fought in Vietnam either opposed the war or did not understand why it was being fought. To be sure, the reasons for the American Civil War were more easily comprehensible to the common foot soldier. But if the pollsters had been busy then, would they have found the understanding and the support so much greater? To understand is not necessarily to support, but not to understand and to leave the exercise of "duty" on the level of blind obedience to the state is that much more tragic. For me, Stephen Crane's youth remains a point of reference.

South Carolina

CROSS the red Savannah River and the vast wildlife refuge that in 1865 was a grid of rice plantations, I set out for the baronies of Pocotaligo. The Sherman of South Carolina was going to be more grandiose and more terrifying than the Sherman of Georgia: that I sensed very soon. In this Low Country, nobility was once a birthright, enough in itself even without being the heart of a rebellion to get up the dander of a ruffian like Sherman. Around 1700, vast tracts of this land were divided into European feudal categories: a barony or seignory consisted of twelve thousand acres; two baronies made a cassique; four baronies created a landgrave. From this last designation were drawn

the representatives of the upper house of the colonial legislature, and this convocation of notables was conceived as
a political body to fall in status somewhere between the
House of Lords and the House of Commons. The grand
and proud titles of the Carolina aristocracy were designed
to distinguish it from English nobility, and some say this
small class of South Carolinians has been aspiring to that
higher station ever since.

After dark, I reached the fork in the road where appro-
priately the choice was to go north to Columbia or cut east
to Charleston. Sherman had made this spot his first objective, so as to confuse his enemy about his intentions.
Throughout his great march he had conspired to put the
Confederates on "the horns of a dilemma." He had
marched toward Macon and Augusta, intending to go neither place. Now he sent one wing toward Augusta and the
other toward Charleston, with Columbia as his real goal.
After Columbia, he would feint toward Charlotte, North
Carolina, to keep Beauregard's sizeable Confederate force
in place there, before he wheeled his armies east toward
Fayetteville. This "indirect approach" (threatening two
points simultaneously and thereby forcing the enemy to
overextend its resources or abandon territory) is much admired by military strategists.

Near Pocotaligo, somewhere not far from the vanished
villages of Coosawatchie or Garden's Corner or Mac-
Phersonville, where Sherman had been a groomsman in a
fancy wedding several years before the Civil War broke
out, I was searching for a "splendid South Carolina estate"
of the old regime, distinctive for its majestic avenue of
moss-draped live oaks. There, Sherman had slept on the
floor early in the new campaign. It had been a very cold
night in February 1865, and he arose several times to rekin-
dle the fire with a mantel clock and the wreck of a bedstead.
In his *Memoirs,* he would call this the only act of vandalism
he *personally* performed in the whole war, as if a com-

mander of vandals can only be held responsible for the vandalism of his own hand. But to what extent had the policy of punishment made the pattern of atrocity inevitable? It was a question Sherman never addressed in his *Memoirs,* nor had Westmoreland addressed it in his, but this episode at a splendid South Carolina estate was a nineteenth-century version of our My Lai debate about command responsibility.

At a wayside store I encountered a green-eyed man, dressed in the long white robes of an unfamiliar African religious sect, peeling shrimp and watching a pro football game. From him, I learned that the Carolina nobility of this area was not quite what it used to be. To be sure, Cotton Hall still exists, but the owner is never there. At another plantation, the only *working* plantation close by, the owner is a refugee from Batista's Cuba. As for the Tomotley Plantation, once the Tomotley Barony, it does still have a majestic avenue of live oaks, but its owner, once an internationally famous polo player, had recently died. The superior ways of plantation life did not seem to interest my informant much. The name of General Sherman brought a wry, unexplained smile to his lips. Somehow we moved to a topic of more interest to him: how slaves had been harbored by swamp Indians through the generations before the war, and how now you could always pick out the product of the mixture. (Indians near plantations had often received escaped slaves warmly throughout the South, but the natives were not always a threat to the establishment. In the Confederate Park in Fort Mill, South Carolina, for example, there is a monument to the "Red Carolinians," Catawba Indians who fought for the Confederacy.)

Why, my storeowner asked, did I not drive down past Garden's Corner and see the ruins of Sheldon Church?

I had planned to do so, although not necessarily this late at night. Why would Sherman's troops set the torch to a church in the middle of the wilderness? The desecration of temples fell into the forbidden area of "gratuitous barbarities," expressly prohibited in all the contemporary doctrines of military ethics. Such profaning was declared to be not only a crime against civilization but against nature, for it was simple, cruel mischief, with no effect on the outcome of the contest. Even if one can imagine the church being used as a Confederate hospital or a clandestine meeting place for guerillas, or the place of worship for the most recalcitrant slave owner, it is difficult to consider it a legitimate target.

There, in the pitch darkness, amid the live oaks draped with moss, the towering brick columns and the crumbling tabby walls present a strong image. They focused my attention on the point that moving into South Carolina, Sherman's troops had finally stepped over the last ethical boundary. Finally, in South Carolina, reality caught up to myth.

Just how far Sherman was now outside the confines of *proportionality* and *discrimination* is plain from the official correspondence. The chief of staff in Washington was H. W. Halleck, who had himself compiled the standard reference book of the day on military ethics entitled *Laws of War*. In Halleck's text, noncombatants were protected, having nothing to fear from the sword of the enemy. They would be treated as friendly so long as they abided by the exactions of the master. The pillage and destruction of towns, the devastation of the open country, "ravaging, setting fires to houses," were termed odious and detestable.

But as the perpetrators of such outrageous deeds may attempt to palliate them, under the pretext of deservedly punishing the enemy, be it here observed that the natural and voluntary law of nations does not allow us to inflict such punishments.

By 1865, Halleck had come a long way from his prewar moralizing. From Washington, he wrote to Sherman in Savannah, anticipating with perverse glee the forthcoming devastation of the cradle of the Confederacy. "Should you capture Charleston," Halleck wrote, "I hope by some accident the place may be destroyed, and if a little salt should be sown upon its site, it may prevent the growth of future crops of nullification and secession."

Here was Sherman's certification. The resident ethicist had overturned his own laws of war. Official Washington sanctioned any punitive procedure that Sherman might devise. Behind Sherman's methods lay a general political complicity. Proportionality and discrimination were dead, dead forever. If Sherman was now, as one writer described him, "a well-oiled machine with his screws loose," those screws were loosened by the entire Union establishment, hungry for victory by any means.

In reply, Sherman promised to keep Halleck's "hint" in mind, but he did not think salt would be necessary. "I look upon Columbia as quite as bad as Charleston," he wrote. The articles of secession after all had been signed in the State Capitol, and today are still enshrined in the bronze tablet in an honored place within its walls. "I doubt if we shall spare the public buildings there as we did in Milledgeville."

It is the local conceit in Charleston, I learned, that Sherman went north to Columbia, rather than east, because from his four years of living in Charleston as a young soldier he had come to love the city so. The head of the South Carolina Historical Society, David Moltke-Hansen, told me this, and I replied that it was most certainly a conceit, for Sherman was so incensed by the talk of secession in 1860 and so infuriated by the possibility of an attack on Fort Sumter that his advice was this: reinforce Fort Sumter and defend it, if it cost ten thousand lives, and if it was attacked, "Charleston must be blotted out of existence."

He did not move on Charleston and exterminate it, simply because, from the military viewpoint, it was a "dead cock in the pit," and he expected it to fall of its own weight, as soon happened, when its communications inland were cut.

Along with his two years in Louisiana, Sherman's four years in Charleston from 1842 to 1846 are, in my view the key to his cruel campaign through the South. Then, at an impressionable age, his attitude of love and hate toward the South's esoteric ways was formed. He meandered through the most overblown, overstuffed, defiant, and pretentious city of the region. Charleston was then a city of thirty thousand, divided equally between whites and blacks. Many of the latter were free, and as a result, police power was enforced as if the city were under siege. A curfew for blacks went into effect at 10:00 P.M., when platoons of bayonet-bearing soldiers marched through the streets with fife and drum. Class divisions were sharper than any place in America, with the upper class peopled from the ranks of the wealthy merchants, the aristocracy, and literary circles. William Gilmore Simms, whose mansion outside Bamberg, called Woodlands, was later burned by Sherman's troops, presided over the literati, writing his popular historical romances about his native state. (Simms's account of the burning of Columbia during the Civil War remains the most graphic account of that event.)

Sherman was stationed at Fort Moultrie on Sullivan's Island six miles from the city. Within the fort, slaves were kept. Braxton Bragg, later the Confederate general whom Sherman faced at Shiloh and defeated at Chattanooga, had his Alfred. Poor Alfred was later struck by lightning, and young Bragg wrote Sherman a pathetic, grieving letter about his servant. Every summer, genteel Charlestonian society shifted to Sullivan's Island to escape the dangerous, contagious "vapors and miasmas," which seeped out of the swamps: yellow fever, malaria, and dysentery. The center of activity on the island was the Moultrie House, a large hotel with grand passages, ornate draperies and chandeliers, an immense piazza for taking the sea air, and an even more immense supper room. Balls went on constantly until November, and the soldiers at Fort Moultrie were expected to perform regularly in dress uniform and to provide their band. Moultrie House became famous for flirtation. The spirited and gallant officers from Forts Moultrie and Sumter generated the electricity.

Amid such dalliance, the wiry ward of an Ohio background, whose trademark would become his wild thatch of red hair, found both delight and disgust. He had graduated sixth in his class instead of fourth, largely because his attention to deportment did not match his academic diligence. This impatience carried over into the social scene. He liked dancing, but was a bit of a wallflower. He liked intelligent conversation, but did not suffer pretense. As a penny pincher, he was overwhelmed by parties where buckets of oysters and cases of champagne and Madeira were consumed in an evening. A year into this sort of thing, Sherman wrote his brother: "A life of this kind does well enough for a while, but soon surfeits with its flippancy— mingling with people in whom you feel no permanent interest; smirks and smiles, when you feel savage; tight boots when your fancy would prefer slippers. I want a relief, and unless they can invent a new Florida war, I'll come back and spend a few months with you in Ohio."

After New Orleans, he found Charleston the most extravagant place in the world, and he had only contempt for the "worthless sons of broken-down proud South Carolina families" whose indolence had become legendary.

"Carolinians boast (they know not what) of this state, this aristocracy, this age, patriotism, chivalry and glory— all trash. No people in America are so poor in reality, no people so poorly provided with comforts of life, and happy it is for them that nature has given them a mild climate."

This memory of youth, suffused perhaps with loneliness,

might have added fuel to his bent for destruction. By the end of his early tour, Sherman was avoiding the social whirl for the solitary hobby of painting, or for hunting trips on the plantations of Cooper's Branch.

As I drove north out of the Low Country into the Piedmont, the yellows, the oranges, and the browns of the late fall again intruded upon the landscape. An occasional cotton field came as a surprise in terrain where drying soybeans, fields dotted with roll bales, shoots of winter grass became the norm. From time to time, a huge tractor-trailer passed, loaded with oak and hickory trunks, and I guessed that the timber came from elsewhere than the River's Bridge swampland on the Salkehatchie. Yankee troops had waded through the three-mile swamp, in water sometimes up to their necks. In the swamp the only notable skirmish took place between the left wing of Sherman's army and the scattered Confederates. But the firing was so intense that the trees were peppered with lead balls. Today, timbering there is unprofitable, for hitting one Minié ball can shatter an expensive sawmill blade.

The towns north of Savannah on the road to Columbia— Hardeeville, Robertsville, MacPhersonville, Barnwell, Blackville, Midway, Orangeburg, and Lexington—were consumed in a carnival of fire. Gradually, the lone chimneys jokingly referred to in Georgia as Sherman's sentinels or Sherman's toothpicks, suddenly seemed no joke. The concept of foraging under tightly controlled, well-commanded parties had disintegrated, as thousands of "bummers" left their regiments for weeks of rampaging. The army of sixty-five thousand had acquired another twenty thousand camp followers. Sherman would later consign the importance of his campaign through South Carolina which smashed the heart of the Confederacy as ten times more important than the March to the Sea, which he considered merely a shift of base. But another observer had a different ratio. Wrote the correspondent for the *New York Herald:*

As for wholesale burnings, pillage and devastation committed in South Carolina, magnify all I have said of Georgia some fiftyfold and then throw in an occasional murder "just to bring an old hard-fisted cuss to his senses" and you have a pretty good idea of the whole thing.

Sherman had created the atmosphere of punishment which had grown, like an inflammation, to disease the whole body of his force.

The few mansions spared along the route had the Masonic story attached to them. When I finally arrived in Barnwell, dubbed "Burnwell" by the Union troops, a prominent building in the town square was adorned by a huge Mason's symbol, as if it were warding off any return of Sherman's evil spirit.

Of all the towns before Columbia, Barnwell's treatment was the most grotesque. The town had the misfortune to be "conquered" by Sherman's cavalry under Gen. Hugh Judson Kilpatrick, known as Kill Cavalry or Little Kil. No subordinate inspired such fear and contempt in the South as he did. Sherman himself had described the diminutive Kilpatrick as "a hell of a damned fool, but I want just that sort of man to command my cavalry on this expedition." Kilpatrick's official mission was to protect the left flank of the army against the only annoyance that remained: the seven thousand Confederate cavalry under Wheeler, but he had issued matches to all his horsemen in Savannah, and exhorted his men to maximum destruction as they moved into "the hell hole of secession." In Sherman's choice of Kilpatrick and in his failure to control his subordinates' wantonness, the charges of war crime receive their weight.

By the account of a brigade commander under Kilpatrick, Barnwell was systematically set fire, and as the flames rose Kilpatrick held a Nero dance at his headquarters in the Hartley House, to which he sent invitations to all the ladies of Barnwell.

"Regarding [the invitations] as orders, [the ladies] like sad ghosts went through the whirling mazes of the dance, while their own dwellings were in flames," wrote Gen. Smith D. Atkins of Illinois. "It was the bitterest satire on social pleasure ever witnessed, and justly stained the reputation of Kilpatrick."

At the tiny Barnwell Museum, next to the town library, I encountered Miss Hildegarde Roberts, a sprightly little lady who pulled reverently from her files a dog-eared monograph on the homes and churches of Barnwell which were lost, "lest we forget." After a brief chat, she took me out to the Hartley House, a two-story, porticoed clapboard structure in a somewhat woebegone state.

"So this is where General Kilpatrick danced while the flames lapped the houses of Barnwell," I said.

"Yes," replied the cheery Miss Roberts, "but the Hartleys were very nice people, and they gave very interesting parties, too."

Not all the ladies of Barnwell had attended Kilpatrick's party, however. Some had "refugeed" to Duncannon, a cotton plantation of twenty thousand acres with one hundred slaves, six miles west of town. Its owner was a colonel in Lee's army, a veteran of the Battle of Seven Pines, and one of his children was sick with a mild case of the measles when Sherman came. Therein lies a tale that a Southerner could ballyhoo. All the family valuables, including the silver, were gathered up hastily and placed under the bed of the sick boy. No doubt the refugees at Duncannon had heard of the general practice by this time, as it is described in one twentieth-century history:

The cavalry galloped up at full speed, dismounted, rushed into the house without speaking to anyone or observing any civilities of civilized life, went upstairs into garrets, cellars, parlors, closets, family apartments, sleeping rooms, breaking open boxes, trunks, secretaries, desks, sideboards, clothes presses, wardrobes—abstracting all desirable articles such as blankets and fine quilts, which in many cases they put on their sore-backed horses, ladies' clothing and gentlemen's clothing and elegantly wrought pillow cases which they converted into flour bags, sometimes strewing the contents of bureaus and of wardrobes all over the floor, and occasionally tearing fine silk dresses into shreds. All decency and civility were ignored. The private apartments of ladies were unceremoniously entered and rummaged and the ladies themselves called by such vile epithets as the Yankee vocabulary contains.

But not at Duncannon! Sad-eyed on the porch, the ladies greeted the cavalrymen with the news that there was a boy in the house desperately ill with contagious scarlet fever. Immediately, a Union guard was posted outside the door of the sick boy guarding the silver, lest the troops contract the vile Southern disease. Unfortunately, the triumph was tarnished by the fact that all the slaves ran off with the Yankees, including a much-loved house servant who rode away on the family's favorite mare, named Ma Lady.

The present owner of Duncannon, Mrs. Suzanne McMillan, told me all this with good cheer, as she showed me around. In the dining room, she pointed out bullet holes where the Yankees had wantonly shot in the ceiling—but with prodding, confessed in a whisper that the Yankees were of the twentieth-century variety and were shooting at wasps. "But we haven't covered up the holes, because it makes such a good story," she said pertly.

◈ ◈ ◈

I pressed on to Blackville, South Carolina, ten miles north of Barnwell. Blackville had been a strategic junction

for Sherman, where the two wings of his army came together at the vital railroad link between Charleston and
Augusta. With the railroad in his control, he ordered fifty
miles of track torn up. No general who did not partly love
war could describe this process with quite Sherman's
ardor:

The track was heaved up in sections the length of a regiment,
then separated rail by rail; bonfires were made of the ties and of
fence rails on which the rails were heated, carried to trees or
telegraph poles, and with great claws, wrapped around the left to
cool. Such rails could not be used again.

Hence, "Sherman's neckties" (also known less color-
fully as a "Lincoln gimlet") and beside Sherman's sentinels, they must have made quite a calling card.

At Blackville, I would again try my hand at schoolteach-
ing. After the flat session in the high school in Gray, Georgia, and a graduate history seminar at Georgia State College
in Milledgeville, I did not have high hopes. In Milledgeville,
a graduate student derived her notion of Sherman not from
the books or from sitting upon grandmother's knee, but
from a Waylon Jennings song on the 1979 *White Mansions*
album. Entitled "They Laid Waste to Our Land," the lyr-
ics are:

> Ain't it enough just to know you got us beat . . .
> The feelings will run as deep as the scars we bear . . .
> What you call justice is plain unfair
> How the hell can you ever claim
> It's been worth all the pain
> Just to have us live together under one flag.

Now it was the Jefferson Davis Academy, where, its
pamphlet announces, education is based on Christian principles, and entrance tests were required to ensure a "hom-
ogenius" student body. Its mascot is the rebel raider, a
plumed horseman in the fashion of J. E. B. Stuart, rearing

on a steed with sword raised high, but the Rebel Raiders never play the integrated Hawks of Blackville High on the gridiron. Under the stern glare of President Davis, I met the history teacher, Bernard "Butch" Bydalek. A light-hearted Tennessean, he is a fulfilled teacher and a frustrated poet. The book on South Carolina history in use here and elsewhere in South Carolina is written by a descendant of William Gilmore Simms. Mary C. Simms Oliphant, who remains a formidable dowager in the Palmetto State, entitled her chapter on the Civil War, "The War for Southern Independence."

Before me sat twenty gangly examples of the modern yeoman class, dressed in their letter jackets and dime-store clothes, their hair teased and blow-dried, expectant pimply faces happy for this break in their drab routine. Talking about General Sherman smelled like a free period to them. They gossiped. They giggled. They all talked at once.

"Show your breeding!" Butch shouted at them to quell their unruliness, but, for some reason, the order did not produce a different result. (Barnwell County has an average annual income of $5,000.) Once again, the symbols of the Confederacy took a beating. They associated the Stars and Bars more with the "Dukes of Hazzard" than with the ragtag remnants of Wheeler's Cavalry. The banners meant squealing tires, beer blasts, and nigger jokes.

It struck me as curious that in the midst of our discussion (slaves were a lot better off in bonds than free, remarked one young lady, because "at least then they had jobs"), Butch Bydalek would blurt out that he had marched with Martin Luther King in Selma. Later, I asked him about this, for I too had been at Selma, and the idea of landing in a white Christian academy from that start smacked of a gigantic retraction or a noble crusade. For Butch, neither seemed the case. His students, he said, were simply incapable of learning side by side with blacks, and he did his best to puncture his students' obsession with race. But his heart did not seem to be in it.

"I think I can be more effective in this setting," he said flatly. But he made no pretense about any heroic mission. Thanksgiving vacation had begun, and he was anxious to get away to Columbia.

So too was I. The afternoon was clear and warm, perfect for a leisurely ramble around the grounds of the State Capitol. I thought of Lt. Col. Walter S. Dillard again, the West Point historian from South Carolina, who had grown up with the Civil War hagiology so evident on the State Capitol grounds, and had not rejected it until after he had commanded a battalion in Vietnam. The six stars marking the spots of the direct hits by Sherman's batterymen as they took the measure of the city from the far side of the Congaree, were meant to perpetuate from one generation to the next a South Carolina bitterness toward all things Yankee. But the trajectory of those cannon balls today would pass over a robust and national city, which has attracted many non-Southerners since World War II. The resoluteness of the state to hold onto its Confederate shrines seems increasingly like an embarrassing concession to the sentimentalists and a provocation to the blacks.

Atop the Capitol, the Stars and Bars fly beneath the Stars and Stripes. Every year, a black caucus in the state legislature pushes to stop the display, but so far it has failed. Before the north front of the Capitol, the Confederate soldier stands high atop a marble shaft. On the south lawn, a huge Wade Hampton equestrian dominates the turf. You can tell that the sculptor (from New York and Paris) loved the South, a Columbia paper once wrote, by the way in the twilight a soft glow passes over Hampton's countenance, showing Hampton "as he is enshrined in the hearts of all South Carolinians. To conceive, to plan, to execute so noble a figure, so kindly and yet so proud a face shows that the heart of the sculptor is good, as well as his mind perceptive."

The same sculptor, F. W. Ruckstuhl, executed the monument to Confederate women at the far end of the State House plaza. It is by far the most interesting statue on the grounds, for it is the antithesis of the heroic, motion-filled equestrian of Sherman at Fifty-ninth Street and Fifth Avenue, New York, so magnificently rendered by Augustus Saint-Gaudens. In the latter, the winged angel of victory holding a palm frond ("Just like a Yank," the Southerner is obliged to quip, "riding, while he lets the lady walk") leads the conqueror. Victor and Victim. Exhilaration and Condolence. To sculptors, there are angels for every circumstance. In the Ruckstuhl rendition in Columbia, the winged angel stands behind a seated figure of womanhood, holding a wreath of protection over her head. On either side of the seated figure is a cherub, one holding a bouquet of roses, the other a scroll bearing the name of South Carolina. Upon the pedestal are words which, for all their old-fashioned floridness, I found unexpectedly moving.

Their unconquerable spirit strengthened the thin lines of gray. Their tender care was solace to the stricken. Reverence for God and unfaltering faith in a righteous cause inspired heroism that survived immolation of sons and courage that bore agony of suspense and shock of disaster. The tragedy of the Confederacy may be forgotten, but the fruits of noble service of the daughters of the South are our perpetual heritage.

The words moved me, because it was the time of controversy over the Vietnam memorial in Washington. What would be the effect of a Civil War monument here, now, which merely listed the names of the 258,000 dead Southerners? After a few thousand, do not the named become nameless? After time, are not names without ideas outdated and simply, in a figurative sense, dead? Here at least was an attempt, right or wrong, to define the spirit of the white slaveholders' rebellion. There was an idea of commemoration against which I could test my current beliefs and sentimentalities. On another side of the statue are these words:

When reverses followed victories, when want displaced plenty, when mourning for the flower of Southern manhood darkened countless homes, when government tottered and chaos threatened, the women were steadfast and unafraid. . . .

Perhaps they were and perhaps they weren't, but somehow, to read that on a memorial as a recognition of universal suffering in war, warmed me. But temporarily. There was an issue here, and it was joined in a dialogue reproduced in William Gilmore Simms's literary ululation over the burning of Columbia. Stilted as it sounds and perhaps a product of Simms's rich imagination, the interchange purportedly took place amid the flames between a distraught woman of the city and Gen. Smith D. Atkins of Sherman's staff, the same Atkins who had been so disgusted with General Kilpatrick's shameful behavior in Barnwell.

"[Sherman] wars on women."

"Yes, and justly," Atkins replied. "It is the women of the South who kept up this cursed rebellion. It gave us the greatest satisfaction to see those proud Georgia women begging crumbs from Yankee leavings, and this will soon be the fate of all you Carolina women."

"How as men you can behold the horrors of this scene and behold the sufferings of these innocents, without terrible pangs of self-condemnation and self-loathing, it is difficult to conceive."

"We glory in it. I tell you, madam, that when the people of the North hear of the vengeance we have meted out to your city, there will be one universal shout of rejoicing from men, women and children from Maine to Maryland."

"You are then, sir, only a fitting representative of your people."

The burning of Columbia was very different from the destruction of Atlanta. Atlanta was a well-defended city in a state of siege; Columbia was full only of elegant, troopless generals, as Mary Chesnut put it in *Diary from Dixie*. This may explain why one hears no lame jokes in Columbia nor sees quaint Sherman etchings on restaurant walls, or why only two roadside historical markers in all South Carolina mention the name of Sherman. Southern cant held for a hundred years that Sherman's actions here were his greatest war atrocity, that regardless of whether the commander issued any direct order, Sherman's guilt was unquestionable. To the extent that the world accepts a broad concept of command responsibility, Sherman must be held responsible for not controlling his troops.

Consider, for example, the American standard of guilt applied to General Tomoyuki Yamashita, of the Japanese army, for the massacre of Filipinos in Manila during World War II. Yamashita was hanged for not controlling his troops, even though he was cut off from them with no communication whatever when the massacre occurred. If such a standard were applied to Sherman, not to mention the Israeli charge of "indirect responsibility" for Jewish political and military leaders in the Beirut massacre, Sherman would certainly be found guilty. But there is ample evidence that as news of the fires filtered to Sherman, he exerted himself to stop them, including fighting the flames himself.

A recent book by a South Carolinian, Marion Lucas, called *Sherman and the Burning of Columbia*, concludes that wind and liquor and flying cotton were the chief culprits in the conflagration, but, of course, liquor consumption is something commanders are supposed to regulate. On the night the city burned, "liquor was drunk with such avidity as to astonish the veteran Bacchanales of Columbia," William Gilmore Simms wrote. Mix liquor with the passion to exact "principal and interest from this cowardly traitor state on its debt to justice and humanity," as one of Sherman's officers wrote, and you have a terrible gladness in contemplating the firestorm. Sherman himself suggested that some malicious soldier may have started the burning, but this "devilish spirit" grew as the fire progressed. To what extent had he contributed to that devilish spirit by his wild statements? In his utter lack of remorse after the war, one finds the rationale only one step away from Hiroshima. "I have said I did not order it nor wish it, but I have not shed any tears over it, for I believe it has hastened what we are all fighting for—the end of the war."

Characteristically, Sherman tried to shift responsibility to the enemy. In his official report, he charged it off to Gen. Wade Hampton. "I confess I did so pointedly to shake the faith of his people in him, for he was in my opinion boastful and professed to be the special champion of South Carolina."

The Lucas book exonerates Sherman personally for the Columbia disaster, but its views could still occasion hot dispute in the local historical society upon its publication in 1976. The distortions do not die easily. Consider, for example, the Centennial supplement that the *State* and the *Columbia Record,* the Columbia newspapers, put out jointly in 1965 to commemorate their city's destruction. As newspaper supplements go, it was commendably comprehensive, but in the headlines and the advertisements the sentimentalities were clear.

"Foragers: Scourge of the South."

"Burning Question I: Yankees Deny and Admit Guilt."

"Burning Question II: Columbians Blame Sherman's Men."

In "South Carolina's Giant in Gray," a heroic portrait of Wade Hampton, scant reference was made to Hampton's actions of ripping open bales of cotton and covering the city with a blizzard of flammable cotton strands. The advertisements were revealing. The Chamber of Commerce asserted that the "invaders very methodically began to destroy the city." The South Carolina National Bank touted how it had loaned the Confederacy millions of dollars and lost more than $3.5 million in its munificence. "Through other years, other wars, other depressions, as in the Lost Cause, South Carolina National Bank has served the financial needs of a confident, courageous people."

Other advertisers in the Centennial supplement, however, avoided such pretense and stuck to what they knew: "Columbia was rebuilt with GUIGNARD BRICK!" . . . "Imagine! In 1865, your great, great, great, great, great-grandmother may have been buying Claussen's bread for 24 years!"

◈ ◈ ◈

Before I left Columbia, I reached James Dickey by telephone. We had met some years ago in Chapel Hill, and I knew he was given, at readings, to cursing General Sherman with a low oath to get a laugh and get a Southern audience on his side before he read "Hunting Civil War Relics at Nimblewill Creek."

> But underfoot I feel
> The dead regroup
> The burst metals all in place
> The battle lines be drawn
> Anew to include us
> In Nimblewill

We shared news of mutual friends, including the elegant Mississippi poet James Seay, who wears a rakish pirate's patch over one eye after a childhood blinding, and has been known to claim that he lost the eye at Antietam. It was the day before Thanksgiving, and "Doctor" Dickey (as his telephone machine identifies him) was otherwise engaged, so a lively exchange about Sherman would have to wait, as well as serious talk about the "strength of fields" with which the poet had enveloped a prospective Southern healer at a presidential inauguration several years before. Besides, I was due in Hartsville at the home of my long-time friend, novelist Elizabeth Boatwright Coker.

On the way out of town, I went to see the columns of Millwood. It would be no more than an image, but, like the ruins of Sheldon Church in the Low Country, an image that lasts. The Millwood estate is surrounded by a commercial jumble. Richway, 15 percent off on all toys and bikes; Food Town, lowest food prices in South Carolina; K-Mart Plaza, with plastic triangular flags flapping from a clothesline. There is Hampton Hills, a condominium development, and Hampton Drive, colonial suburban homes one after another, and—barely visible—amid untended undergrowth, by the peeling green paint on the fenceboards of the entrance, the marker: "Millwood, boyhood home of Wade Hampton III, burned by Federal troops in 1865."

I had called ahead. The last descendant was not well . . . he was in the hospital. The maid did not think he would mind if I came to see the columns. Down a pebble driveway, not well cared for anymore, woods overgrown. . . . In the distance, a loudspeaker blares from a commercial horse stable.

Three columns rise before me. There are pedestals for six. A huge live oak cradles one of the columns between two branches, so that one cannot be sure which way the mansion once faced. Honeysuckle hangs from the branches, "tendrils hanging like bait," to borrow a line from Dickey. "Millwood . . . a place of yore for its charm and elegance of society, its frank hospitality and the lavish bounty of its successive hosts," wrote Simms. "The destruction of this family seat of opulence, grace, and hospitality will occasion sensation in European countries." But

Mary Chesnut had suggested that the Confederates gutted the place before the Yankees could have a chance.

From Columbia to Cheraw, the last leg of Sherman's punishment, the tales take on a grinding sameness. Winnsboro, Chester, Camden were all left smouldering. Toward the end of my journey, it had gotten harder to take note even of such perversities as a coffin exhumed and its occupant dressed formally and placed in the pulpit before the torch was brought, or a mule riding away with the mistress's bridal veil tied to its ears. But in Hartsville I could expect memory to be filtered through the novelist's imagination.

Elizabeth Boatwright Coker's nine romantic novels have centered on the Civil War and its aftermath. If one can believe the blurbs on the back of the paperback editions, these "torrid" novels of the South, along the lines of "the tempestuous saga of a ravishing beauty torn by divided loyalties and consumed by passion in the war-ravaged South . . ." have made her the best-selling historical novelist in America.

I was returning for my favorite Hartsville occasion, the annual Thanksgiving feast of the Damon Hunt Club in the Pee Dee Swamp. Late in the afternoon, I turned into Elizabeth Boatwright Coker's driveway on Home Avenue with great anticipation. I had not been back for two years. She greeted me open-armed between the columns, decked out in a flowing chiffon tunic, carefully coiffed for me and the guests later, and the cheery news that she was deep into her latest novel, a departure for her, about "an old Lady called Miz Elizabeth who lives on Home Avenue and is kidnapped by teenage drug smugglers." I knew as a master storyteller she was only half kidding, for she might just pull off something of the sort, but before it was over the drug smugglers might become blockade runners in Savannah around 1862.

Before we went off to feast in the swamp the following morning, Elizabeth had promised me a talk about *La Belle*. Her 1959 novel was about Marie Boozer, the legendary Columbia beauty who with her cigar-smoking, Union-sympathizing mother, had followed Sherman out of Columbia along with the other hangers-on, and eventually married a French count. A true story had inspired the book, but, as she acknowledges in her author's note, the truth "has been so lacquered by gossip, legend, and anecdote that it has been difficult to separate the real woman from the mythical one"—a situation, in short, tailor-made for the historical novelist. It was a process, she conceded, that applied equally to General Sherman. "To this day people in Columbia still speak of Marie and her mother with as much current curiosity, envy, admiration, and opprobrium as they do of the fiery General Sherman."

For Elizabeth, it is a matter of principle that the historical novel must stay within the spirit of known fact, for within those confines she has always found plenty of room for passion, conflict, and imagination. (This is in contrast to playwright Thomas Babe. In his play *Rebel Women,* produced at New York's Public Theater in 1975, Babe stopped reading about Sherman when he felt the facts began to "overwhelm" or "terrify" him, interfering with his imagination. In Sherman, he felt he had a figure about whom enough, but not too much, was generally known, so that he was "free." But for my taste, Babe stopped reading too soon, because in imagining Sherman's cruelty, he had the play's climax be a scene of Sherman forcing sex upon a pregnant Southern lady on the promise to save her prisoner husband later. The result, even in the theater, was to embellish further Sherman's ghoulish reputation.) On such weighty subjects as the relation of history and art, I knew it would not be easy to turn Elizabeth Coker "serious."

"Every time someone asks for a serious talk," she quipped, "I feel as if I'm about to get a whippin'."

From her ancestry, one might predict purple passages about Sherman whenever he turned up in her novel. Her great-uncle, James Boatwright, was the mayor of Columbia when the Civil War broke out, and when her late husband's forbear, Maj. J. L. Coker, returned to find the appalling ruins of his region, it was as if he laid a moral burden on his descendants. "Someday, [Sherman's] barbarous practices and spirit will be execrated by the good people of every section," Major Coker wrote. But I had been struck in *La Belle* at its matter-of-fact treatment of Sherman himself. The storyteller painted her heroine with a great passion for the Confederacy, and let events simply swirl around her.

Sherman had always fascinated Elizabeth. She sees him as the idealistic schoolteacher who thought he was brandishing the sword of the Lord, and, curiously, that is also how she sees the Edgefield orators of South Carolina like Preston Brooks, and even John C. Calhoun. Inevitably—I could almost feel it coming—she found a place to quote me again the remark of Calhoun: "The North says to the black man, God Damn You and be free. The South says to him, God bless you and be a slave." It was a remark she had quoted to me eighteen years ago, when her somewhat less enthusiastic son, James, and I were marching to desegregate a North Carolina movie theater. Now, it flashed briefly through my mind that she saw me in the same vein: the idealistic, self-righteous schoolteacher bent on massive social change. To her, it is the Sherman seed.

Before she cheerfully showed me the sword slashes from Sherman's men on the Chippendale chest of drawers in her dining room (was this her version of the Yankee bullet holes in the ceiling at Duncannon?), or before I let her get too far about how they stole Aunt Martha's trousseau, lace petticoats and all ("You know we hate 'em," she said right on cue. "Why shouldn't we remember!"), I wanted to read back to her a passage from *La Belle*. It contained the patriotic ardor that the Vietnam veteran in Savannah, Roger Durham, so longed to feel and found so mystifying. The heroine was now in New York at about the time of Appomattox, when her mother looked out a window of the Astor House to see Marie leading a band down Broadway:

[T]here was Marie, waving a small flag of the Stars and Bars (where had she kept it hidden on the voyage?) and she had pushed the big thick politician off the cracker barrel and was standing on it herself waving the Confederate flag and singing Dixie at the top of her strong lungs, and she looked so bold and valiant that the whole street was cheering and clapping and urging her to sing—sing—sing.

With the fury of fervent patriotism Marie sang every verse and at the end, as the drum ruffled off, she looked around at the crowd with the fierce eyes of a demon and waved the little Confederate flag as ferociously as if it were an avenging sword. Riffraff and respectable citizens alike shuddered and the ones in front moved back until there was only one person left very close to the box—a Union Naval officer. As valiant in his patriotism as she, he reached up and jerked her down and she struck him in the face and left a red scratch down his cheek. But he took the flag roughly away from her and snapped it in half and flung it into the crowd.

Then he turned and himself disappeared into the midst of the goggling people who were avid for any kind of new sensation and were wishing the girl would jump at him again like the wild woman she appeared to be and they'd have a good fight to excite them higher.

But at this point a black man came through the crowd and began speaking sharply to her. She made as if to strike him but he shook his head and took her firmly by the arm and struggled to make a way for her through the mob that broke and divided for them to squeeze through.

There were so many currents in that; I marveled at a modern person being able to write such a passage.

"Well?" I said, my look suggesting that she justify herself.

"Oh," she replied, "I made all that up." I would get no more.

We gathered up her contribution to the swamp feast (the women are allowed at the hunting lodge only this one time in the year; they bring the food) and piled into her yellow Corvette. I wanted to detour through Darlington, for I guessed the town had changed since Elizabeth grew up there and I wanted to see the sycamore tree where they hanged Amy Spain. The road to Darlington cuts through the flat, sandy cotton and soybean fields. What once was the captivating domain of Elizabeth's prototypes is now merely a figure on a balance sheet, perused by faceless managers in faraway boardrooms. West Germans are the cotton barons now, attracted by cheap labor that turned out to be more cheap than efficient. After a huge investment, the Germans are reportedly disillusioned and looking for a way out. Cottonseed oil, once the profitable base for Wesson Oil and Crisco, is becoming less profitable than soybean oil. Increasingly, the elegant and charming patricians of the area, who supported their style of life over the years from the land, are being forced to choose between "agribusiness" and selling out.

So, too, did Elizabeth have to face a Darlington very different from the one of her childhood. The Piggly-Wiggly Food Store, the Funeral Home, the Hardee's Hamburger joint have replaced the sites of childhood bliss. The Opera House on the town square is gone, as is the grand hotel built in the fashion of Palm Beach. A pinkish, five-story courthouse now overwhelms the town square, around which fire engines used to race. The old town clock is gone, and so are the massive sycamores, on one of whose branches Sherman's cavalrymen found Amy Spain hanging —the final desperate warning—the harbinger of the secret war of white sheets and night riders to come.

In 1976, in the historical journal called *Darlingtoniana*, the old controversy was revived. That a seventeen-year-old black girl named Amy, the slave of Confederate Maj. A. C. Spain, was hanged in the Darlington town square on March 10, 1865, six days after Sherman's men came and went, is not in dispute. The issue is whether she was "a martyr of Freedom" or an uppity, thieving, disobedient wench—in short, a bad girl. It is an issue with which I am very familiar, for the arguments are not far afield from those in the 1975 Joan Little case in North Carolina, about which I wrote a book.* How North and South perceive a racial Donnybrook fair has not changed very much in a hundred years.

In the September 30, 1865, issue of *Harper's Weekly,* under the sketch of a lynching, an article described a "colored woman named Amy Spain" who could not restrain her exuberance as Sherman's men arrived, for she saw the "long night of darkness which had bound her to slavery" about to end. In irresistible Victorian parlance, the article concluded that her persecutors would be forgotten, but "Amy Spain's name is now hallowed among the Africans who, emancipated and free, dare, with the starry folds of the flag of the free floating over them, speak her name with holy reverence."

The *Harper's* article was considered then, and apparently by a few still today, to be a libel upon Darlington's good name. Major Spain was quick to respond. He declared that Amy, "his female," had a "hot, hasty, and ungovernable" temper, and she was hanged in clothes stolen from his daughter. In her, and the African race generally, the major wrote, there were "contradictory and opposite elements." "In the future let us all hope the Ethiopian may change his traditional and actual characteristics even though his skin may retain its glossy black." On the night Sherman's men came, Amy went berserk. She stole valu-

---

* *The Innocence of Joan Little, a Southern Mystery,* New York: Times Books, 1977.

ables from her masters and cursed them to their face and, as always in these matters, a sexual, race-mixing element was present. Major Spain charged Amy with the remark: "I intend to set up for myself and take a white Yankee for a husband."

With Sherman gone, a Confederate military commission convened. It was deemed that an example "sudden and violent" was necessary "to curb an uprising spirit of insurrection." Amy Spain was condemned. In jail, she was visited by a Methodist preacher to whom, according to her tearful master, she recanted her wickedness and conveyed the message to her colored congregation not to follow her example. Thereafter, an "orderly and kindly" execution was performed, followed by a "decent" burial, to which, Major Spain reported, his children went and wept over the corpse.

At last we arrived at the hunting lodge. The hunters stood around in their camouflaged fatigues, their rifles safely away in their padded cases, looking a bit crestfallen. For on this Thanksgiving no deer hung from the eaves, as in years past. The hunters mingled with their friends in fancy Fifth Avenue attire and waited for the blessing to be given to the smoked goose, venison, and even wild boar that awaited us amid the different renditions of caramel cake. (The hunter who carved the boar confessed that presenting his trophy at this feast was the only way he knew to get the thing out of his freezer.)

The Pee Dee River will always be associated with this Old English feast for me. Sherman viewed the river differently. Crossing it uneventfully was his last hurdle. The next major river was the Cape Fear in North Carolina, which he expected would be in Union hands after the capture of Wilmington. After the Pee Dee, he wrote, he had no concern for the future.

The Bennett Place | 7

AT BENNETT PLACE, outside Durham, North Carolina, I came upon the empty room in the new visitor's center. But my impulse to be a museum director was waning. There, I met the superintendent and the chief "interpreter" for state historical sites. They complained of an "identity crisis" in relation to Appomattox. Even in the history textbook for North Carolina high schools there is a sketch of Lee surrendering "the Confederacy" to Grant in Virginia, and Bennett Place is not mentioned. I did not know how to help them.

After South Carolina, Sherman fought one last battle. At Bentonville, North Carolina, in a bold and well-conceived attack, Johnston threw everything he had left (a mere 14,100 men by his own account) at the exposed left wing of the invading army. The result was inconclusive, with Sherman fighting defensively as he waited for reinforcements. With his superior force facing the rapidly disintegrating Confederate Army, Sherman knew that he could afford more casualties than his enemy. It was a battle of attrition now, to use the modern phrase. But a battle of attrition is one thing, a war of attrition another. Of his war of attrition, General Westmoreland would write: "Since the World War I battle of the Somme and Verdun, [war of attrition] has been a strategy in disrepute, one that to many appeared particularly unsuited for a war in Asia with Asia's legendary hordes of manpower. Yet the war in Vietnam was not against Asian hordes, but against an enemy with relatively limited manpower. . . . In any case, what alternative was there to a war of attrition?" On April 24, 1966, in a speech at the Waldorf Astoria in New York, the commander had answered his own question. "The only alternative to a war of attrition is a war of annihilation," he said. Perhaps that was what Sherman's war had finally become. In any event, the major consequence of the Battle of Bentonville was simply another 3,947 casualties.

Thereafter, as Sherman resupplied his troops and made ready for a final push to encircle Lee's army at Petersburg, he journeyed by steamer to City Point, Virginia, for a conference with Grant on March 27 and 28, 1865. By chance, Abraham Lincoln was there, and the commanders had two conferences with the president that would guide Sherman's controversial role as a peacemaker at Bennett Place a few weeks later.

To the end Sherman maintained his contempt for politicians. He saw an anarchical strain in the American populace that made their governance virtually impossible by democratic means. Perhaps that was the tyrant in him. Lincoln had done little to allay the feeling from afar. But Lincoln and Sherman shared one strong, emotional bond. Each had had a son named Willie who had died a youth. Willie Sherman had come to his father after the fall of Vicksburg in 1863. Like Willie Lincoln, he was his father's favorite and was a great favorite of the troops, as he donned a uniform and was referred to as Sergeant. At Vicksburg, Willie Sherman contracted typhoid fever and died a few days later in Memphis. His father never forgave himself for bringing the boy into "that sickly region in summertime."

At City Point, Lincoln was intensely nervous at Sherman's absence from his army at this critical juncture and beseeched his commander to return to North Carolina quickly. By the by, Sherman inquired if the President was ready for the end of the war. The kindliness of Lincoln's response swept Sherman away. It was as if the brutality of the terrorist was suddenly brushed aside by the charitable magnanimity of the giant before him—as if Sherman's great passion for total war could be magically transformed into a great passion for total peace. Both Grant and Sherman supposed that one more great battle between their combined armies and the combined army of Lee and Johnston might be necessary. Lincoln pleaded with them to avoid the carnage if it were humanly possible. By the account of a witness, Lincoln authorized Sherman to secure the surrender of Johnston on *any terms*.

This was general conversation, perhaps even idle chitchat, not a formal policy session. What Lincoln wanted from his military leaders was the complete surrender of the rebel armies and the return of soldiers from both sides to their farms and their shops. He, almost alone, was the voice of charity, for in his whole wearied deportment, he manifested the pain of a generation of Americans, as if he had taken the collective pain into his own body. Neither Lyndon Johnson nor Richard Nixon, William Westmoreland nor Henry Kissinger ever seemed to undergo any such transfiguration over the pain of Vietnam. In the banal language of modern politics, Lincoln alone was "soft" on Confederates; all others were "tough" on traitors. The tide of retribution against the treasonous South was already strong, but the need for a social transformation of the region after the war was clear. How to handle that transformation was a delicate, political question, and by the City Point meeting with his commanders Lincoln had not declared himself definitively. He was in the throes of political maneuver. He had given only hints about his approach to reconstruction. Magnanimity for the suffering of the South would have to be balanced against punishment for overt treason. Blame for that treason would have to be carefully considered at the same time as the war-torn region was put back on some footing . . . without its crutch of slavery.

But there was no reason to air these subtleties with Sherman and Grant, for they had plenty of purely military matters to fill their heads. It was a critical moment, far more critical than any of the three men could imagine. In twenty days, Lincoln would be dead. The possibility for misunderstanding was great, as the politician loosely instructed the military men, avoiding the political fine points that he may have supposed Sherman and Grant would not understand or appreciate.

But to Sherman, civil and military matters were often united. In 1863, he had written a brilliant analysis of Southern ante-bellum society and given many thoughts on how it might be transformed after the rebellion into a more industrial, less stratified New South. So impressed had Lincoln been with the document that he not only applauded Sherman's thinking but asked that his paper be published (which Sherman declined). In Atlanta, in 1864, when a feeler about a secret meeting with Governor Joseph Brown of Georgia and Alexander Stephens, the vice-president of the Confederacy, reached Sherman, Lincoln excitedly encouraged Sherman by telegram to go forward with the meeting (though it never materialized). In Savannah, Sherman and Stanton had discussed civil matters for hours upon end: what was to be done with seized cotton?; what was to be done with fifty thousand liberated slaves who had followed his march?; whether the Union economy could sustain many more months of war before it collapsed?

It was only natural then for Sherman to raise with Lincoln an immediate matter where military and political areas were inseparable. What was to be done, Sherman asked, with the political leaders such as Jefferson Davis (who was then in Greensboro)? Should they be allowed to escape? If caught, would they be tried and condemned as traitors?

Lincoln's response was . . . well, Lincolnesque. Small wonder that in the movies or the theater today there has never been a believable performance of this demigod. Neither Gregory Peck in the television movie *The Blue and the Gray* nor Roy Dotrice in the play *Mr. Lincoln* seemed more than caricatures. The walk, the hat, the melancholy eyes, the right, wise, homey riposte to every situation, are too firmly fixed in the popular mind for an actor ever to bring it off. Lincoln appears a caricature of himself even in the history books.

Lincoln had a tough political problem in his meeting with Sherman at City Point. Sherman had won the war for the president, but in such a manner that would make the reconciliation of the nation more difficult. Sherman had outlived his usefulness; he had been hard to control in the war and would be even harder to control in peace. Now, it was time to come down hard upon him.

Lincoln replied that he once knew a man who had taken a total abstinence pledge. In a visit with a convivial friend he was offered a drink, but refused, citing his pledge. So the friend proceeded to fix lemonade, and along the way gestured to the brandy bottle, pointing out that lemonade could be made more palatable if it were sweetened with a little brandy. The flexible teetotaler replied that if it could be done "unbeknown" to him, he would not object. Sherman inferred that if Jefferson Davis and the other political leaders should escape "unbeknown" to the president, Lincoln would not object.

(Neither Nixon nor Ford nor even Jimmy Carter would ever exhibit this same desire that in postwar healing, the problem of what to do with the Vietnam dissenters should be quietly discarded, unbeknown to them.)

The politician had bowled over the military man—reversing the current fashion. In his *Memoirs*, Sherman recorded just how deeply he had been touched by this last glimpse.

I know when I left him that I was more than ever impressed by his kindly nature, his deep and earnest sympathy with the afflictions of the whole people, resulting from the war, and by the march of hostile armies through the South; and that his earnest desire seemed to be the end of the war speedily, without more bloodshed and devastation. In the language of his second inaugural address, he seemed to have "charity for all, malice toward none" . . . When at rest or listening, his legs and arms seemed to hang almost lifeless and his face careworn and haggard; but the moment he began to talk, his face lightened up, his tall form, as it were, unfolded, and he was the very impersonalization of good humor and fellowship. . . . We parted at the gangway of the River Queen, about noon of March 28, and I never saw him again. Of all the men I ever met, he seemed to possess more of the elements of greatness, combined with goodness, than any other.

And after Vietnam, few dare take on the role of Lincoln. He could not *live* on the stage or the screen or in the halls of Congress. There has been no voice among our politicians to speak "with earnest sympathy" to what Vietnam had done to the generation that either had to fight the war or reject it. If Lincoln had become a caricature, so the *Lincoln impulse* was discredited.

◇ ◇ ◇

On April 11, 1865, Sherman approached Raleigh and received news of Lee's surrender at Appomattox. His announcement to his troops caused a furor. "A little more labor, a little more toil on our part, the great race is won, and our government stands regenerated after four long years of war." The government regenerated after four years of war? The conclusion was hasty.

At that point a new specter terrified Sherman. He could not compel Joseph Johnston to fight his vastly superior army, but neither could he catch the Rebel in the open country of the North Carolina Piedmont. Johnston might easily disperse his army into guerilla bands. (History now tells us that Lee had considered and rejected this very possibility before he surrendered to Grant.) By Sherman's analysis, the Southern cavalrymen were better horsemen than their Northern counterparts. With hit-and-run tactics, bands of renegades might fight over the entire area of the South that Sherman had supposedly conquered, and prolong the war indefinitely. Thus, Sherman's position vis-à-vis Johnston was markedly different from that of Grant and Lee. Lee's army was trapped and surrounded. Johnston's army as a cohesive body was merely spent, but the Confederate general was not compelled to surrender.

On April 14, in Raleigh, Sherman received an invitation to talk with Johnston. Peace, as we now say, was at hand. On the morning of April 17 he arrived at the Raleigh depot, where a locomotive waited to take him to Durham's station. From there he was to proceed along the Hillsborough Road by horseback for the meeting. As he prepared to board the train, a telegraph operator rushed to him excitedly, saying an important cipher message was then coming in from the secretary of war. Sherman held the train for nearly an hour, while the news of Lincoln's assassination was decoded.

For Sherman, this moment must have required an almost superhuman effort at self-control. For him, the war had been fought upon a simple principle—that anarchy must be crushed. More than any man, he had come to the point of resolving that issue by military means. Now, assassins and guerillas presaged a new process, a new predicament for the nineteenth and twentieth centuries.

If Sherman's mission was official revenge, what better justification for a firestorm could there be than this? If it was to be his fate to be charged with wanton pillage anyway, who would blame him later for dropping all pretense now at controlling his troops? But the vision of Lincoln at City Point checked him. He turned to the telegraph boy and asked if the corporal had told anyone else of the content of the message. Receiving a negative, he swore the soldier to secrecy and proceeded to the meeting with Johnston.

Five miles out on the Hillsborough Road from Durham's station, the commanders met and proceeded together another mile to a small farmhouse owned by a farmer named Bennett. The farmer was invited to retire to an outbuilding. Once in Bennett's spare living room, Sherman handed Johnston the dispatch from Stanton, without comment. As the older man read, Sherman watched closely, searching Johnston's face for any hint, however remote, of prior knowledge or even complicity in the diabolical plot. By Sherman's account, beads of sweat broke out on Johnston's brow. The Southerner proclaimed the act to be a disgrace to the age and cried out that the South had finally come to realize that Lincoln was the best friend it had. Surely, Sherman did not hold the Confederate government responsible. Perhaps military men such as he or Lee could not be involved, Sherman replied, but he was not so sure

of politicians like Jefferson Davis and "men of that stripe."
One "ill-placed" comment might infuriate his troops, Sherman warned, and "a fate worse than that of Columbia
might befall Raleigh." Johnston sought to assuage his vol-
canic adversary. Sherman had fought "hard and clean," he
said soothingly; and he compared the Union conqueror to
Caesar and Hannibal.

In due course, they moved to the issue at hand. Sherman
proposed a straightforward surrender along the lines Grant
had accorded Lee. This is what he had promised Washington and had even written in a dispatch upon his departure
for the conference with Johnston that he would be careful
not to "complicate [the truce with] any points of civil policy." Johnston was not quick to accept, underscoring the
difference in his military situation to Lee's. Still, he conceded, further fighting would be murder. He cited the
words of Napoleon to the Archduke Charles at Wagram:
the civic crown earned by preserving the life of one citizen conferred more glory than the highest military
achievement.

With that, Johnston countered with an offer of universal
peace. Let them "make one job of it," a peace that would
embrace not just his own army but all the remaining Confederate armies, a peace from the Potomac to the Rio
Grande. It must be remembered that after Appomattox,
one hundred thousand Confederate soldiers were still under
arms, and Johnston had only forty thousand of them.
Strong forces remained in Tennessee and central Alabama.
None of these forces were surrounded as Lee's army in
Virginia had been. Sherman leapt at the idea. He spoke
excitedly about his City Point meeting with Lincoln. He
was, he proclaimed, abreast of Lincoln's views about
the war's aftermath (even though Lincoln was no longer
president).

It was as if Sherman suddenly felt possessed by Lincoln's spirit. The angel of vengeance would now become the angel of mercy. He would carry forward the magnanimous program of the martyred president almost as a mystical act. His new mission had the cast of heavenly design. Sherman must now *become* Lincoln, before the vindictive petty politicians in Washington took the great man's place. I think it was more. This was his one fleeting chance for atonement. In one bold stroke he could sweep away all he had done before, all that had been said of him as the barbaric warrior and all that would be said of him when history took over. He would go down as the great conqueror and the great peacemaker together. After Vietnam, only Robert McNamara would have the same impulse.

But not so fast. While Johnston announced that further conflict was pointless and would be murder, he spoke of the anxieties of his officers about the terms of surrender. What about their political rights? Were the Southern people to become slaves of the Northern people? Would there be persecutions or military exactions? What about their property? "To gain so cheaply this desired result" of universal surrender, Johnston asked what concessions Sherman was prepared to give, for only with reassurances about political rights, could Johnston promise that he could hold his army intact for a complete surrender, preventing it from dispersing into uncontrolled guerrilla bands.

But could Johnston speak for Confederate forces other than his own? The Confederate commander promised to secure that authority overnight. Curiously, Sherman did not feel he needed authority from Washington to speak for Federal armies in the field other than his own. He felt himself in no need of special instruction from the hysterical capital.

With universal surrender on the table, the two men parted, Sherman for Raleigh, Johnston for Hillsborough, to secure overnight the authority from Jefferson Davis to speak for all Confederate armies. At Raleigh, Sherman drafted his announcement to the troops of Lincoln's murder. If one single word from him could turn the city to ashes and render its population homeless, as he had warned Johnston, the words he did use were hardly detached. "We have met every phase which this war has assumed and must now be prepared for it in its last and worst shape, that of assassins and guerrillas; but woe unto the people who seek to expend their wild passions in such a manner, for there is but one dread result!" That result, he left to the imagination.

That night, meeting with his staff, Sherman seemed not to comprehend the consequences of the assassination. He had no impulse to wire Washington with the news of Johnston's overture and to wait for instructions. He had become Washington, Lincoln's Washington, a kind of twilight authority dedicated to a noble purpose of his own definition. From a military standpoint, he wanted to hold Johnston to some surrender, any surrender, or at least locked in negotiation, for he needed a few days to resupply his army. Later, as if writing for the record, he asserted, "Without exception all advised me to agree to some terms, for they all dreaded the long and harassing march in pursuit of dissolving and fleeing army—a march that might carry us back again over the thousand miles that we had just accomplished. We all knew that if we could bring Johnston's army to bay, we could destroy it in an hour, but that was simply impossible in the country in which we found ourselves."

They had arrived at the moment where the organized Southern armies might have dissolved into guerrilla bands —and prolonged the war indefinitely. With Jefferson Davis as Ho Chi Minh, the head of a fast-moving underground mobile government, fighting harassing operations against the occupying Union garrisons throughout the hospitable homeland, the conflict could have gone on indefinitely. If

Sherman could make the populace, young and old, feel the hard hand of war, the population in turn could make Sherman feel the hard hand of occupation, bankrupting the already shaky Federal treasury. Eventually, the Union would have had to come to an accommodation. Such a peace movement had been just barely averted seven months earlier, only because Sherman had captured Atlanta immediately before the 1864 election and thus ensured a resolute second term.

On the night of April 17, the discussion between Sherman and his staff moved quickly to political questions. Should they permit the escape of Jefferson Davis, as Lincoln had wanted? Not only should they do so, one of his generals argued, but they should even provide a ship to take Davis and the other top Confederate political leaders from Charleston to Nassau.

The following morning, at Bennett Place, Sherman and Johnston reconvened. Johnston had received authorization to proceed with a universal settlement. If agreement could be reached, the other Confederate armies would surrender on the same terms. But what assurances could Sherman give Confederate officers concerning their political rights, Johnston wanted to know. Sherman cited Lincoln's amnesty proclamation of December 8, 1863. Upon laying down their arms and swearing allegiance, officers could receive a pardon and resume full rights of citizenship. At Appomattox, Grant had extended amnesty to officers *above* the rank of colonel, including General Lee himself. Johnson was skeptical. He sensed, better than Sherman, that prior representations by the slain Lincoln might now be moot. A Confederate political leader was summoned into the farmhouse, and Sherman was presented with a handwritten draft containing a long preamble and wordy surrender terms that included a total amnesty for all Confederate civilian authorities, including Jefferson Davis.

Sherman read it quickly and tossed it aside. It was too general and verbose, he declared. But before he tried his own hand at peace terms, he pulled out a bottle of whiskey from his saddlebag, and, by his account, the gesture occasioned an almost beatific expression on the face of his hard-pressed adversaries.

Taking pen and paper, Sherman withdrew to a small table with his whiskey bottle and began to write furiously. He receded into his private world, the surrogate Lincoln, the merciless conqueror possessed by Lincoln's kindly spirit and by guilt for the desolation he had brought to the region he once loved. The guilt was unconscious—the term in those days would certainly have been "unmanly"—but I believe it was central to his actions.

What emerged, between slugs of whiskey, were seven points. Beside the standard provision for disbanding armies, these remarkable five points stood out: (1) the recognition of state governments before the Union government had a chance to restructure itself; in short, no Reconstruction; (2) the guarantee of political rights before the Federal government had a chance to weed out the highest traitors; (3) the guarantee of the rights of property, with no mention of slaves as an exception; (4) a distribution of arms in the state arsenals that might easily be repossessed by recalcitrant rebels, if they regained political rights too easily; and (5) a general amnesty.

Sherman finished his document with a flourish of satisfaction. Upon reading Sherman's document, the Confederates "readily" accepted, no doubt with unseemly speed. Why not? One can imagine them exchanging euphoric glances and mightily suppressing whoops of joy. The Confederacy lived, in all but the name! The Old South endured! Long live the Confederacy!

◈　◈　◈

The war was over, but what had it been fought for? Lincoln wanted to be charitable after so terrible an ordeal, but would he have allowed the Union casualties to feel their sacrifices had been for nothing, as a century later so many Vietnam casualties did? After divisive war, whether it be a civil war where a generation takes arms against one another, or a pointless immoral war where a generation is divided between soldiers, resisters, and shirkers, reconciliation is only one moral imperative. The cause of the victorious North had been this preservation of the Union, and by the right of victory, it demanded that the vestiges of rebellion and secession should forever be expunged. With the Emancipation Proclamation in 1863, the abolition of slavery had been officially folded into the struggle of the North, and that institution, too, by rights, had to be smashed in fact and in spirit in the new nation. But for so passionately fought a cause as the South's, protecting "a way of life" as the romantics still refer to it, but surely, protecting one's hearth from armed invasion, the impulse to rebellion and the habit of enslaving the black man could not be magically waved away. A social revolution was necessary, and it would have to be imposed from without. It too would require a moral fervor, as strong as the passions of the war itself, which would treat discrimination and disunion as scurrilous evils.

Thus, at the Bennett Place, reconciliation and reconstruction were opposites: to bind up the nation's wounds would leave the issue of the war unresolved. To tackle the remaking of the South immediately was to prolong the state of war.

But one option was not open to Sherman or Andrew Johnson, or to Lincoln had he lived. That was to do nothing. General Johnston had to surrender on some terms to Sherman, and if those terms did not contain some concession to political rights, the recalcitrant Confederate officers were not going to surrender, because, from the military point of view, they did not have to. Even a year later, when Andrew Johnson settled into his role as naysayer to the radical Republicans and protectors of the very Southern gentry he had at first promised to impoverish, his "restoration" (restoring the Southern states to the Union, regardless of how many secessionist leaders were involved) required *some* action.

For ten years after Vietnam, another restoration took place. But it followed no reconstruction that involved hard grappling with how and why American men were sent to a jungle ten thousand miles away, or with how and why America lost. No Vietnam policymakers have been disgraced, as Confederate leaders were, nor have the evils of their thinking been clearly defined, so those evils would not be repeated. Nor have the many diverse casualties of that policy been properly cared for. As a consequence, the United States drifted into a similar situation in Central America and the Middle East, thinking many of the same thoughts, applying many of the same theories. Nor has there been, apart from what the mere passage of time provides, any real reconciliation: no generous amnesty to the dissenters; no broad program to meet the special, indeed unique torment of the surviving Vietnam veteran; no broad recognition of the contribution of dissent and civil disobedience to ending the war. By contrast to the aftermath of the Civil War, reconstruction and reconciliation were not contradictory in Vietnam's aftermath. They were joined, one meaning nothing without the other, and intertwined in that neither was undertaken. Binding up the nation's wounds after Vietnam was stiff medicine: a series of punitive clemencies for Vietnam resisters, no equalizing of Vietnam veterans' benefits to the benefits of World War II veterans, endless studies on Agent Orange without legislation to compensate the victims, no reconstruction aid for Southeast Asia. Two positive measures alone mark the ten-year period: ninety-one "readjustment centers" for veterans, put into operation seven years after the Paris Peace, and a monument in Washington.

Lincoln charity has been absent. Sherman atonement has been absent. Time has simply elapsed, and people wonder why, for those who had to choose, the wounds do not heal.

For ten years after Vietnam, evasion and psychological repression dominated the country's thought, as it tried to forget its longest and most expensive war and its first Lost Cause, as if Vietnam was a parenthesis in our history. In 1983, Ronald Reagan could still talk about "the Great War," the war of his youth, World War II, as if no other subsequent war deserves mention. That sentiment is the malady of his generation, but Reagan is hardly unique. Every president since 1945 has shared this fixation with "the big one," America's one great heroic war, the war against Hitler. In Reagan's cause, this is heavy with irony, since the closest he ever came to combat was in 1969 when as governor he commanded the California National Guard in its assault on Berkeley protestors with clubs and tear gas and rubber bullets. Politicians continue to find a willing audience in celebrating pre-Vietnam, prenuclear, broad-shouldered Americanism, and in touting an America that never lost a war and stood for the "forces of Good and Liberty," to use Reagan's phrase.

In short, Vietnam has not been integrated into American history. Only ten years after the Paris Peace Accords, is the national effort at cleansing and clarifying about to begin.

◈ ◈ ◈

Assassination is a reality of modern political life. It has spawned an army of secret service men, a science of investigation and crowd control, a technology that only the modern policeman can know or understand. In my adult life, which has known six presidents, all have been the targets of assassins, three have been shot at, one has died. A U.S. Congressman, Leo Ryan, has been slain; a black prophet, Martin Luther King, murdered; and an Alabama governor and presidential candidate, George Wallace, has been paralyzed by a bullet. The man with a pistol, lurking in the shadows or in the faceless crowd, has become a familiar character of modern film and literature, and the act of political murder, if not quite commonplace, has lost its element of terrible shock and surprise.

It was not so in April 1865. Lincoln's single guard at Ford's Theater, who moved away from the presidential box to get a better view of the play, is an adequate symbol of law enforcement in that day. The Secret Service had been established only weeks before, comprised a handful of men, and was headed by a notorious liar and rogue named Lafayette Baker. Sherman's peace terms to General Johnston sped to a Washington frazzled with hysteria and consumed with the passion for revenge over America's first and most shocking assassination. The document sped not by telegraph, but in the hands of a single military aide, Maj. Henry Hitchcock, who had been instructed by Sherman to be careful of spies who might importune him. Hitchcock's trip, by locomotive from Raleigh to the coast, and by steamer to Washington, took two days. He arrived in the early evening of April 21.

In the twilight transition, with the country not quite comprehending that Lincoln was gone, and His Accidency, as Andrew Johnson came to be known, not quite appreciating that he had ascended to power, the secretary of war, Edwin Stanton, was the man in charge. Through him the search for Booth was carried forward, and it was a disorganized fiasco altogether. Ten thousand Federal troops scoured southern Maryland, steeping on one another's toes, with no set plan of investigation, and the absence of immediate results only sent Stanton into greater spasms of anxiety. The war secretary tried an offer of a reward, $10,000, for Booth, but this only intensified the competition among troops. In the end, it took the rogue, Detective Baker, to come up with a plan to catch the murderer, and he accomplished it with twenty-five men and "a little bending of the rules." Later, Baker would write a book about the Secret Service and congratulate himself for his own "keen discernment and profound knowledge of men, bred of many secret and perilous adventures and many hairbreadth adventures," and he proceeded to attribute to himself confidences and heroics that could not possibly have been true. In one, he had President Lincoln whispering to him confidentially several days before the president's death, when Baker presented the president with details of assassination plots:

"Well, Baker, what would they want to kill me for? If they kill me, they run the risk of getting a worse man."

The agitated, frightened, judgmental Stanton leapt to the conclusion that the assassination was a conspiracy, hatched from Richmond, "planned and set on foot by rebels under pretense of avenging the rebel cause." Booth, Stanton was sure, was headed back to Richmond for his just rewards. This was scarcely Stanton's opinion alone. General Grant's first wire to Richmond after the assassination was to arrest top Confederate officials and all high officers who had refused to take an oath of allegiance. How many assassins might still be loose, no one knew. In his message to Sherman about the assassination, Stanton had mentioned a man named "Clark" who was supposed to have designs on Sherman, but Sherman replied flatly, "He [Clark] had better be in a hurry or he will be too late."

It is another of the modern injustices that modern entertainment foists upon the American public that a Hollywood film in the 1970s entitled *The Lincoln Conspiracy* suggested that Stanton himself had been the linchpin of a conspiracy to kill Lincoln, but there is no evidence whatever for it. Stanton's admiration for Lincoln bordered upon worship. In Lincoln, Stanton saw the qualities of grace and sensitivity and leadership that he himself lacked. He had uttered the immortal words, when the president's breathing stopped, "Now he belongs to the ages," and he had been unable to control himself when he viewed Lincoln's body lying in state in the Capitol. To this distraught cabinet member had been left the unenviable task of seeing that Mrs. Lincoln's request that there be no commercialization of the murder be honored.

Into this Washington, with this unnerved war secretary at the helm, Sherman's peace terms arrived at the War Department at 6:00 P.M., April 21. Grant saw them first and felt instinctively that his friend had overstepped his authority. Stanton rushed to the War Department, and Grant, now the man in the middle, tried to soften the reaction as he handed the war secretary the Sherman document. The terms, said Grant, were not exactly what "we hoped for"; they went beyond what he had accorded Lee at Appomattox; on the other hand, Sherman had achieved a universal surrender.

Stanton's first glance at the document sent him into a soaring rage. Sherman was wild and uncontrollable. Now, at the moment of victory, Sherman had turned traitor. With one stroke of his pen, he had given away all the war was fought for. The old persistent rumors about Sherman's insanity inevitably surfaced. The general was imperial Stanton ranted, an antidemocrat who had expressed his preference for a monarchy over a republic only weeks before, wasn't that so? and now, by God, there was a military coup afoot. Its plans were broader than the simple assassination of Lincoln. Suddenly, in Stanton's mind, Booth and Sherman were coupled.

Beneath Stanton's frenzy lay the timeless problem of civilian control over the military, a precept which military commanders, occupying hostile territory or being presented with the chance to compel a ceasefire, often find complicated. But Stanton was shepherding the delicate area of the administration's Reconstruction policy. At the last Cabinet meeting over which Lincoln presided, Stanton had put forward a plan for the "temporary" military occupation of the South after its unconditional surrender, as the first step toward Reconstruction. Under military protectorship, Southerners would have to prove their loyalty by an oath of allegiance before they could resume a part in the political life of the country. After Vietnam, war resisters were invited to prove their loyalty in a similar fashion. Since 1863, Lincoln had experimented with loyal legislatures in Louisiana and Virginia, with disappointing results. Throughout the war, a loyal Virginia legislature—it was a precious vehicle altogether—had met in Alexandria. In Louisiana, Lincoln had hoped for a ten percent solution: ten percent of the populace who would take a loyalty oath would elect a legislature, and it would become a "tangible nucleus" around which the supposedly remorseful rebels would rally. "Such a government is only to what it should be as the egg is to the fowl," Lincoln wrote, "but we shall sooner have the fowl by hatching the egg than by smashing it."

But at the Bennett Place, Sherman had produced the fowl itself, and the bird, with its scarlet and blue plumage, looked distinctly like the gritty menace that the Union had been trying to exterminate for four years. The Sherman truce was an appeasement by the total victor and the very sort of accommodation that Lincoln's opponent in the 1864 election, General George McClellan, had proposed and the country had rejected.

In his excitement, Stanton seized pen and paper and wrote a note for all cabinet members. "By the order of the President," a cabinet meeting was announced for eight o'clock that evening. The messenger dispatched, Stanton dictated a memorandum to his secretary, "sentences tumbling from his lips in an impetuous torrent," and then the secretary of war and the general rushed off to find President Johnson and inform him of the cabinet meeting the president had just ordered.

The meeting convened promptly at eight o'clock. General Grant, trying to keep the brakes on, read Sherman's dispatches to the cabinet. With Stanton leading the charge and President Johnson following, the action was roundly condemned. All agreed with some self-satisfaction that mere generals in the field had no authority to decide political questions. The terms were promptly disapproved, and Grant, at his own request, was authorized to take the disapproval to Raleigh personally.

Then the meanness began. Stanton directed Grant not only to deliver the president's disapproval but to take with him a directive from President Lincoln to General Grant, dated March 3, 1865, in which Lincoln expressly forbade Grant to discuss any political question with General Lee in a surrender negotiation. Although Sherman had never seen the March 3 communiqué, Stanton's purpose now was to imply that Sherman had directly disobeyed a presidential command at the Bennett Place, and was in effect launched upon a mutiny. As a result, Grant was ordered, upon reaching Raleigh, to relieve Sherman of command, to inform the enemy of the disapproval, and to resume hostilities in forty-eight hours.

From the governor's palace in Raleigh, Sherman turned his mind to resupply and to rebuild bridges for his railroad, taking what iron "on the branch" that he needed for the process. He was confident that his terms would sail through Washington, so confident that in his covering letter he had even instructed the new president not to vary the terms at all, for *he* had considered everything. He could see no hitch, as he wrote his wife. Sherman, the brutal warrior, was now Sherman, the tender peacemaker, and the opposites thus latched together would assure for him a place unique in history. Amid his military activity, he found time to write a friendly letter to General Johnston, congratulating them both on their good work, two old adversaries from the same club making one job of it. He thought they would have no trouble from Washington in recognizing existing state governments, he wrote, although the lawyers might want to introduce some technical language here and there. As to the blacks, Sherman set the tone for the next hundred years. "I believe if the South would simply and publicly declare . . . that slavery is dead, you would inaugurate an era of peace and prosperity that would efface the ravages of the past four years of war. Negroes would remain in the South and afford you an abundance of cheap labor, which otherwise will be driven away; and it will save the country the senseless discussions which have kept us all in hot water for fifty years."

While Grant steamed along the coast to North Carolina for the purpose of diluting Sherman's conceit, Stanton was hatching his scheme. His passion had been taken into an even higher orbit by a telegram from Richmond that had arrived after Grant's departure. It passed on the rumor that millions of dollars in gold from the Richmond banks had been taken by the fleeing Confederate leaders, and the rebels hoped to use the loot as a bribe to General Sherman as the price of escape. Grabbing a map and misreading the troop movements of Sherman's commander below Greensboro, Stanton divined that Sherman was at that moment opening up an avenue of escape for Davis. The bribe was already in effect!

To take on Sherman now was a formidable risk, for the general was now at the height of popularity, the most successful officer in a Union army famous for failures. Sherman had in reality reëlected Lincoln with his victory in Atlanta and broken the back of the rebellion with his march. His brother, John Sherman, was a powerful senator from Ohio. But great issues as well as careers, were at stake, and Stanton took on the task with relish. He summoned the reporter from the *New York Times* and gave him for publication an official War Department dispatch, heavy with innuendo about traitorous motives on General Sherman's part. The worst possible construction was put on Sherman's actions; the March 3 Lincoln-to-Grant communiqué forbidding political discussion was quoted in full, implying that Sherman had the communiqué at the Bennett Place and went ahead anyway on his mystical mission; the Richmond rumor about Davis's bribery horde was also quoted, alongside the false report that Sherman had cleared the railroad between Greensboro and Charlotte. "The orders of General Sherman . . . will probably open the way for Davis to escape to Mexico or Europe with his plunder which is reported to be very large, . . . Johnston's negotiations look to this end." The terms and Stanton's ten reasons for disapproving them (which had not been shown to Sherman) followed. The dispatch in the *Times* concluded cryptically with the news that Grant had gone to North Carolina to direct operations against Johnston's army.

But Stanton was not finished. His new commander in Richmond was H. W. Halleck, the erstwhile ethicist, whose prewar book on military ethics set out the rules for the protection of property and the humane treatment of civilians, and who as army chief of staff had invited Sherman to level Charleston and pour salt on it. Halleck had assumed command only several days before. Now, Stanton instructed Sherman's subordinate commanders to disregard Sherman's orders and ordered Halleck to move into Sherman's area of command to cut off Jefferson Davis's escape. Thereby, Union army was set against Union army, and it is well that events quickly passed these orders by. For this last act, the march of Union troops behind Johnston's army while the Confederate commander held his own army in place in good faith accordance with his armistice, reflected directly on Sherman's honor as a gentleman and a soldier.

Grant had come to North Carolina, so his affectionate biographer wrote, to soften the blow of Washington's scorn, but he could have softened it better in Washington had he spoken up more forcefully for Sherman. He could have refused to supersede Sherman or argued for a more temperate tone to the disapproval, for the entire Union was in Sherman's debt. But Grant was treading his way between two highly volatile characters. He was also caught between duty and friendship. In the end, he neither did his duty by relieving Sherman of command, nor upheld his friendship by supporting Sherman against the political wolves, and somehow, it turned out all right. He saved his friendship with Sherman without jeopardizing his position as supreme commander.

The style of management had changed in Washington, and Grant was trying to cope with it. Later in his memoirs, commissioned and shepherded by Mark Twain, Grant compared the contrasting styles of Lincoln and Stanton.

They [Lincoln and Stanton] were the very opposite of each other in almost every particular except that each possessed great ability. Mr. Lincoln gained influence over men by making them feel that it was a pleasure to serve him. He preferred yielding his own wish to gratify others, rather than to insist upon having his own way. It distressed him to disappoint others. In matters of public duty, however, he had what he wished, but in the least offensive way. . . . Mr. Stanton cared nothing for feelings of others. In fact, it seemed pleasanter to him to disappoint than to gratify.

It is generally supposed that these two officials formed a complement to one another. . . . [But] it is not a correct view in my estimation. Mr. Lincoln was not timid, and he was willing to trust his generals in making and executing their plans. The secretary was very timid, and it was impossible for him to avoid interfering with the armies. . . . He could see our weakness, but he could not see that the enemy was in danger. The enemy would not have been in danger, if Mr. Stanton was in the field.

At this juncture, Stanton had mastered his timidity and let loose his practice of disappointing in the most offensive way.

Had the facts come to Sherman all at once, rather than piecemeal, in the days that followed, this reunion in Raleigh between himself and Grant might have been a far more sour affair. Together, they had won the war. The emotional bond between them, forged by trust and respect and hard fighting, had made one nearly the reflection of the other, as opposite as they were in personality. Grant did not commit his emotions to paper, partly because he was not a learned man, but Sherman did so often and had even employed his pen in defense of Grant. After the battle of Shiloh, a withering attack on Grant's generalship appeared in an Ohio newspaper, charging Grant with stupidity and negligence and reporting a "general feeling" that the commander should be court-martialed or shot. The diatribe was written by the Ohio lieutenant governor, Benjamin Stanton (no relation to Edwin). Sherman rushed in. He was not surprised, he wrote, when newspapermen lied, because "it is their trade." But men in public life should not stoop "to this dirty work." To assert that Grant was surprised at Shiloh is "the most wicked falsehood that was ever thrust upon a people sad and heartsore at the terrible but necessary casualties of war."

If you have no respect for the honor and reputation of the generals who lead the armies of your country, you should have some regard for the welfare and honor of the country itself. Our whole force, if imbued with your notions, would be driven across the Ohio in less than a month and even you would be disturbed in your quiet study where you now in perfect safety write libels.

But the pen was not sufficient. During the tempest over Shiloh, Sherman found Grant, drooping upon a stump, and preparing to go away for a while. "You know I'm in the way here, Sherman," he said. But Sherman prevailed upon him to stay. After the victory at Chattanooga in March 1864, Grant was appointed lieutenant general and shifted to Washington. And Sherman, in glory as in despair, wrote to him what he felt:

I believe you are as brave, patriotic, and just, as the great prototype [George] Washington; as unselfish, kind-hearted and honest as a man should be; but the chief characteristic in your nature is the simple faith in success you have always manifested which I can liken to nothing else than a faith a Christian has in his Savior.

This faith gave you victory at Shiloh and Vicksburg. When you have completed your best preparations you go into battle without hesitation, as at Chattanooga—no doubts, no reserve; and I tell you that it was this that made us act with confidence. I knew wherever I was, that you thought of me, and if I got in a tight place you would come—if alive.

Now, Sherman *was* in a tight spot, and Grant was coming, acting as subtly as he was able, and honestly as a man had to be . . . but no more so. No doubt, there was a large, freewheeling welcome before they settled in with hearty coffee and Grant told Sherman what he must; that his terms were disapproved, and that he was to give the enemy notice to surrender on a military basis pure and simple. Otherwise, hostilities were to resume in forty-eight hours. By Grant's account, Sherman took the news quietly, but later in letters and testimony, Sherman sought to justify himself. He denied that his terms recognized Confederate governments or abrogated their debt; he asserted that his certification of rebel institutions was a temporary measure, a military means to an end, "the commonest thing for military commanders" in times like these. Occasionally, he argued, military commanders had to seize the moment to secure surrender, when constant communication with civil authority was not possible—(a point which overlooked the fact that General Johnston had delayed overnight to obtain that very negotiating authority). Washington's action would surely now mean that Johnston's army could dissolve into bands of desperados, and Washington could deal with them. He would not. In Sherman's mind, the image of Lincoln at City Point was engraved. If Sherman talked of Lincoln, Lincoln, Lincoln, as if to justify his Bennett Place terms, Grant must have wanted to shout at him, "But you are not Lincoln"; since Lincoln had been murdered, the rules in Washington had changed . . . changed forever. The impulse toward revenge had overwhelmed the impulse toward reconciliation. Besides, he had not come to North Carolina to be persuaded by arguments, but to convey a simple order from civilian authority.

At each juncture in this difficult mission, Grant stripped away the passion to keep the situation in control. He made nothing of his order to relieve Sherman of command, but rather expressed satisfaction at the state of military affairs. He downplayed Stanton's torrent of abuse and wild language and imprecations of a Sherman political design. He kept his presence in Raleigh as much a secret as he could, partly because he did not want the Confederates to know of his presence, mainly because if events proceeded toward their main objective of a simple military truce, he meant to slip out of town quietly, leaving his friend "free and untrammeled" and still very much in command. And in his first communication to Washington, he wired Stanton that Sherman was "not surprised" at the disapproval, a useful dissembling, and had obeyed orders exactly in informing the enemy of Washington's position.

The following day, as the Union generals waited for Johnston's reply, Sherman wrote to Stanton directly, admitting his "folly" in negotiating nonmilitary matters, but citing Stanton's own instigation toward that very thing in Savannah . . . to bend the rules to gain victory at the earliest moment. He still believed Washington had made a mistake, but that was not his affair. He reassured Stanton that he would follow orders.

Sherman's mood was still on the level of bruised sensibilities, for the *New York Times* would not publish Stanton's skewed version of events for another three days. The matter, so far as Sherman was aware, was being handled in official communications, deemed sacred and confidential. But his response never questioned the supremacy of civilian authority, and in this he differed from Douglas MacArthur. Even in the coming days, as the full extent of Stanton's insult became clear, and umbrage turned to unbridled rage, the matter stayed on the level of honor and decency as shabby treatment for the South's conqueror.

General Johnston, on the other hand, had become the hub of the expiring Confederate cause, and it was not to his liking. The peace process had only been initiated by the Confederate commander because Jefferson Davis was sure an overture by the Confederate president would be spurned. For the Union had consistently denied the legitimacy of the Confederate government. To negotiate with its civil authorities now would be tantamount to recognition. Still, the initial note to Sherman from Johnston hoped for Jefferson Davis to be involved. It stated the purpose of the military conference as arranging an armistice, so that the *civil authorities* might enter negotiations to end the war. But at Bennett Place, Sherman rejected that scheme out of hand in accordance with his government's policy. He would neither receive nor transmit to Washington any message from the renegade Confederate functionaries. If any negotiations were to take place, it would have to be strictly between military men, with the subject surrender.

As the Bennett Place terms made their way slowly to and from Washington, between April 18 and April 24, the anxieties within the Confederate ranks rose markedly. Johnston had advocated surrender going strictly on the numbers: he had 25,000 soldiers in tatters but still in arms, and he faced three Union armies fresh and resupplied: Grant's 180,000 in Virginia, Sherman's 110,000, and Canby's 60,000 in Alabama. That made a ratio of eighteen to one. Now, in the six days he awaited Washington's answer, he lost another 8,000 in desertions.

The Virginian received Washington's response and immediately communicated the disapproval to Davis, who had made it to Charlotte. To the Union demand for an unconditional surrender, Davis's reply was defiant: surrender the infantry, he ordered Johnston, but send to me all the remaining cavalry and any other soldiers who could be mounted on horses from the wagon trains. The order was Sherman's nightmare, "the tangible nucleus" not for a loyal government to which contrite rebels might rally, but for a mounted guerrilla force for the uncontrite.

Only one thing stopped this from happening: the disobedience of an old-fashioned man. General Johnston objected to Davis's order for ethical reasons, for the order met only one of his great duties as he then perceived them: the protection of the Confederate executive. But what of his army and his region? He decided to disobey this last order as a Confederate officer.

"The belief that impelled me to urge the civil authorities to make peace, that it would be a great crime to prolong the war, prompted me to disobey these instructions," Johnston wrote in his memoir. "They would have given the president [Davis] an escort too heavy for flight and not strong enough to force a way for him and could have spread ruin all over the South by leading three great invading armies in pursuit. In that belief, I determined to do all in my power to bring about a termination of hostilities."

And so the tables were turned fully upside down. It was Johnston now who, in insubordination and far more conscious than Sherman of being on a mission solely of his own, sued for surrender on the enemy's terms.

Within twenty-four hours, Johnston requested another meeting at Bennett Place, and the following day Sherman ventured again to the modest farmhouse. General Grant expressly remained behind in Raleigh. By nightfall, Sherman returned with Appomattox terms signed. Peace had come, not universally from the Potomac to the Rio Grande, for hostile forces remained in Alabama and Texas, but at least from the Potomac to Mobile Bay and the Sabine River. Grant was satisfied with his three days in North Carolina. He slipped away unnoticed the next morning. And Sherman, in turn, would later take comfort that during their time together Grant had not evinced "in his language or manner one particle of abatement in his confidence, respect and affection that have existed between us through all the varied events of the war."

On his way back to Washington, as he stopped at Goldsboro, Grant received a copy of the April 28 *New York Times,* and he was horrified. "I fully realized what great indignation [this treatment] would cause Sherman, though I do not think his feelings could have been more excited than were my own."

Sherman did not see the paper until May 2, and his passion welled to gale force. But rather than express his outrage to his devoted troops, who as they marched one hundred thousand strong on Washington, would have done anything for him, Sherman repaired, characteristically, to his writing table to defend his personal honor. In his peace terms, he maintained little pride, understating his hopes for their adoption now. He wanted them ratified for military reasons solely, to accomplish the orderly dismantling of the Confederate army and to relieve his nightmare of guerrilla bands set upon infinite mischief. The terms suddenly became "skeletal" and, after all, submitted to the proper authority for action. Then they became mere "glittering generalities," meaning much or meaning little, which had the effect of holding the enemy intact and in place until Washington could decide upon its peacetime course. Adequate precedent, at least in so far as the authorities had deigned to inform him, existed for each point in his truce, he argued, in the form of instructions both from Secretary Stanton and President Lincoln, and he rightly felt victimized by the vacillation of civilian authority over the involvement of military leaders in political questions which impinged upon a commander's role. But nowhere in the literature that Sherman spawned in May 1865 over this confrontation is there the least hint of a desire to impose his own solution. Everywhere, he accepts implicitly the supremacy of civilian control. He was, in short, never dangerous. To the end, he believed, naively, that Lincoln would have sustained him, had the president lived, or at the very least, not treated his awkward effort at peacemaking with such contempt.

What galled him was the assault on his soldier's code: the sanctity of official correspondence, published in part to the world without his knowledge or consent; the charge of insubordination; the orders to move troops of another command into his own, as he was trying to effect an honorable surrender; and the directives to his own subordinates to disregard his orders. On these points, he was unforgiving, and he vowed revenge upon Stanton in a most Victorian fashion.

On disregarding his orders, he wrote, "This is too much; and I turn from the subject with feelings too strong for words, and merely record my belief that so much mischief was never before embraced in so small a space as in the newspaper paragraph headed 'Sherman's Truce Disregarded.' "

On the publication of his official correspondence, together with directives he had never seen, he wrote, "As the editor of the *Times* has logically and fairly drawn the inference from this singular document that I am insubordinate, I can only deny the intention. I have never in my life questioned or disobeyed an order, though many and many a time have I risked my life, my health, and reputation in obeying orders, or even hints, to execute plans and purposes not to my liking. It is not fair to withhold from me plans and policy (if any there be) and expect me to guess at them. . . . [My men] will learn with pain and sorrow that I am deemed insubordinate and wanting in common sense, that I, who have labored night and day, winter and summer, for four years, and have brought an army of 70,000 men in magnificent condition across country deemed impassable, and placed it just where it was wanted almost on the day appointed, have brought discredit on the government."

And on the civilian control over the military, he wrote with manifest hurt, "It is true that non-combatants—men who sleep in comfort and security while we watch on distant lines—are better able to judge than we poor soldiers, who rarely see a newspaper, hardly can hear from our families, or stop long enough to get our pay. I envy not the task of reconstruction and am delighted that the Secretary has relieved me of it. . . . I will therefore go on and execute your orders to the conclusion, and when done, will, with intense satisfaction, leave to civil authorities the execution of the task of which they seem so jealous; but as an honest man and soldier, I invite them to follow my path; for they may see some things and hear some things that may disturb their philosophy."

◈ ◈ ◈

The empty room at Bennett Place.

Was there a way to make it more than *pure* history? As

161

just another historical monument, it could never compete with Appomattox. Not enough happened here. The challenge was to make it *applied* history.

How might Sherman's march be rendered into a parable for modern time? How might Sherman at Bennett Place be made into a monument to peacemaking?

The inevitable glass case or the audio visual display can not contain the lessons, for the lessons are ideas and concepts. Sherman's pen or the whiskey bottle from the medical stores or even examples of his frantic, illegible penmanship . . . such trinkets are trivial and beside the point. The official correspondence between Sherman and Stanton? Newspaper clippings from the *New York Times?* For a figure so modern as Sherman and a process so universal as making peace, clippings and correspondence are static. Sherman's terrible gifts are his notions of honor and necessity in war.

The place needs a treatment that can be every bit as exciting as a war reënactment. It needs to be a place of reflection every bit as interesting as a battlefield park. To imagine peace? How can that ever be made as exciting as imagining war? It needs a great, quiet spectacle with this torn, rich, fascinating character as its central figure who will sharpen the modern connections: the degree of permissible terror against a wartime foe, the widening license of war, reconciliation after divisive war, political control over the military. It needs a show that can make the past live as prelude and warn the present of the coming finale.

The empty room at Washington.

Names of fifty-five thousand soldiers etched upon black marble carving a *V* into an earthen depression. A congressman and a combat veteran called it a "black gash of shame." A Vietnam policymaker called it, in quiet resignation, a testament to suffering in an unworthy cause.

Many heralded a long overdue recognition of the Vietnam veteran.

Recognized for what?

Others say its emptiness makes it a place of quiet reflection.

Reflect upon what?

The names of the dead are not enough.

PART II
Present as Finale

The Sherman Parable 8

GENERAL Sherman had done the dirty work for the Union. To him had fallen the duty to break the spirit of the rebellion, to punish the rebels, whatever their sex or station. His unsparing, relentless hand had given the Union victory. The dirty work of the Vietnam war was consigned to a small percentage of the Vietnam generation: the poor, the uneducated, and the youth who fought, who were wounded, who died. Most who went to Vietnam, the studies show, saw moderate to heavy combat. It is only the glories of modern medical science and the speed of the helicopter that prevented the names on the

Vietnam Memorial in Washington from being etched in much smaller print.

The dirty work in the Vietnam aftermath has been done to all members of the Vietnam generation, not just those who fought and those who resisted, but also to the majority who avoided the nasty business altogether. In 1971, a Vietnam veteran who had turned passionately against the war, put the matter starkly. Wrote veteran and poet Jan Barry:

With the conviction of Lieutenant Calley, the real dilemma of my generation has finally been brought unmistakably home. To kill on military orders and be a criminal, or to refuse to kill and be a criminal is the moral agony of America's Vietnam war generation. . . . Every last Vietnam [veteran] is guilty along with Calley of committing war crimes. Because a "free fire zone"—where anything that moves can be shot—is by definition a violation of the Geneva Convention of 1949 with respect to the treatment of civilians; because "a search-and-destroy mission"—where anything living is destroyed or removed—is also a violation of the Geneva Conventions; because massive defoliation, reconnaissance by fire, saturation bombing, mad moments, and forcibly relocating villagers are all violations of international law, and therefore, war crimes. . . .

Our dilemma is that no matter what we do—go to Vietnam or refuse—either action is criminal, against some law, and therefore, "wrong." . . . Going to Vietnam is a war crime, refusing to go is a domestic crime and just sitting still, somewhere in exile or limbo, is a moral crime. It is a terrible time today to be American and young. In fact, it apparently is a crime.

A whole generation has been scarred by the war and immobilized in its aftermath. The choices it had and it lives with, nobody wanted to think about, not even they. Its veterans were treated first as suckers and monsters, a dangerous combination altogether, and ten years later, as lost souls, jittery and uncontrollable wrecks who dissolve pathetically before the wailing wall their government had given them, remembering God knows what, grieving for their friends and for themselves. The country has not and may not ever look to them for leadership, certainly not in the way it turned to the brash, upright young World War II heroes like John Kennedy, Richard Nixon, Lyndon Johnson, Gerald Ford, and Jimmy Carter—men who ran for office proudly displaying themselves in their veterans' uniforms and waving their war records.

Its vocal protestors and its conscientious objectors continue to bear the stigma of disloyalty. And worse: they take the blame for shaking the political will of the leaders to prosecute war and seize "victory." To the resisters went the scorn for official restraint, and we are asked to believe, that restraint "lost" the war. Such ideas can take hold only in a country that has either forgotten why the Vietnam war could *never* be won in the conventional sense or confounds reality by embracing the war as a "noble cause." In the rush to forget Vietnam, it was forgotten who checked the violence of two presidents, and who exposed the bottomless demands of the military, and to whom went the laurels for forcing the country out of the war. There has been precious little nobility for the protestor, except in his own mind, except in his assurance that historians will note who stood up against the madness. No memorial will be erected to his sacrifices and achievements, unless in privacy, he wishes to enter the empty room of the Vietnam Veterans Memorial in Washington and make it a protesters' memorial as well, taking comfort in his personal efforts to stop the carnage that the memorial forces one to reflect upon.

As for the well-dressed malingerers, the best educated, the most cunning, the most creative of the generation, they live with their little secret: their citizenship came of age on a note of avoidance, an avoidance without apparent prejudice to themselves which in turn bred a profound cynicism toward their responsibilities in a free society. Their man-

169

hood began in failing to answer the call, either to arms or to resistance. Their alienation is quiet and opportunistic. They blend well into the society. Their careers often became those specialties that could ensure a refuge from the fray. Because of early deferments for husbands and fathers, often they formed marriages that never should have been consummated, and they sired children who never should have been born. If the cruel charge of substitution is valid against any group, it is valid for the sixteen million who avoided Vietnam legally. By their avoidance, the country had, de facto, reverted to the practice of the Civil War, where a man could buy a substitute. This forced the American army to lower its standards and turn the war into a working-class enterprise. Had it not been for this overall turpitude, a Lt. William Calley could never have been an officer in the U.S. Army. And it created a formidable, muted contempt within the ranks between the few well educated and the many uneducated. Because the avoiders are the brightest, as well as the majority, of the generation, their cynicism in the aftermath is especially damaging to the country. The luster went off public service and the political career after Vietnam and Watergate, and the talented young pursued strictly private careers. As for congressional duty, some who might otherwise have been motivated to serve, shied from the risk of exposing a non-existent war record.

Sherman's dirty work ended in victory, and the victory swept away in the North any preoccupation with the manner of victory. Victory sealed over for the Union veteran his memory of theft or wanton destruction in Dixie. In Vietnam, defeat and atrocity are fused. It is sometimes said that a veteran's own narrative of what happens to a man degraded by ignoble, impersonal violence has an authenticity that only the veteran can have. But in our first television war, the degradation was no secret, and a young man did not have to experience it to know it. For ten years, most veterans could not or would not talk about Vietnam, for the mere telling had a profound psychological danger of its own. The society disavowed responsibility for the war and separated itself from the warrior's actions. As a result, the veteran was left on his own to come to grips with what he had done personally in Vietnam. Most have yet to digest their experiences and come to terms with them, and thereby to seal them over. Now some are beginning to talk, and the society has suddenly decided to listen.

A new and quite different heroism for the Vietnam veteran has suddenly become possible. The veteran who can articulate his experience in war and his emotions in the aftermath, and who has made his way through a painful self-renewal, could be the best agent for a Vietnam reconstruction. In coping with what happened to him in Vietnam, he can turn that agony to a positive force. In doing so, he must know that he is not unique in the American annals of war. The wanton violence of Sherman's bummer and Westmoreland's grunt differs as looting differs from killing, but neither time nor morals are static. Stealing the jewels from a peasant's hooch in Vietnam would be a precious little crime today. The patterns of behavior in both armies were encouraged by the official policy and extended the rules of permissible conduct in the same degree. The burning of Columbia and the slaughter of My Lai were exceptional only in their dimensions. The formal order for civilized behavior contrasted with the informal message toward atrocity in precisely the same way.

◇ ◇ ◇

The weak remembrance of the nation needs strengthening.

In the last years of America's involvement in Vietnam, the young were being asked to risk their lives for the "cause" of gradual disengagement. As the prospective re-

171

cruit saw it, the supreme sacrifice for so modest and abstract a principle had become unacceptable. The very basis of the disengagement was a tacit admission of defeat. The young man was asked to contemplate his own death, if that was to be his extreme fate, so that the defeat might be slow rather than abrupt, so that the country's agents rather than her own troops might suffer it on the battlefield.

The war made the whole nation howl, as surely as Sherman had done it to Georgia and South Carolina. Those who howled during the Civil War were the Southern women; they carried their bitterness most luridly into the aftermath. During the Vietnam disengagement, it was the young. The young had mobilized the protest, spearheaded from the college campuses, coming to its most noble flowering in the mass of half a million around the Washington Monument in 1969, and to its symbolic apocalypse in the killing of four students at Kent State University in May 1970. That killing was occasioned by a protest against the invasion of neutral Cambodia—yet another precedent-setting episode of the Vietnam war that widened the license of war by deceiving the American public through official denials of the illegal incursion.

By 1971, the standing of the government to ask men to serve in that war had been shattered. Its call to the youth had become untenable. In that year, the Supreme Court had decided in *Welsh v. United States* that mere moral and ethical disapproval of *this* war apart from any religious belief or general pacifism was sufficient to avoid service. The consequence was that in 1971 the government was certifying conscientious objectors as fast as it was inducting men into the armed forces. By some astonishing breakdown in the national health, half the young men were failing their preinduction physicals. A friend of mine, for example, was rejected by the army and went on to play for the Philadelphia Eagles for eight years. In one month, April 1970, twelve thousand did not report for their induction physicals.

And Richard Nixon faced a deadline. In the summer of 1973 the authority for compulsory conscription would run out. Given the nature of the war and great opposition to it, it was unlikely that the power to draft would be renewed. Thus, based upon the accommodating recommendations of the Gates Commission, the notion for an all-volunteer army took hold. If Nixon wanted to spread the disengagement over the life of his first term, any large-scale presence had to end by the summer of 1973.

In these years from 1969 to 1973, the youth faced the prospect of being among the last to be drafted and perhaps among the last to die, as the country slowly conceded the cause. To defuse the protest, to set one youth against another, and thereby to carry on with its "manpower" needs to the bitter end, the "lottery" was instituted in 1969. This was a dark comedy, a cruel and cynical spectacle, gussied up in the form of a vast bingo game and televised to the nation. If one's number turned up, the prize was not cash, but to be cashiered. It was not so much a lottery as roulette, American style, but it was in the nature of the general depravity of the day that the strategy did work. If one's number did not come up, his passion for protest ebbed. Service to one's country became a matter of bad luck.

In 1971 another proposal sought to disperse the alienation of the young and solve the problem of the summer '73 deadline. The National Service Act of 1970 proposed to broaded the concept of one's obligation to embrace eleemosynary work in forests and hospitals as an alternative to the warfare in the jungles of Vietnam. In the words of its sponsor, Rep. Jonathan Bingham of New York, "By allowing young men to decide for themselves if their convictions are sincere enough to commit themselves to a period of civilian service rather than face the possibility of a military

173

draft, the impossible task which is now thrust upon local draft boards to review applications for conscientious objector status would be eliminated.'' Implicit in the proposal was the fact that the Selective Service System had tired of its task of judging the sincerity of youthful convictions and was desperate to get out of the business, somehow or other, altogether. With the *Welsh* decision by the Supreme Court, there ceased to be a measurable ''objective'' standard by which to judge conscientious objection. If one simply didn't want to go to Vietnam—and who did?—it required only the wit to articulate the feeling as ''conscientious.'' In due course, the notion of national service was recognized as wallpaper, and it quietly died.

By 1970 the opposition of American youth had become an awesome force, and it seemed that among its diverse elements only the Vietnam soldier himself could be taken for granted by the political establishment. In the language of the day, the soldier had answered the call of his country, and, as Nixon himself was given to say, ''It was not an easy choice.'' The warrior had pulled his time, a phrase often uttered as if it were something akin to a jail sentence. But in 1970 trouble began to brew even in this seemingly safe quarter. A sizeable group of veterans banded together and began to talk openly of the atrocity that they believed was general in Vietnam and was particular in their own experience. That these utterances commenced while the war was still in full swing made them especially shocking and unprecedented in American history. Curiously, the trial of William Calley in Georgia sparked the antiwar veterans' movement. To these veterans, the pudgy-faced little rube was not the exception, but the symptom of the rule, and, therefore, the rule's ultimate victim. His conviction was the policy convicting itself. The body count, the free-fire zone, the search-and-destroy mission made William Calley inevitable, and he existed, said the veterans, in

every American platoon and in every byway across Vietnam. The antiwar veterans proceeded with a shocking and
unique symbolism, piercing to the essential guilt of the
country over the war effort. There was a terrifying quality
to their protest: their tales had an authenticity no one could
bear. It began in earnest as scores of veterans "turned
themselves in" for the same crimes that Calley was charged
with, and proceeded with such actions as the occupation of
the Statue of Liberty.

The history-making quality of this lay in the violation of
a time-honored soldier's code. For veterans to bring back
not the glories but the horrors of war and to bring them
back while those horrors were still happening was unprecedented. It was as if a cadre of Kilpatrick's cavalry convened in New York in March 1865 to speak of their wild
dance amid the flames in Barnwell, South Carolina, and to
display the jewels and the trousseaus of the Hartley House.
In February 1971, in Detroit, veterans convened the Winter
Soldier Investigation into American war crimes. One
hundred twenty-five veterans testified to a gamut of battlefield outrages, including the clean, impersonal atrocities
from cockpits of a jet fighter or a B-52. The purpose of the
Winter Soldier Investigation was to underscore the filth of
the war.

These men were the advance guard of what the country
would wake up seven years later to discover as a "social
problem." The early voices were the true exceptions; most
would come to feel the same way—and there were tens of
thousands of them—but they would repress their feelings
and their conscience for years to come. For the most part,
in 1971, the veterans remained numbed, intellectually and
morally, like the B-52 pilot from Atlanta who said:

Our base in Thailand was a very nice base. I felt lucky to have
been stationed at Karat. I really didn't think much about my

bombing of Vietnam—it was a job. In the airplane it was sort of a sterile environment, you weren't really part of the war. . . . I really didn't know the effect of the war on the Vietnamese. . . . The Vietnam War didn't really affect my life. I have not changed, no, nothing significant. My beliefs may have changed somewhat. But that is probably because I am older.

The press ignored the Winter Soldier Investigation, and those who took note sloughed the occasion off, dismissing the soldiers as bad apples. But the movement of veterans grew, and in late April 1971, twelve hundred veterans descended on Washington to make their case to their government and before the television cameras. Though the terms were not used, the soldiers came to witness how far their country's military had moved from the historic standards of proportionality and discrimination in warfare. The term they did use was a last mission of national conscience.

It was a remarkable event, in some ways the most effective antiwar protest of the Vietnam era. For veterans could say things with umimpeachable authority. This was a new Army of the Potomac, a new Lincoln Brigade, who huddled in darkness under the far-off glow of the Lincoln Memorial, because the government had banned an encampment on the Mall, and campfires were grounds for arrest. Between them there was a reverent respect for one another. They possessed a terrible earnestness about their mission. Though they had belatedly acquired the shaggy look and hard-edged rhetoric of protest, they did not want to be lumped together with the "peaceniks" of their generation. They had not come to be arrested. At first, they were desperate *not* to be arrested. Rather, they had come to lobby for an immediate, unilateral, and unconditional withdrawal from Vietnam, an end of further war appropriations, a full amnesty to all war resisters, and full public hearings into Vietnam war crimes with complete immunity for those who testified. They wanted government action in the spirit of

Lincoln's words inscribed on the entrance to the Veterans' Administration: "To care for him who shall have borne the battle and for his widow and for his orphan," words from the Second Inaugural Address in the paragraph which began, "with malice toward none, with charity for all" and which immediately followed the phrase about binding the wounds of the nation.

The mere thought of these modern bummers put the government into a frenzy, and it overreacted. Several days before the veterans' arrival, the Justice Department sought a ban on sleeping on the Mall, fearing an unruly mob of dangerous men who would secure slumber rights for much bigger mobs in the future. The ban was quickly overturned by the U.S. Court of Appeals, which recognized the "symbolic" importance of the Mall bivouac to the soldiers whom their government had required to sleep in much less comfortable turf. But Chief Justice Warren Burger overturned the order by the Court of Appeals. As the fit and the lame began to arrive, the judiciary was arrayed against them. But the police were hesitant to throw the cripples off the Mall and into the street, and so the order of the chief justice slid along unenforced for a few days. The veterans laid out their bed rolls, and some of them slept in "body bags" for the effect, dramatizing, unwittingly perhaps, the classic nightmare of the combat survivor.

On the first day of the protest, a file of three hundred veterans marched silently to Arlington National Cemetery for the purpose of laying a wreath, but the gate to the cemetery was slammed in their face. That occasioned a debate as to whether they should get ladders and storm the resting place to underscore the "insensitivity" of their government, but the suggestion was voted down. On the next day, as they awaited the enforcement of the chief justice's order, they held their first Vietnam reënactment. Over the steps of the Old Senate Office Building and the east steps of the

177

Capitol, squads of deadly serious GIs in fatigues, bearing plastic M-16s, fanned out on a mock search-and-destroy mission. At the Capitol, three women wearing coolie hats attempted to run away from the infantrymen.

"Waste 'em! Waste 'em!" a soldier screamed, and with calm deliberation crouched and squeezed off a burst of automatic toy clicks. The coolies fell, screaming, as they burst stage blood over themselves and the Capitol steps.

"It's disgusting! It's horrible!" a Capitol Hill secretary said contemptuously, and turned away.

"Get the body count!" another GI screamed.

Another soldier grabbed a woman roughly from the crowd.

"Why are you here!" he shouted at her.

"This is my home," the woman said plaintively, before she was dragged off for her interrogation as a V.C. Later, another search-and-destroy operation took place in front of the posh Julius Garfinkel department store in downtown Washington. Noonday shoppers found that invasion of their privacy obscene as well, and scattered for cover in the lingerie department. To an observer, the soldiers had strange, unseeing eyes as they went about their theater with a terrible seriousness. It was as if they moved somnolently behind glass.

The bulk of the veterans were less interested in theater than in lobbying their congressmen. "There's a real parallel between this camp and the Nam," said one. "There in the daytime, we'd go out on patrol and do distasteful duty. At night, we'd come back to camp and try to forget it. You'd drink and smoke and tell stories. It's the same thing here. Talking to congressmen is distasteful duty. But at night, we have each other."

The congressmen, in turn, did not know quite what to make of the invasion. When squads of veterans turned up at the House Armed Services Committee, Rep. Sonny

Montgomery of Mississippi chided their manners, and said more than he realized.

"These young men are only hurting their cause with this," he said. "They are going to have to learn to respect the rights of others."

But it was quickly understood that some forum for this astonishing anger and bitterness had better be provided, and Sen. George McGovern secured a Senate auditorium. Story after shocking story poured from the veterans, and a few congressmen were stirred. One was Sen. Philip Hart of Michigan. Later, he would write that World War II veterans like himself could not escape the contrast. They had returned from "that great popular adventure" buoyed by accomplishment and support. "We joined veterans' organizations, not because we wanted to forget the war, but because we wanted to remember it." Conversely, the Vietnam veterans had melted back into the society, "each with his own private measure of pride or bitterness . . . no one really knew which." Vietnam was a great enterprise of very doubtful morality, the senator observed. "Americans have discovered that their government can lie, that allies can be corrupt, that their sons—under the confused pressures of guerrilla war—can casually rape young women at a country crossroads or shoot children in a ditch. The anguish of veterans is no tribute to the foresight and intelligence of those holding government offices—myself included among them—when this war was getting cranked up." Senator Hart prophesied, without then knowing that he was talking about future President Ronald Reagan, that there would be much rhetoric after the war about Vietnam as a noble venture.

"Obscure achievements will be dusted off and cited as justification for the sacrifice. None of it will be easily believed. Maybe historians will conclude that it was worthwhile. But I doubt it. It just looks to me like something

we'll have to live with and—if we're lucky—learn from."
Senator Hart died before he saw his prophecy come true.

As the week wore on, this modern Lincoln Brigade began
to realize that it was not going to force a full-scale debate
in Congress on the Vietnam involvement. In the meantime,
they were getting an object lesson in what interested re-
porters. The press paid a great deal of attention to the familiar mode of Vietnam protest: upside-down flags, long
hair, marijuana joints, arrests. At the Supreme Court, eight
veterans were arrested before all the doors to the courthouse could be locked. Demanding that the Supreme Court
declare the unconstitutionality of the war, they were led
from the building by police, with their hands behind their
heads in the classic pose of the prisoner of war. That image
made all the papers. Fifty veterans marched to the Pentagon and were met by a brigadier general, standing disap-
provingly as if he were George Wallace at the schoolhouse
door.

"We'd like to turn ourselves in for war crimes we've
seen or committed," a veteran said.

"We don't take prisoners here," the general responded,
trying to shoo them away. "We've got business to conduct
here."

These minor rhetorical and public relations victories
gave the veterans little heart. What they demanded was
the ear of Congress. Nothing infuriated them so much as the
idea that they had no right to oppose the war, or
even the right to initiate a dialogue about it. They were the
good sons, they felt, the patriotic ones, who went to war,
and now earnestly believed that Congress needed to hear
from them how the war had degenerated.

Grudgingly, toward the end of the week, the Senate Foreign Relations Committee agreed to witness formally the
testimony of John Kerry, a twenty-seven-year-old navy
lieutenant who headed the Vietnam Veterans for Peace
(and who twelve years later was the only antiwar figure of

the Vietnam era, along with SDS leader Tom Hayden, to achieve modest political success. He would become the lieutenant governor of Massachusetts). Earlier in the week, Kerry had been interviewed on the television program "Meet the Press" and had been asked what many Americans considered the ultimate question.

"We are told repeatedly by the Administration that one of the basic reasons for continuing the war is to justify those 53,000 deaths," began a *New York Times* reporter. "It seems to me that what you are saying is that the country withdraw from Vietnam regardless of the consequences to Vietnam itself. Doesn't this make meaningless the sacrifice of those 53,000 lives?"

Kerry pointed to the families of the dead and the imprisoned who had joined the protest. "[We] are coming here to say to the people of this country: We have lost our sons. We have lost our husbands. We have lost our buddies. I lost a leg. But the important thing is not that *that* happened. Let's not keep killing people to justify my loss. Let's not glorify the dead. Let's try and glorify the living. Let's do something for the living. Therefore, we say, don't let it happen to any more people when it doesn't have to. Don't let it happen to someone else."

With that sentiment, it was recognized that Kerry spoke for the mass of Vietnam veterans, not just the membership of his group or those who approved of his politics. In the years after the war, the determination that Vietnam never happen to another generation, regardless of whether it was a noble cause lost by a failure of will or lost because it was wrong and obscene, became the fundamental meaning of the war for the casualty of it. Before an awed and silent committee, Kerry delivered a powerful statement:

We are here to ask, where are the leaders of our country? Where are they now that we, the men whom they sent off to war, have returned? These are the commanders who have deserted

181

their troops, and there is no more serious crime in the law of war. These men have left all the casualties and retreated behind a pious shield of public rectitude. This administration has done us the ultimate dishonor. They have attempted to disown us and the sacrifices we have made for this country. . . .

We wish that a merciful God could wipe away our memories of that service as easily as this administration has wiped away memories of us. But all that they have done and all that they can do by this denial is to make more clear than ever our own determination to undertake one last mission—to search out and destroy the last vestige of this barbaric war, to pacify our own hearts, to conquer the hate and the fear that have driven this country these last ten years, so when thirty years from now, our brothers go down the street without a leg, without an arm, or a face, and small boys ask why, we will be able to say "Vietnam" and not mean a desert, not a filthy obscene memory, but mean instead a place where America finally turned and where soldiers like us helped it in the turning.

In that last line lay the poignancy and the optimism of these soldiers, but Kerry could not imagine that in just ten years, rather than thirty, the young could ask a paraplegic on a college platform which side America fought on, North or South Vietnam. The political leaders he besought to speak then would have been speechless for years, and the country would seem to have neither a memory of an obscene place or of a turning point, but virtually no memory at all.

Off the veterans went for their last, unprecedented, heart-wrenching ritual. General Westmoreland had embraced Napoleon's maxim that "a bolt of ribbon will win many battles," and had put great emphasis on conferring battlefield decorations. Now, before a temporary restraining fence erected on the west terrace of the Capitol, and before a bronze statue of Chief Justice John Marshall, who stood for the exercise of personal liberty, the veterans stretched in a long, orderly line back to the Mall. The first, a marine sergeant named Jack Smith, made the opening statement: "We now strip ourselves of these medals of courage and heroism. We cast them away as a symbol of dishonor, shame, and inhumanity." One by one, the veterans stepped to the microphone, some in anger, most in terrible anguish, identified themselves, and then threw their ribbons and medals over the fence. Of all the actions in the entire era of Vietnam protest, this was the most searing image.

Thus it fell to the Vietnam veteran himself, the lower-level instrument of the policy, not the policymaker, to articulate the concern about the widening license of war, as practiced by the American military. It was far from a remote consideration of an abstract principle. The warrior's testimony was about his own dehumanization and brutalization by the environment of Vietnam, and it was testimony, galvanized by guilt and shame at what he had seen, reported, and watched be covered up by the vast protective military system. The testimony was a painful and courageous effort at self-regeneration, and at its core was a personal atonement. It was the Bennett Place impulse.

At the conclusion of the encampment of more than a thousand veterans in Washington in April 1971, congressional hearings were held to investigate the allegations of war atrocity. The hearings were *ad hoc* and were convened by the congressman from California, Ronald Dellums. Backed by twenty-one fellow congressmen, Dellums had tried to get the Rules Committee of the House to hold full, *official* hearings into the repeated charges and to get the House leadership to back the effort. Other congressmen had pressed the hawkish Armed Services Committee to consider the charges. In entering the full testimony of the Detroit Winter Soldier Investigation into the *Congressional Record* several weeks before, Sen. Mark Hatfield of Oregon urged various congressional committees to conduct hearings on the relation of American conduct of the Vietnamese war to international treaties like the Geneva Convention, ratified by the United States, which set out rules of warfare. Additionally, Senator Hatfield proposed a special commission to assess the "moral consequences" of Indochina involvement for the nation and the American public.

"We as a nation must find the proper way to honestly confront the moral consequences of our actions and to turn ourselves away from the thinking and the policy that has degraded our moral posture and to recognize that out of contrition and self-examination can come a genuine rebirth of the ideas we hold as a people."

But, *de rigeur,* the real powers in Congress would have nothing of it, and the *ad hoc* hearings became the precious spectacle of the converted listening intently to the convinced.

This was another stitch in the great pattern of avoidance by the political establishment that left the war unresolved in its aftermath and leaves it undigested today. With the abrogation of responsibility, the Vietnam experience became a matter of personal witness. Sixty percent of the Vietnam veterans (according to the seminal 1981 Veterans' Administration study, "Legacies of Vietnam") went to Vietnam either opposed to the war or not understanding it. In 1971, soldiers testified to their atrocities, not because they held any hope that the atrocities would stop, but because they were driven by a private imperative. There is perhaps only one example of a young man's personal witness that led to an important institutional response. That was the action of Ron Ridenhour, the soldier who began hearing the tales of massacre from his old buddies in a place called Pinkville, and who finally, after much agonizing wrote a letter to the secretary of defense.

Exactly what did, in fact, occur in the village of "Pinkville" in March 1968 I do not know for *certain*, but I am convinced that it was something very black indeed. I remain irrevocably persuaded that if you and I do truly believe in the principles of justice and the equality of every man, that this country is founded on, then we must press forward a widespread and public investigation of this matter with all our combined efforts. I think that it was Winston Churchill who once said "A country without a conscience is a country without a soul, and a country without a soul is a country that cannot survive." I feel that I must take some positive action on this matter. I hope that you will launch an investigation immediately and keep me informed of your progress. If you cannot, then I don't know what other course of action to take.

That letter led to the investigation into the My Lai massacre, the prosecution of Lieutenant Calley, and the Peers Commission Report which detailed the cover-up in the aftermath.

In later years the searing internal debate over morality within the Vietnam veteran would be played out not within the forum of politics or history, but within the forum of the psychiatrist's office or the confessional booth . . . if it was played out at all. The shame was the most terrible for the veteran who served after 1968. To kill or be wounded in the war of disengagment, which lasted longer than the American Civil War, left a profound residual. The combat veteran after 1968 was the first American soldier in history to be openly deprived of the battlefield mythology of gallantry and victory. "Post-traumatic stress disorder," prison, alcoholism, drugs, joblessness, lack of direction, addiction to violence were problems that took their most virulent course in the veteran after 1968. And, therefore, bitterness remains the greatest for the Nixon-Kissinger part of that war, leaders who used the first thirty-one thousand dead in Vietnam to justify the second twenty-four thousand. Only once does a veteran have to hold up a crumpled hand, paralyzed by a bullet that passed through his watch and wrist, as one did for me in the summer of 1983, and say, "I was lucky. I carry this around," to know how soul-shriveling the experience was. The crumpled hand assuaged the guilt. It was his dues, his "pay-back" . . . not enough perhaps, but helpful nonetheless, for the spastic member enabled him to *function* in the civilian society after the war. And for him, the wound was received not while he fired a weapon in anger but in the innocuous act of taking a battlefield photograph. Had the bullet not hit his well-made Japanese wrist watch, it would have passed through his wrist and into his brain.

In the Dellums hearing, the first five witnesses were West Point officers with extensive combat experience, dark-eyed, haunted men who came before the committee in the single greatest act of bravery in their careers, ensuring the scorn of their career-oriented peers, to testify to what the institution that had shaped them had become to them. Capt. Fred Laughlin, West Point 1965, spoke of soldiers who like himself went to Vietnam as "blank pages" and came to know quickly, in the nuances of official training, what the difference between official, written orders and unofficial, encouraged practice was. "I think America needs to undergo a bout with reality," Captain Laughlin told the congressmen, "for in the long run, America is the one, not the people who fought in Vietnam, not the Calleys nor the Westmorelands, but America in the long run that has to carry this stigma."

Capt. Greg Hayward, West Point 1964, bolstered his fellow officer. Of the "body count mania," Captain Hayward said, "When we intentionally violate the rules that we have on our MACV cards, they represent a policy of treating Vietnamese as less than human." That was too tepid for Capt. Robert Johnson, West Point 1965, who said, "With search and destroy policy, I couldn't help but view these Vietnamese as little less than human. We went in and destroyed their homes, they weren't really homes. They were hooches. I wouldn't have had the same zeal if we were destroying red brick homes or split level houses in suburbia." He had never had any meaningful training in the rules of land warfare at West Point, Johnson told the committee; indeed, he did not know what the law of land warfare really was until he returned from Vietnam. A slow, gradual process had worked on him. "It became clear to me that the free fire zone and the search-and-destroy tactics, where we systematically destroyed villages and routinely bombed the countryside, that we were waging war not against any abstract ideology but waging war against the Vietnamese people." Echoes of General Sherman. Speaking of interrogation techniques such as electric shock to the genitals or throwing prisoners out of flying helicopters, tactics which were routinely promoted or acquiesced in by high American officers, Maj. Gordon Livingston, West Point 1960, said, "This is a direct violation of the Army Manual which makes the commanding officer responsible for observing the Articles of War."

"So the system itself tends to discourage the assumption of responsibility for preventing war crime?" a congressman asked leadingly.

"The system is so large and well organized that even an individual who finds what is happening to be morally repugnant is led to question his own values. The question always arises, am I crazy or is what is going on here crazy? When the system is so large and so well organized, it is very hard for the individual to assert himself."

With one voice these professional officers contended that My Lai had been the inevitable consequence of the overall policy, and Lieutenant Calley "the ultimate victim of the institutional structure of this country." If there could be amnesty for all soldiers who would come forward to testify to crimes they had committed or witnessed, Congress could know the full scope of the degradation. Even to that clutch of sympathetic legislators, such an amnesty was unthinkable. "It is beyond the power of the United States to waive the provisions of the laws of nations which make it a crime to execute and maltreat civilians," said one. So the matter would be left to individual conscience, and, for most, driven deep into the soul. The rush to forget Vietnam took shape in the veteran as the rush to deny that he had done those things.

Toward the end, a congressman asked of Capt. Robert Johnson the ultimate question, but the question that no civilian of whatever persuasion had any real right to ask of a Vietnam veteran. "Within the acts of individuals, there are moral judgments that are made. I wonder if you in the course of your service made any moral judgment to kill innocent children, women, old men, as did Lieutenant Calley?"

The shift from collective responsibility to individual guilt was abrupt. It was as if time had reverted a hundred years, and the witness was General Sherman at the Tomotley Plantation, confessing to the smashing of a mantelpiece as the only act of vandalism that he personally committed in the entire campaign. Captain Johnson's agony was manifest, and after a long moment he sought refuge in cynicism. Holding up his hands, his lips curling in a smile without joy, he said, "My hands are clean, you see, because I had a radio and could call in napalm strikes."

Parades for Victory and Defeat

IN EARLY May 1865, Sherman's army made its way toward Washington. In the hands of a different man, it might have been a terrifying instrument, for it was flushed with victory and livid at the treatment of its chieftain. Within his own army, "Uncle Billy" was already a legend. In Columbia, before the flames took hold, a Union prisoner had composed a song, as he awaited his liberation, and he had given it to Sherman. Now, his troops took up the air as they moved, sixty-five thousand strong, on Washington for their final show. "Then sang we a song of our chieftain, that echoed over river and lea; / And the stars of our banner shone brighter, when Sherman marched down to the sea. / Then cheer upon cheer for bold Sherman went up from each valley and glen. . . ." Halleck in Richmond and Stanton in Washington had publicly insulted their chieftain. The troops meant to back Uncle Billy in any way he saw fit to have his satisfaction.

As the troops marched north, the reasons for Halleck's and Stanton's actions receded in memory. On the day Johnston had surrendered for the second time on simple Appomattox terms, Booth had been shot dead in a burning tobacco barn near Port Royal, Virginia. The corpse had been brought to Washington and was kept below deck on the naval vessel *Montauk,* while the slippery Detective Baker informed Secretary Stanton. The diligence of the Secret Service notwithstanding, a rebel sympathizer managed to snip a lock of Booth's hair as a treasured relic of a sectional hero, before Baker could snatch it away from her. Baker told Stanton this, as he laid before him with melodramatic distaste Booth's belt and pipe, knife and compass, two pistols and a diary describing his flight in graphic detail, including how the lame, hunted assassin had killed his horse and slept between the dead animal's legs for warmth several nights before he was shot down. Stanton understood how martyrs were made. He thought every· hair on Booth's head might turn into a valued souvenir for Southern sympathizers and he ordered Baker to find a fit spot for the villain—a grave, secret, unmarked, and unhallowed. Clandestinely, Baker did so, in the floor of a warehouse in the Arsenal Grounds at Greenleaf's Point (where the grave stayed until 1869, before Booth's remains were taken to Baltimore and given a fit burial in the family plot with a number of his fellow actors performing as pallbearers). The terror over a continuing wave of assassination was dwindling, but Stanton still kept his house under a heavy military guard, fearing Sherman's troops now as much as anything else.

As Sherman's army approached Richmond, Halleck sent a consoling letter to Sherman, inviting him to parade through the streets of the rebel capital, but Sherman was fermenting his resentment and declined. He could not be responsible for what his troops might do. Densely, Halleck issued a peacetime echo of his wartime insult by ordering a wing of Sherman's army to parade anyway, but this gave Sherman the opportunity to forbid it. He overrode Halleck, and thereby asserted his control over his army once again. The troops bypassed the capital and made for Alexandria.

Grant's Army of the Potomac was already drilling hard on the parade grounds for its grand review down Pennsylvania Avenue. It had been agreed that the smart easterners with their kepis and the colorful Zouaves would have the first day, and Sherman's western strangers the second. Sherman and Grant would compete in the greatest military pageant ever witnessed in Washington. The throngs awaited in anticipation of the contrast that would be presented to them, but Sherman was the real object of interest. What would be the deportment of a force that could burn so wide a swath across the South? Would the soldiers look the part of barbarians, unkempt, fiercely wild-eyed, ragtag? Would they be boastful or secretive about their ravages? And what would be the appearance of this Tecumseh?

While his army camped at Alexandria. Sherman crossed over to Washington to visit his friends. President Johnson sought to assuage Sherman's anger, professing not to have know of Stanton's shenanigans until he read the New York newspapers. If Sherman did not believe the protestations, he made no mention of it. Grant offered his good offices to arrange a reconciliation between Sherman and Stanton, but Sherman refused. He would take an apology from Stanton directly and personally, but if it should not be forthcoming he was "resolved to resent the insult, cost what it might, as publicly as it was made."

With the Civil War as with Vietnam, race always seemed to lurk in the background. Even at this moment, Sherman saw their differences over the freed slaves as the nub of his dispute with Stanton. In the parlors of Washington, he complained that Stanton wanted to destroy him because he had not favored making blacks into soldiers and now did not favor enfranchising them. Stanton was trying to fashion blacks into so much "pliable electioneering material" (even if it was to counteract the votes of petulant rebels in the South). To make Negroes loyal voters in the South would produce new riots and war—and anyway the simple souls did not want the vote. But now Sherman would have his revenge.

The morning of May 24 broke clear, and the dirt streets of Washington were dry for Sherman's triumphant parade. He meant to bring a fresh odor to the streets of the city, making sure that not just his men but his bummers with their Southern spoils of war paraded their prizes—the official prizes like the Georgia milch cows and Carolina pigs. In an instant the bummers were transformed, both for the public and for themselves, from thieves and barbarians into colorful folk heroes. (A similar process would happen when the Vietnam Veterans Memorial was dedicated in 1982). Not just the men but the manner of Sherman's victory was to be paraded for the applause of the joyous North.

Before each division marched its corps of black pioneers armed with picks and shovels, and alongside some companies, families of freed slaves merged with the column. His magnificent horse garlanded, Sherman himself rode at the head of the column. Behind it came the troops, ten abreast, garbed in their slouch hats and battle-worn uniforms that had faded to a hue somewhere between Union blue and Confederate gray. Division upon division uncoiled down Pennsylvania Avenue, as one journalist put it, "like a tremendous python." At the Treasury Department, at the bend of the avenue north, Sherman paused to look back upon his creation. Later, his description of it took off in lyrical flight.

The column was compact, and the glittering muskets looked like a solid mass of steel, moving with the regularity of a pendulum. . . . It was, in my judgment, the most magnificent army in existence—65,000 men in splendid physique, who had just completed a march nearly two thousand miles in a hostile country. In good drill . . . the steadiness and firmness of the tread, the careful dress of the guides, the uniform intervals between the companies, all eyes directly to the front, and their tattered and bullet-riven flags, festooned with flowers, all attracted universal notice. Many good people had looked upon our men as a sort of mob, but the world then saw that it was an army in the proper sense, well-organized, well-commanded, and disciplined. It was no wonder that it had swept through the South like a tornado.

How quickly in victory is atrocity forgotten! In one great victory parade, all death and filth and thieving were painted over with the brush of glory. In one day, the warriors became noble again. Bummers suddenly became colorful folk heroes. One grand celebration sealed up personal secrets about robbery and wanton burning. No one would ever require their secrets to be revealed, and they certainly felt no impulse to reveal the secrets themselves.

On the spot where Sherman turned to regard the pageant, at the intersection of Fifteenth Street and Pennsylvania Avenue, now stands the elaborate Sherman monument. Guarded by four life-size sentinels on its corners, the pedestal for the great equestrian rises fourteen feet and engraved upon it, in recognition of the delicate minuet between war and peace, is the Sherman quotation: "War's legitimate object is a more perfect peace." Below Sherman and his horse are two conceptual statues known as the War and Peace groups. Peace is represented, predictably, by a serene, half-naked woman and three children, the boy holding a bird, the woman, an olive branch. On the White House side of the statue, War is a more interesting work of art. Its grotesqueness suggest Goya: again, a woman is the central figure, this time, bound, her clothes torn aside by her own hysterical hands baring her breasts, her mouth huge and distorted, her eyes oversized empty sockets, and she stands upon a dead soldier with a rifle whose body is preyed upon by two vultures.

Sherman rode on. As he approached Lafayette Square he was asked to notice Secretary of State William Seward, who had been placed in the second story of a brick house on the Square. Seward had sustained dreadful injuries in a fall from his carriage a month and a half before, dislocating his shoulder and breaking his jaw on both sides. The fall had saved his life. For on the night of Lincoln's assassination, Booth's adoring accomplice, the half-wit Confederate deserter Lewis Paine, had entered Seward's house and attempted to butcher the bandaged and immobile secretary of state with a knife, slashing him around the face and the neck. But the iron brace supporting Seward's jaw protected his throat, and Paine raced out into the night shouting, as all modern assassins seem to, "I'm mad! I'm mad!" Sherman, guerrilla fighter and progenitor of the new total war, acknowledged the feeble salute of the assassination victim, and in their exchange it was as if the modern age had been ushered in.

At the reviewing stand, Sherman dismounted before the cheers of the highest officials in the land. He moved to President Johnson and warmly shook hands, then to General Grant and the others in the cabinet. When he came to the war secretary, Stanton extended his hand cordially, and Sherman refused it.

"I do not shake hands with clerks," he was heard to mutter contemptuously. To Sherman's immense satisfaction, his rebuke was universally noticed. How civilized, even for Sherman, scorn could still be!

Amid this glorious military pageantry and this juicy grist for Victorian parlor gossip, it is not surprising that the appearance of General Sherman at this time before the Committee on the Conduct of the War was overshadowed. But it was the last time for Sherman the peacemaker to play the surrogate Lincoln, and it showed that he had acquired a measure of political skill since the Bennett Place. The committee was dominated by Radicals, who were soon to be busy in remaking the South, and it called Sherman to account not for the flames of Columbia but for his tenderness at Bennett Place. The committee's real agenda was to tie Lincoln to Sherman's actions and thereby discredit the dead president along with his impulse to charity. But Sherman would not go for it. He strode before the committee, defiant and magnificent. He made his case and supported it with his voluminous and eloquent documents. He laid his embarrassing lapses into sacrosanct civil areas to promptings from Stanton rather than Lincoln. Stanton had encouraged him to involve himself in civil matters in Savannah . . . Stanton had not wanted Jefferson Davis caught, etc. Before the committee his untenable concessions became glittering generalities, dashed off in haste to keep the Confederate Army from splintering.

But how had Lincoln instructed him at the City Point conferences? What about amnesty? About slavery? About punishment for high rebel officials? What did Lincoln say about the manner in which Sherman should negotiate peace?

"Nothing definite," replied the bold-faced witness. "it was simply a matter of general conversation, nothing specific or definite." It was a congressional dissembling that in Watergate days was usually phrased: "I don't remember . . . I don't recall . . . not to my knowledge."

As Sherman left the committee room to the cheers of the audience, his aide-de-camp collared him. Why had the general not been more forthcoming? Why had he not told the lemonade and brandy story? Describing the details of his City Point conversations, Capt. Dayton said, could only exonerate Sherman now!

"I'm no politician, Dayton, God knows I've proved that in the last few weeks," Sherman replied dryly. "Don't you see what they're trying to do in there? If I had testified that the terms with General Johnston were dictated by Lincoln, then the obloquy I now bear will shift to the dead President. He and all he stood for will be discredited, and the radicals can impose whatever Carthaginian terms on the South that suit them. I will not be used in any such scheme. Never in my life have I engaged in throwing off on any man, regardless of who he is. Never for whatever gain."

◈ ◈ ◈

On January 23, 1973, Henry Kissinger and Le Duc Tho initialed the cease-fire accord in Paris "to end the war and bring peace with honor in Vietnam and South East Asia." Peace at last had come after three months when, despite the Christmas bombing which had involved more ordnance tonnage than had been dropped on Germany in the entire Second World War, peace had supposedly been "at hand." The January agreement was essentially the same as had been on the table the previous October, and the *New York Times* prophesied that for years it would be debated whether essentially the same agreement might not have been hammered out four years earlier.

Reconciliation was the word that seemed to be on every tongue. Under the Paris agreement, elections were to be supervised by a coalition of South Vietnamese, neutralists, and Communists, known as the Council of National Reconciliation and Concord. In his speech to the nation on January 24, President Nixon said to Hanoi: "As we have ended the war in negotiation, let us now build a peace of reconciliation. . . . All parties must now see to it that this is a peace that lasts, as well as a peace that heals." Chapter

VIII, Article 21, of the accord contemplated an "era of reconciliation" with North Vietnam, where the United States, suggestive of the Marshall Plan, would "contribute to healing the wounds of war and to the post-war reconstruction of North Vietnam." Later, Kissinger would write in his memoirs, "We stood, I fervently hoped, at the threshold of a period of national reconciliation that would be given impetus by the unique opportunity for creativity I saw ahead. America had found a way to merge the idealism of the Sixties with the sterner pragmatism of the recent past."

And at midnight on January 23, many hours after the initialing in Paris and many hours before the president's speech to the nation, Nixon called Kissinger from the Lincoln Sitting Room in the White House, where the president had been brooding. Whether malice or charity ran through Nixon's mind as he gazed upon the Lincoln etchings at this critical, creative moment must be left to literature.

The moment had come which was in historical terms the neck in the hourglass for the Vietnam era. For the Civil War that decisive moment between war and Reconstruction was dominated by the agony of Lincoln's assassination and the scandal of Sherman's blunder at Bennett Place. The assassination had stoked the fire for revenge. The Bennett Place episode had given definition to charity. What would be the equivalents for Vietnam? What would dictate a tone of healing or of recrimination for this postwar period? Who would be the Sherman to argue that the only meaning to America's longest war could be found in forging a more perfect peace? All over America the church bells rang and the flags flew and prayers were said. At the Twenty-first National Prayer Breakfast at the White House, three thousand government leaders joined the president to give thanks, and Sen. Mark Hatfield, a profoundly religious man, besought his political audience to ask collective and individual forgiveness for *their* role in the war. The war was a fact of American history. It should be regarded, prayed the senator, as an "exile of love from our hearts." By asking forgiveness, "we can soothe the wounds of war and renew the face of the earth and mankind." Could the political leaders acknowledge complicity in an American disaster? Could they tolerate the notion that they too must be supplicants?

For me, this moment of transition was intensely personal. I had poured three years of my life into the military in the dangerous years of 1965 to 1968, when the build-up had taken place and most lives were lost. Only through the caprice of the computer had I ended up with a comfortable stateside assignment in intelligence rather than as a hard-eyed interrogator of suspected V.C.—an area notorious for both the commission of war crimes and the acquiescence in them—or worse: as a quiet American in civilian clothes searching for raging hate of Communists in some Oriental that would lead to his recruitment in a suicidal intelligence mission or paying Vietnamese to dress up like Viet Cong and go on rampages in jungle villages, or the ultimate—volunteering myself for missions along the Cambodian border—an activity that friends with the same training became involved in and to which I would have been very suggestible. I could have ended up very easily like my friend Mister Reynolds. (See Chapter 14.)

For I recognized then, and I still acknowledge, that my fascination for the war was at least as strong as my abhorrence of it, and it was, after all, ours. Part of me pushed inexorably toward involving myself deeply—the writer's impulse, no doubt—for I wanted to have something to say later about the central experience of my generation. The other part checked me and guided me into safer waters that were both service and avoidance at the same time. My passion for the amnesty cause was my reparation, for I realized that this fragile equipoise between fascination and abhorrence redounded to the benefit of the warmakers. Unless abhorrence was total, one could easily be enlisted. They got me. They used me. When our contract was fulfilled, they released me unharmed, with "honor and distinction." I admired those who had not been lured by war's fascination or swept along in some half-cocked generational romance . . . who had simply used their heads. My four-year obsession with amnesty was my belated tour in the abhorrence of war, after my three-year tour in the fascination for it. I could articulate my feelings early because I had not been maimed. Nor had I been thoroughly alienated by protest. The mere awareness of the potential criminal within me was enough of a prod. Given the sanction of my government and the general depravity of the Vietnam scene, I would have been a willing participant. It would not have taken much to brutalize me. This dark perception led me to a profound respect for the resister and a profound sympathy for the warrior. And in the case of some warriors, sympathy became respect as well, as I watched the lonely struggle, unaided by his society, to come to grips with what he had done in Vietnam, to take responsibility for those actions, and, finally, at long last, to seal them over and move on. There has been no parallel process for the society at large.

In the week of the Paris agreement, I published a book that chronicled the torturous exile of the Vietnam combat veteran who had deserted the army when he was ordered back to the war for a second time. By all standards, John David Herndon was a sad case, not a particularly attractive subject to become a test case on the morality of the Vietnam war, although in his seedy halting working-stiff way, he had the true spark of courage and moral heroism too. He was certainly representative of the Vietnam victim, for in him was fused the warrior and the deserter. The book was a political tract full of youthful passion, that argued for universal amnesty for all war resisters. I had special standing to make the case. As one who had served, I could speak for those who had not. While I did not appreciate it at the time, the Madison Avenue advertisement for the book set the tone for the months ahead. It carried a picture of a hand, fashioned in the V-sign for peace, as if it were a poster, and riddled with bullet holes. "The Cease Fire Has Been Signed," read the copy. "Now the battle begins."

The ad pleased me, for it was eye-catching and effective, and it validated me finally as part of the "peace movement." I was primed for "the battle," for we had all developed an adversarial relationship with our government, as it had with us, and it had become a habit that neither the government nor the Vietnam generation found easy to break, even now that the rules had been changed. It did not take me long to tire of this combat. For as I traveled around the country to talk about the book and the cause, the television carried the moving story of the return of American POWs, and I was stacked up against every flag-waver and right-wing nut who could be roused out of the bushes to oppose me. Objective journalism and all that. No doubt, the fireworks that resulted made me reasonably lively entertainment.

If it did not occur to me that the habit of confrontation should change now that peace had come, it evidently did not occur to Nixon either, as he sat there on the first night of peace contemplating Lincoln. At least, no mystical transformation was evident in his official conduct in the coming few days. On January 31, he held his first full-scale press conference. The first three questions dealt with the subjects that might suggest the first steps of reconstruction: the rebuilding of Indochina, the return of the American prisoners, and amnesty.

For some months the dimensions of a rebuilding program

had been in the air. Nixon himself had mentioned a figure of $7.5 billion, a third of which was to be earmarked for North Vietnam. In Chapter VIII, Article 21, of the Paris Accord, these reparations were defined as consistent with "traditional" American generosity after the war. The day before Nixon's press conference, it was announced that Kissinger would go to North Vietnam in twelve days to discuss the machinery for funneling the aid, and Kissinger had expressed the hope that the relationship with North Vietnam would move from hostility to normalization and from normalization to conciliation and cooperation. But, said Kissinger, as if he were given his cue to the naysayers, any aid would go to North Vietnam only after the implementation of the agreement was "well-advanced."

At his press conference, Nixon underscored the incentive of the lucre, and said nothing of its moral necessity or the grand American tradition of postwar generosity. He, too, seemed to invite opposition to the idea.

"I have noted that many Congressmen and Senators and many of the American people are not keen on helping any of the countries in that area . . . but I look upon such help as a potential investment. In peace, to the extent that the North Vietnamese participate with us in the reconstruction of North Vietnam, they will have a tendency to turn inward to the works of peace rather than turning outward to the works of war." The actual dollar figure for American generosity would have to be negotiated, Nixon said, and the Congress would have to support it.

In the Paris Accord, the enemy agreed to return the 566 American prisoners within sixty days. This was the immediate emotional issue, and their return was one of the few undisputed accomplishments of the war. The manner in which they came home was of major psychological importance, akin to a national catharsis. Homecoming could take on the quality of understated gratitude, but it was rich in opportunities for political demagoguery and exploitation. This last, tiny group of Vietnam victims would have a significance way out of proportion to their numbers.

"This is a time that we should not grandstand it," Nixon told the press. "We should not exploit it. We should remember that it is not like astronauts coming back from the moon after what is, shall we say, a very spectacular and dangerous journey, but these are men who have been away for years. They have a right to privacy." But rights to privacy sometimes had to be weighed against needs for political haymaking. The first signs of political scandal had begun to eat away at the foundations of the Nixon presidency.

If Nixon's cautious stance on reparations and his understated promise on POWs was not histrionic or Lincolnese, neither was it bellicose. It would take the question on amnesty to bring out the pronounced flavor of revenge.

"Mr. President, do you have anything specifically in mind to help heal the wounds of this country, the divisions over the war, and specifically, down the road, much farther in terms of amnesty?" a reporter asked.

Nixon began with what amounted to major medical news: "It takes two to heal wounds," he said. He had sympathy for anyone who had made mistakes. "We have all made mistakes. But it is a rule of life, we all have to pay for our mistakes." Given the fact that he was at that moment desperately trying to hold the Watergate cover-up in place, after the conviction of two senior officials of his 1972 reëlection campaign the day before in a widening scandal, this observation would later take on a certain poetic prophecy.

We finally have achieved peace with honor. I know it gags some of you to write that phrase, but it is true, because it would have been peace with dishonor had we bugged out and allowed what the North Vietnamese wanted: a Communist government in

South Vietnam. . . . The war is over. Many Americans paid a very high price to serve their country . . . serving in a country very far away in a war that they realized had very little support among the so-called better people, in the media, and in intellectual circles . . . [men who served] despite the fact that they were hammered night after night, day after day, with the fact that this was an immoral war, that Americans should not be there, that they should not serve their country, but should desert their country.

This was rich fare for Nixon psychohistorians later, for all his animosities, large and small, were on display. As he scoffed at the notion of a higher morality, so he sought to reduce the proportion of the problem. Suddenly, the exile numbers of over forty thousand (not to mention the half-million deserters and quarter-million bad discharges) became "a few hundred." It was an example of what Nixon biographer Fawn Brodie called his tendency to tell "unnecessary lies." And then the bottom line.

We can not provide forgiveness for them. Those who served paid the price. Those who deserted must pay the price, and the price is not a junket in the Peace Corps or something like that. The price is a criminal penalty for disobeying the laws of the United States. If they want to return to the United States, they must pay the penalty. If they don't want to return, they are certainly welcome to stay in any country that welcomes them.

When a year and a half later Nixon would be driven into his own exile and himself become a candidate for forgiveness, the argument was quickly made that he had suffered enough. In accepting his pardon—was it a tacit admission of guilt?—he would acknowledge his "mistakes and misjudgments," but he would not remember his own maxim that the price for disobeying the laws of the United States was not a junket at San Clemente, but a criminal penalty.

For the psychology of forgiving and forgetting in the war resisters' case and in Nixon's was remarkably similar. Indeed, from this moment in early 1973, the two situations would be linked for the rest of the decade.

By setting the tone of malice at this grand, creative moment, Nixon invited malice against himself later. I know I felt it. As David Frost's Watergate advisor in the Nixon interviews in 1977, it would give me immense satisfaction to hear Nixon refer to himself as the last casualty of Vietnam; he had at least widened the notion of Vietnam casualties beyond the battlefield to include himself. And I would have a role in forcing the exiled president's only real statement of contrition. ("I let down my friends. I let down the country. I let down our system of government and the dreams of all those young people who ought to get into government but think it's too corrupt.") Even then, in 1977, the combative Nixon would protest that he did not really intend a Watergate cover-up. If he had, he would have simply declared, after the 1972 election, executive clemency for the Watergate figures and coupled it with an amnesty for Vietnam war resisters and deserters in one grand gesture of mock generosity. That, he thought, would have been the end of it, and he would have gone on to fulfull his dream of "building a lasting peace." Perhaps. But in 1973 he asked the war resisters to grovel; in 1977, when his time came, he would not do so, and there seemed to be something universal at work here.

"People didn't think it was enough to admit mistakes," Nixon told Frost. "Fine. They want me to get down on the floor. No. Never. Because I don't believe I should."

◈ ◈ ◈

If American history has its fruitful moments when presidents feel safe in reaching for posterity at whatever political cost—the beginning and end of presidencies, the end of wars and the like—it must be hoped that the moments can be months in duration. That Nixon in January 1973 was flushed with the "triumph" of Paris, which allowed for the total American withdrawal from Vietnam and a return of the prisoners, is understandable enough. That he was combative and sensitive when the need for his four-year war of disengagement was questioned is also understandable, given the great vulnerability of the argument on its face. Did Nixon and Kissinger really expect a long-lasting "peace with honor" . . . or were they simply buying a "decent interval" before the final collapse. That is for others to debate. In any event, between January and July 1973, the totality of the Vietnam defeat was not yet clear. The will to believe honor had been achieved was compelling, as strong as was the will to believe later that Vietnam veterans were heroes in a noble cause. But honor in modern America, like shame, is a concept that has grown murky since the days of Alexander Hamilton and Aaron Burr. During the middle 1970s, I used to ask college students to define single instances of honor and shame, both on a personal and national level, and the request always led to an embarrassing silence.

In the first six months of peace, the country comforted itself in its illusion of honorable peace, but it made no pretense to the inevitable corollary of reconciliation. In fact, the very absence of reconciliation pointed up the illusion of honor. The return of the POWs shoved all other considerations aside, and it was carefully staged. Eighty military public relations men deployed from the Philippines to Travis Air Force Base to shepherd "Operation Homecoming." Five hundred sixty-six soldiers made up the complement. They were the most enthusiastic of the American warriors. The majority were officers and fighter-bomber pilots who had made the military their career, who had waged the war from their sterile cockpits, and wasted years of their lives in prison camps. The senior commanders among them had missed the national protest and disavowal of the war. They were, as one of the physicians who examined them put it, "patriotic anachronisms." A contingent among them, those to be shot down in the first American air strikes on North Vietnam in 1965 and 1966, had come very close to being tried as war criminals by Ho Chi Minh. Using the Nuremberg Tribunal as precedent, Ho proposed to charge the fliers with wanton destruction of villages and inhumane acts against civilian population. (When Pope Paul VI and United Nations Secretary General U Thant interceded with a strong protest, Ho Chi Minh relented.) It is hardly profound to say that their will to believe their president was stout-hearted and that their years of captivity had not been in vain was overwhelming.

The tragedy of "Operation Homecoming" was not so much personal as national, for the extravaganza that took shape killed Vietnam reconciliation. Perhaps this was an accident of history, but it was an accident that was allowed to happen. Nixon was not Lincoln, to be sure, but it did not take a giant to recognize what the national priority should now be, nor did it take a genius to see that the POWs could become agents of savage recrimination against those who opposed the war. Perhaps the need for a few Vietnam heroes was understandable as well, even if the prisoner as hero, like the hostage as hero later, would become a new fixture in American folklore. It was all a far cry from the beach at Iwo Jima. But before the last POW was back in the United States two months later, reconstruction aid to Indochina was dead. The true experience of the two and one-half million Vietnam veterans was severely distorted. Amnesty was untouchable. And the POWs were at one another's throats. Over the whole process, Richard Nixon stood attorney.

On February 13, as Henry Kissinger was in Hanoi finalizing the reconstruction agreement for a Joint Economic Commission, the first 169 American POWs arrived in the

Philippines. At first, they were carefully shielded from the press, as they were examined physically and psychologically and pronounced to be in relatively good health, considering. In Washington, Nixon ordered the flags raised to full staff (they had been at half-staff after Lyndon Johnson's death on January 22) as a tribute to the heroism of the POW families (who supported the president) and to all who had helped "win" peace with honor. In New York a crab apple tree was planted in City Hall Park as a tribute to the POWs, probably an appropriate symbol with its spectacular, short-lived spring blossoms and its small, bitter, and inedible fruit that follow. Everywhere "God Bless America" was the theme song.

Over the next forty-seven days, a national melodrama was played out. The proud, grateful, unsteady survivors came down the ramp, along with the lame and the bedridden, and their very survival was a moving testament to human endurance. Their black pajamas exchanged for new starched uniforms, the gaunt men delivered, bold, nervous salutes and knelt to kiss the American soil. It was as if these few hundred suddenly became the American soldier at large: proud, professional, brave, tough, undaunted by indescribable hardship, representative of the best in America.

To them went the parades, while the Vietnam grunts watched in the crowd and the politicians repaired to the hospitals that would receive them. At one in Queens, New York, conservative Sen. James Buckley chose the spot to draw the contrast to the Vietnam shirkers. He would fight amnesty to the end, for amnesty was "tacit support for the proposition that young men who elected to escape service in the Vietnam War are somehow morally superior to the vast majority of young Americans who understood their responsibilities and shouldered them." The Big Lie of that statement went unnoticed amid the emotion.

On March 29, the last sixty-seven prisoners were flown

out, and on March 31 one of the few parades for *all* Vietnam veterans took place in New York. It was significant for what it was not, more than what it was. There was no blizzard of confetti. No high government officials were in attendance. It was organized not by the government but by an *ad hoc* group calling itself the Home with Honor Committee. No solid mass of steel uncoiled like a tremendous python down Broadway, as it had for Sherman down Pennsylvania Avenue more than a hundred years before; no soldiers, in good drill, eyes straight forward, with a steadiness and firmness of tread, about which all could say, "This was an army in the true sense." Instead, it was a motley group, with boisterous, bearded antiwar veterans rubbing shoulders with the fat, comical contigents from the local VFW and American Legion posts who turn out for any parade. If anything attracted universal attention, it was the medal of war winner, who did not stride, but was wheeled up the Great White Way as if he were the modern version of Secretary of State Seward. And a few POWs were in attendance. Cardinal Terence Cooke pronounced the benediction, but his request to pray with him in the spirit of gratitude and reconciliation did not meet the temper of the day.

For that morning, with all the prisoners back, the Pentagon authorized the POWs to speak openly about their captivity, and the gruesome details filled the newspapers. Beatings, shacklings, torture, solitary confinement, disease, starvation: "the catalogue of abuse read like an index to Marquis de Sade," wrote one news magazine. The scene turned ugly instantaneously, and the immediate casualty was economic aid for North Vietnam. Congressman Joel Broyhill of Virginia said: "Accounts of torture convince me that not a cent of American money should be spent rehabilitating a country apparently run by savages." Congressman Jerry Litton of Missouri suggested that the aid problem be solved by sending draft evaders to North Vietnam. "If those in America loved the North Vietnamese too much to fight them, perhaps they still love 'em enough to help them in their reconstruction program." And Rep. John McCollister of Nebraska said of the North Vietnamese: "To hell with 'em. I would not vote a bus token to North Vietnam. If the North Vietnamese want the money, they could get their good friends Ramsey Clark and Jane Fonda to take up a collection for them." This presumably played well to the home crowd, and the lefty gadfly, Jane Fonda, accommodated the attention by charging that the POW stories of torture were exaggerated. Immediately a resolution to declare Jane Fonda unwelcome in Colorado was introduced in that state's legislature, and on April 6 a similar censure measure passed the Indiana legislature. On April 5, the U.S. Senate passed a resolution, sponsored by Sen. Harry Byrd, Jr., of Virginia, by a vote of 88–3, to bar any reconstruction aid to North Vietnam unless Nixon received congressional support for it. Since it was clear that no such support would ever be forthcoming, this in effect ended the idea. For some weeks, the administration continued to speak of the possibility perfunctorily, presumably to tide along the meetings of American and North Vietnamese in Paris for a while longer. But the opportunity had unraveled. In July, Nixon found in the continued presence of North Vietnamese troops in South Vietnam the pretext to exclude North Vietnam from an Indochina aid package. The Paris talks were suspended. On this score, then, the admirable American tradition of postwar generosity, so rooted in the Marshall Plan, was dead.

Against the political pyrotechnics during the first week of April, an editorial in the *New York Times* was a voice of reason. It pleaded for the POW tales of hardship to be contrasted with the many stories of American and South Vietnamese abuses. Citing the tiger cages for Communist

POWs in Con Son, the large and small My Lais, torture of prisoners, bombing of civilian areas, and the use of chemicals, the *Times* called these violations of the spirit if not the letter of international law. The primary concern of the United States at this moment should be strengthening the rules of war which the country had "historically championed," said the newspaper, "and the highest U.S. authorities could not escape responsibility for the abuses that had tragically taken place." In this, the *Times* echoed the sentiment of the chief prosecutor at the Nuremberg Trials, American Robert Jackson, who had said that the tribunal did not propose to lay down laws of conduct that the United States would be unwilling to apply to itself. But in 1973 the country was in no mood to think of broader accountability. Another American tradition was dying. The *Times* plea was, as Sherman put it, a passing breeze of the sea on a warm summer day. Geneva Conventions, it seems, are only convened after American victories.

In the first week in April, the carefully staged harmony among the POWs unraveled as well. With an appearance on "60 Minutes" by Navy Capt. Walter B. Wilber, who had been in captivity for five years, the old Korean War issue of POW collaboration with the enemy surfaced again. Without being tortured, Wilber had made antiwar statements for North Vietnamese propaganda, as had other Americans, and now on American television he attributed his change of mind during twenty months in solitary confinement to the pressure of conscience. "I had time to think of what we were doing and the big bugaboo of conscience and morality began to show itself," Wilber said. Several days later, Maj. F. H. Kushner of the army, while testifying to animalistic conditions for Americans held in South Vietnam by the guerrillas and a mortality rate of 50 percent, said his antiwar statements had been forced in captivity, but in freedom he would not repudiate the substance of them. Suddenly, the Pentagon campaign of "forgive and honor" was shattered, as rumors flew that senior POW officers planned to prefer court-martial charges against the POW doves. Finally, on May 30, Col. T. W. Guy, the senior POW officer, went through with the threat by charging eight POW enlisted men for collaboration. Before the charges could be dismissed, on July 3, one of the eight, Sgt. A. L. Kavanaugh, committed suicide.

Through the spring of 1973, the country clung doggedly to its illusions. Even as POWs turned on one another over the issue of collaboration, they took time out to toss out the first ball in various pro baseball stadiums around the country. Their statements about the American peace movement they never knew grew more frequent and bitter. The peace movement caused the North Vietnamese to misinterpret American policy and to prolong the war, they said in remarks that might have been crafted in the White House shop. Meanwhile, Dallas followed New York with a three-day binge sponsored by H. Ross Perot, the computer magnate. Speaking for the four hundred POWs in attendance, the ranking POW, now Brig. Gen. John P. Flynn, told the crowd of thirty thousand, "It is more than fitting that we salute you, the People. We will stand by the people, should they or the President ever need us again. God bless you all." It was the way all wished it might have been before and might always be in the future. Meanwhile, the Reverend Carl McIntyre, the tub-thumping forerunner of the Moral Majority, promised to stage a war crimes tribunal of North Vietnam's leaders.

By early April, however, POW stories were competing on the front pages with stories about Watergate and the Pentagon Papers trial in Los Angeles, and Richard Nixon needed every distraction he could find. Unfortunately for him, exploiting the POW bathos did not suffice. During April–May–June 1973, seven out of ten covers of *Newsweek* were related to Watergate.

But on May 24, in a tent on the White House lawn, the

president threw a banquet for 610 former POWs. The guest list ran to 1,300, and it was called the largest and most spectacular gala in White House history, excepting perhaps the time that Andrew Jackson turned the place over to the street mobs. Nixon called them the most distinguished audience he had ever addressed (a few days later a former nurse in Vietnam would ask how many extravaganzas Nixon would give for the permanently disabled Vietnam veterans), and they in turn gave him sustained cheers on their feet when he said about the Pentagon Papers, "It's time to quit making national heroes out of those who steal secrets and publish them in the newspapers."

That the "secrets" Daniel Ellsberg had stolen were the documents that portrayed the pattern of deceit and error fed to the youth of America about why they needed to risk their lives in Vietnam, seemed to occur to few. Nor did the POWs seem to be aware that they were being used one last time. Several days before, the Pentagon Papers episode turned full circle when the trial against the thieves was dismissed over the revelation that the White House had initiated a burglary against Daniel Ellsberg's psychiatrist. The "plumbers" were searching for material to smear the turncoat.

So the president made the war, and the war spawned pacifist thieves (once intrepid spooks) whole stole the government's secret lies. The president sent his own thieves to burgle the pacifists' personal secrets, so the pacifists would be discredited. The government tried the pacifist thieves in court, but the case was dismissed and the government itself discredited when the president's own thieves were found out. But not before the same thieves were caught in another burglary called Watergate, which later not only discredited the president, but brought his government down.

It sounded not so much like a fable, but a sloppy farce.

A Sort of Charity | 10

IN LATE February and early March 1972, Sen. Edward Kennedy of Massachusetts held the first hearings on the problem of amnesty for Vietnam war resisters, even though the war was still very much in progress and would go on for another ten months. By general agreement, the Kennedy hearings were merely educational rather than directed toward immediate legislative action. The chairman himself defined a modest goal of illuminating the complexities of an issue that in the past two years had been subject to much simplification and distortion, as well as passion.

Amnesty after Vietnam was the first and, in many ways, the most important symbol of reconciliation, but it would not be the last. Richard Nixon had won the 1968 presidential election on the theme of reconciliation and peace. By that election year, the war had claimed thirty-one thousand lives. The voters were told of a secret plan for ending the war, and Nixon made "bringing the country together again" a centerpiece for his campaign. But his national security adviser, later secretary of state, and presumably the custodian of his secret peace plan, felt, as he later wrote in his memoirs, that the Nixon administration could not simply walk away from an enterprise involving thirty-one thousand dead "as if we were switching a television channel." Thus, Nixon and Kissinger were waving the bloody shirt (as it was known in the post–Civil War period) well before the conflict ended. Indeed, waving the bloody shirt became the pretext for the slow tune-out of the war, and the Nixon/Kissinger team did not switch channels completely for another four years and another twenty-five thousand American dead.

In his opening statement to his Senate subcommittee, Senator Kennedy spoke of the intense emotions that amnesty aroused in the country and he framed the issue as follows: "How, some ask, can amnesty be offered to those who fled when others fought? But, others assert, how can amnesty not be offered to those who were right about the war before the rest of us?" Some doves like himself, he said wryly, were asking amnesty for their own previous support of the Vietnam war.

The tone was gracious, for it recognized that the political Left, including President John Kennedy, was implicated in the decisions that sustained the war effort for so long. But the senator nevertheless missed the point and gave credence to a fallacy that would plague reconciliation for the next four years. He posed the problem of amnesty as one of fair play, which pitted the agony of the Vietnam veteran against the agony of the exile—one set of victims against other sets of victims. It was as if a complicated chart of moral righteousness had been devised. At the top were those who believed, who fought, who died. Across from them were those who criticized, who resisted out of pure moral principle, and who were jailed. Despite the willingness of the peace forces to lend themselves to this kind of balancing, both categories within the Vietnam generations were small. Who is to say in what state of mind the 55,000 died? Many speak for the dead, but the dead can't talk, as Dalton Trumbo once observed. And only 8,800 men went to jail in the Vietnam era for conscientious resistance. Thus, after the pure cream, the categories got murky—like those who fought but did not accept or understand what they were fighting for or those who evaded the draft or deserted for less than purely ethical motives, or the substandard draftees who were rushed into uniform to meet Pentagon manpower needs, when high-quality draftees were unavailable. Nowhere in the debate was it mentioned that of the twenty-six million draft-age men from 1964 to 1973, sixteen million never served, and most took positive steps to avoid service. During the Vietnam era, the law encouraged legal draft evasion, and the society, especially for the privileged classes, condoned it. Secretary of Defense Robert McNamara, for example, had written two personal letters to draft boards supporting the conscientious objection claims for sons of his Defense Department aides. The legal draft evaders were quite content, of course, to stand on the sidelines of the amnesty debate, as they had stood on the side of the war. The debate had nothing to do with them.

Nonetheless, the very peace forces that might have become the healing forces after the war, accepted unquestioningly at this early drill for reconciliation that moral balancing must guide the postwar period. While the Kennedy hearings were preliminary and purely "educational," they did much to form the liberal congressional thinking on reconciliation. The transition period between war and peace had, again, like Bennett Place, become critical.

That not much might be expected from the president in 1972 is scarcely worth mentioning. His secret plan for ending the war had turned out to be the slow domesticizing of it, a Vietnamization that had taken four years and another 25,000 American lives (not to mention another 184,000 South Vietnamese killed), and it had involved a practice of bombing which extended the permissible boundaries of total war equally as much as General Sherman had in his time. So, it was hardly surprising that Nixon would not countenance the notion of an amnesty which his opponents interpreted, incorrectly, as certifying the injustice and even immorality of his war.

Three months before the Kennedy hearings, at a November 12, 1971, news conference, Nixon was asked if he foresaw granting amnesty to expatriates who considered the war "immoral." The question had been framed incorrectly, and it gave Nixon the chance to reply with a flat single word, "No." On January 2, 1972, the president was asked on television to elaborate, and replied: "As long as there are Americans who choose to serve their country rather than desert their country, and it is a hard choice, and [the troops] are there in Vietnam, there will be no amnesty for those who deserted their country. As long as there are any POWs held by the North Vietnamese, there will be no amnesty for those who deserted their country."

This would seem to have marked in time when the era of reconciliation after Vietnam would commence. The modern parallel to Bennett Place would be the moment in time when the last American soldier and the last American prisoner of war was returned home. Later, this moment was postponed until the time when conscription ended. Sometime, an agenda for peace had to assert itself, but that time kept getting put back. Even at this juncture, Nixon reached for a Civil War analogy, although characteristically he sought to confuse the amnesty debate by speaking of a minor Lincoln amnesty to Union deserters rather than Confederate rebels.

"You remember Abraham Lincoln in the last days of the Civil War, as a matter of fact just before his death, decided to give amnesty to anyone who had deserted if he would come back and join his unit and serve out his period of time," Nixon said. (It was true that on March 11, 1865, Lincoln had promised that any Union deserter who returned to his unit within sixty days would not lose his citizenship or suffer any other loss of political rights. But this was a simple ploy to beef up the Union Army for the last battle and had nothing to do with the grand issue of binding up the wounds of the torn nation after peace.) "I, for one, would be very liberal with regard to amnesty but not while there are Americans in Vietnam fighting to defend their country, and not when POWs are held by North Vietnam. After that, we will consider it, but it would have to be on the basis of their paying a price, of course, that anyone should pay for violating the law."

Paying the price became the call of the warriors. It was a way to say in peace that their war was not wrong or immoral. Resistance had to remain a crime in peacetime, for if it were executed it undermined the need for the grand sacrifice. At least, that was how the policymakers saw it. There was no slackening in peace in justifying their war: it had been fought, so the American word would be taken seriously abroad; it had been fought to honor an American commitment; it had been fought to demonstrate American "resolve" to check the contagious spread of world communism. Staunch opposition to amnesty was the necessary corollary to the belief that American involvement in Vietnam had been just and noble.

217

The only problem with this was that the less educated and lower classes of the Vietnam generation had paid the price both by fighting the war and resisting it, and they would continue to bear the price in the era of vindictiveness that followed. In his initial statements, Nixon echoed the first words of Andrew Johnson when he assumed the presidency on the eve of peace: "I hold that robbery is a crime; rape is a crime; treason is a crime and crime must be punished. Treason must be made infamous and traitors impoverished." But Andrew Johnson would learn that the price of vindictiveness was high, too.

So it was that Nixon and Edward Kennedy, conservative warrior and liberal dove, came together a year before the Vietnam war was over on certain assumptions. First, an amnesty must balance the price of the Vietnam soldier against the pain of the Vietnam expatriate. Second, there should be a penalty for violating the law, with the liberal speaking for a more lenient penalty. But harsh or lenient, punishment for the *wrongdoing* of resistance was appropriate. Third, the American Civil War was a valid parallel for the postwar period, and Abraham Lincoln the moral mentor for the Vietnam aftermath. And, fourth, the exit of all American troops from Vietnamese soil was the first moment when the government could begin to think about a policy of reconciliation. Only if a staunch opponent of the war were elected in 1972 could the second Reconstruction of our history be possible.

The first witness before the Kennedy hearings in February 1972 was Curtis Tarr, the director of the Selective Service System, who for years had had the thankless task of determining the sincerity of conscientious objection. In the first few years of the war the task had been relatively easy, for religious affiliation was the sole test and could be easily verified. But in 1965, in *United States v. Seeger,* the Supreme Court broadened the test for conscientious objection by disavowing "religious training and belief" as the sole requirement for conscientious objection. In 1971, with *Welsh v. United States,* the court broadened the test still further by stating that purely moral and ethical beliefs, quite apart from religion, were sufficient to achieve an exemption from military service. The result was that in 1971 the Selective Service System was processing more applications for conscientious objection a month—twelve thousand to fourteen thousand—than were being inducted into the armed forces. Nevertheless, even under the two broad Supreme Court decisions, draft boards still had to judge the sincerity of a registrant's opposition to the Vietnam war. To judge moral belief on such a vast scale had never before been conducted by the American government. It was a process that Curtis Tarr hoped would stay unique with the Vietnam war. He hoped it would end soon, and never again be attempted.

Senator Kennedy asked Tarr about amnesty after the Civil War. Had relief not been granted then to persons charged with treason?

"But it was a civil war, you see," Tarr replied, as if that separated the conflict from all other American conflicts, including Vietnam, and made it irrelevant, rather than made the crime of the Southern rebels the most heinous, and the amnesty to them so much more charitable.

"I do not know if any of the people thought they had committed treason at the time it was granted," Kennedy replied.

"If we use the Civil War [as a precedent]," Tarr said, "we are still going to have to determine ways appropriate for 1972 or 1973 or 1974."

In discussing the Civil War precedent, Tarr's testimony had underscored an important principle of the reconciliation process: the common foot soldier, the youth of Stephen Crane or the youth of the Vietnam era was always

219

given relief for treason or desertion or, for that matter, any wartime transgression, and the relief was given instantly after the divisive conflict was over. The need to end discord was far greater than the need to punish technical wartime offense. If any persons were to be excepted from relief, it was decision makers, or persons in positions of political influence, like leaders of a rebellion above a certain rank or station, but not the youthful soldier or the youthful dissident.

It was not long into this discussion before a shrill Southern voice cried out in protest. Sen. Strom Thurmond hailed from Edgefield, South Carolina, which spawned the rabid "Edgefield orators" of the pre–Civil War days like Preston Brooks, who had caned abolitionist Sen. Charles Sumner nearly to death on the Senate floor in 1856. The town had also become notorious in the Reconstruction days for its night riders and its massacre of disarmed black militia during an attempt to protect the Negro right to vote. Thurmond's grandfather, George Washington Thurmond, had been a corporal in the South Carolina Volunteers, and his Senate staff proudly announces that the good corporal had been with Lee at Appomattox. With the passage of generations, it appears that nearly every Confederate ancestor who survived was with the noble Lee at the end. Actually, Corporal Thurmond surrendered to Sherman at Greensboro. There is no record of Corporal Thurmond ever signing an oath of allegiance to support the Constitution of the United States and to respect the emancipation of slaves after the war, as was required for political rights to be restored. Now, Senator Thurmond rose boldly to defend Southern mythology, for he shriveled at the comparison between the nobility of his corporal grandfather and the seediness of the Vietnam resisters.

"Did I understand you to hint or suggest that those who fought against the Union in the so-called Civil War were traitors?" Thurmond asked Kennedy.

"I said they were labeled as such, as violating the laws," Kennedy replied judiciously.

"And you would call them traitors?" Thurmond pressed.

"No, I would not."

"Well, I wanted to debate that with you, and I wanted to remove any insinuation, because I got the clear impression that you said they were traitors."

In the face of this smouldering Southern passion, Senator Kennedy skedaddled, and Sen. Philip Hart of Michigan jumped in to play the Yankee foil. "Senator Thurmond, are you saying that the Confederates were responding to a deep moral conviction?"

"I am saying that the Confederates were fighting for the rights of states. The states joined the Union voluntarily, and they felt they had a right to withdraw voluntarily, and they fought for the states where they lived, most of them. There were a few that fought on the other side, and to call those people traitors would be entirely out of order. There is no such thing as a grandson of a Confederate veteran who fought in that war being a traitor. I would deeply resent that [insinuation] and you know I would."

"I respect the conscience of your grandfather," Senator Hart replied wryly, "and I'm glad he was granted amnesty."

"Well, I want to say, [the War Between the States] was a different situation from now. In this Vietnam War, the states are still a part of the Union. Back then, they withdrew from the Union and were fighting an entirely different cause. There is no comparison at all between the two."

Senators Hart and Kennedy may be forgiven for letting Senator Thurmond's provincial version of history and law sink itself. Few subjects have less chance of accommodation than a replay of the Civil War with a chauvinistic Southerner who really does admire the old Southern slave aristocracy and really does care about his ancestry. Generally, such passion is considered harmless. But here it had consequences. Within the Book of Perfidy, if one were to exist, surely this is clear: refusal to fight the country's war (especially if the refusal is based on high principle) is less of a sin than taking up arms in violent struggle against the American government. But if on the eve of peace in Vietnam even this could not be agreed upon, then charity after Vietnam was going to be hard in coming.

At that moment in 1972 the dignity of his forbears occasioned more passion in Senator Thurmond than did the problem at hand, and he came back to it on the next day of the hearing with renewed vigor. For him, this was no sport, at least, if his public posture could be judged sincere. It is an endearing irony that Southerners who had been the greatest beneficiaries of official charity in American history now became the shrill voice of retribution. Senator Thurmond set the tone for the rest of the Southern delegation in Congress. The double irony would come four years later, when it took a Southern president to offer the first genuine act of healing.

"[Confederates] did not just secede and run off to some other country," Senator Thurmond proclaimed. "They seceded and fought for what they believed in. That is far different from today. Those men who ran to Canada or Sweden fought for neither side. They have just evaded military service. There was an honest difference in men who were willing to fight during the War Between the States. I cannot imagine anybody today calling those people traitors. It is an outrage. And I think anyone who called those people traitors are cowards themselves, and I do not care whom it applies to."

For Thurmond, refusing to fight was to be joined with cowardice; manliness with the fighting instinct. If there was a point worth discussing here, it was treason itself. Vietnam was an undeclared war, and therefore technically under the Constitution no one who refused to fight the Vietnam war could be charged with treason. And no one was so charged between 1964 and 1973. High treason involves only acts constituting a serious threat to the stability of the state. The high incidence of draft evasion and desertion during the Vietnam era had not undermined the ability of the government to fight the war, only made it lower its standards for cannon fodder. Only the Southern Rebellion falls squarely into the category of overt treason.

"No people of this country underwent the sacrifices [Southerners] did after [the War Between the States]," Thurmond lumbered on. "They were under military rule for ten years. They suffered enduring hardships. Yet they supported this country and supported its government and provided fighting men in every war this country has fought. Today the South is the heart of patriotism. When anyone refers to those who fought on the Southern side as traitors . . . they do not know history."

Amid this stentorian posturing, it would be left to one who really did have a sense of history to clear the air of heavy fog. Henry Steele Commager, the distinguished American historian, came on to illuminate the real record. Commager would state definitively that the Civil War possessed the best model for a Vietnam reconciliation. The desertion from the Union and the Confederate armies ran at roughly 10 percent, Commager pointed out, and together desertion and draft evasion had threatened the very viability of the Confederate Army, whereas the Union cause, drawing upon a greater manpower pool, had never been so threatened. In 1864, as Sherman cut his great hook around the Appalachian range, there were more Southern deserters and draft evaders in the mountains of the Carolinas than in Lee's entire Army of Northern Virginia. No action was ever taken against any deserter in any section after the war. The Constitution defined treason as simply bearing arms against the United States, pure and simple, the scholarly Commager said, not looking at Senator Thurmond.

But it was the historian's summation that one might profoundly have hoped to hear from a man in political power.

"For almost a decade now, our Nation had been sorely afflicted," Commager said. "The material wounds are not as grievous as those inflicted by the Civil War, not for Americans anyway, but the psychological and moral wounds are deeper and more pervasive. Turn and twist as we may, we come back always to the root cause of our malaise, the war. If we are to restore harmony to our society and unity to our nation, we should put aside all vindictiveness, all inclination for punishment, all attempts to cast a balance of patriotism or of sacrifice—as unworthy of a great nation. Let us recall rather Lincoln's admonition to judge not that we be not judged, and with malice toward none, charity for all, strive to bind up the nation's wounds."

The senators listened courteously to these noble words, but would they be translated into political action?

"Can you tell us as a historian what kind of atmosphere we would have in this country if we do not take a tolerant view of these young people who left the country as a matter of deep conscience?" Senator Kennedy asked.

"I am inclined to think that the consequences would be deeply disturbing and that we would later deeply regret them. . . . They would be consequences that would leave a stain on our history. It is always better to forgive than to take vengeance, and our society is now deeply torn. It is torn not only on the issue of war, but on the issue of race, which closely connects with the war. It has torn hostilities within our great cities. We should be ready to pay any reasonable price to restore harmony, to win once again the confidence of the American people in the wisdom and the generosity of their government, to reknit a society which is in danger of unraveling. I do not think granting amnesty to all deserters and draft evaders alike, however unfair it may seem to be to some, is too high a price to pay.''

But in pondering such thoughts, the feet of the modern politicians would turn to clay.

◇ ◇ ◇

When Gerald Ford ascended to the presidency in an accidental manner, unique in American history, he seemed to understand intuitively that he must be peacemaker to the nation. But what genuine act of healing could he deliver? How could he manifest a true Lincolnian impulse? What would give him real standing to be remembered as a healer and a peacemaker. Nine years of Vietnam and two years of Watergate had implanted so deep a strain of disillusion with government in the American people that only Lincolnian effort could root it out. Trust had been shattered. The assumption of dishonesty at the highest level had become the prevailing attitude. The generation that had been asked by its country for the act of supreme love had dropped out.

Despite his pedestrian career in the House of Representatives, despite his reputation as a party stalwart and bland personality and unfailing supporter of the Vietnam war effort, there seemed to be potential in the man for rising to the call. He had the feel of heartland America about him. His fumbling speech had the tone of straightforwardness. "Ford is everything Nixon pretended to be,'' my father wrote of the transfer of power, but with time, genuineness would not suffice. One of Ford's first acts as president was to move the portraits of Lincoln and of Truman into the Cabinet Room, for they were the presidents he most admired. (Nixon had chosen to pray with Kissinger in the Lincoln bedroom on the night before he resigned, but this homage to the Great Emancipator for Nixon came late.)

The inherent contradiction between trying to be Lincoln and Truman at one and the same time soon manifested itself in the Ford presidency. It was the conflict between mercy and justice, between charity and tough talk, between peacemaking and the old jingoism that had been so consistent in Ford's previous public life and had gotten the country into the Vietnam quagmire at the outset. And Ford had been asked to preside over contradictory events: both the reconciliation of the nation and the final defeat of Western colonialism in Vietnam. The denouement, with its humiliating image of Vietnamese clients clinging to the skeds of American helicopters as they lifted off the roof of the U.S. Embassy would come months into the Ford term. By his "voluntary impeachment," as he put it in the David Frost interviews, Richard Nixon had avoided being the first president to preside over an American defeat. On April 30, 1971, Nixon had proclaimed that he would rather be a one-term president than to suffer that humiliation. With the eye of history, his escape is a technicality.

Gerald Ford, this accidental president, came with a special debt: he was beholden to his predecessor for his rise above his station, and the manner in which the transition was made from Nixon to Ford remains, if not a historical mystery, certainly a psychological one. It has never been adequately clarified whether or not Ford came into office on August 9, 1974, by virtue of a Nixon expectation that a full, unconditional pardon would soon be forthcoming. Like General Johnson at Bennett Place, Nixon was not compelled to surrender in August 1974. Overwhelming hostile forces were arrayed all around him. His troops had deserted him long since, and his followers had dwindled to a few tired die-hards. To fight on, through a full impeachment debate in the House and a trial in the Senate, would have been *political* murder, but he could have chosen to do so. At the time, I was in Washington, following the impeachment events closely, transfixed by the greatest political drama of our time, and I was reminded of an entry in the diary of Georges Clemenceau as he pondered Andrew Johnson during his last days in office.

"Mr. Johnson, like Medea, stands absolutely alone. He is his sole remaining friend. Unhappily, he does not suffice."

But Nixon still had a few friends (Senator Goldwater would estimate about fifteen senators), and the open country of endless legal wrangling was there to retreat through.

Attention has focused on the actions of Alexander Haig on August 1, 1974, as Haig went to Ford, supposedly to "brief" him on Nixon's "options" after the revelation of the "smoking gun" tape. The Bennett Place dynamic was surely at work: Nixon would be anxious about his political rights and criminal charges after resignation, and what concessions might his vice-president be willing to give. The only bargaining chip that remained to Nixon was a stubborn vow to prolong the political agony indefinitely. A different man might have offered concessions himself, some act of largesse that might make a Ford pardon more palatable. An amnesty for Vietnam dissidents was his natural choice, perhaps his only choice. Nixon would boast, unpersuasively, to David Frost two and a half years after his resignation that he might have swept all his problems away, even at this late juncture, by one grand gesture of mock charity: a pardon to all Watergate conspirators, to all Vietnam resisters, and to himself.

Universal amnesty for Southern rebels had, after all, been one of Andrew Johnson's last acts. As Georges Clemenceau wrote of that act on Christmas Eve, 1868, "his proclamation allows him to crown his career with a final act of clemency and magnanimity." But there is no evidence of Nixon considering anything of the sort at the time. To think of such a gesture was probably not in his nature. Ford was left to make the concessions. He, in turn, might have thought to offer only some of Sherman's "glittering generalities,'' meaning much or meaning little, but meaning enough to wrest Nixon's signature on a resignation document. But instead, Ford came through with a unilateral surrender. Richard Nixon was pardoned of all past crime, real or alleged, immunized against any future prosecution, and sent off to his comfortable exile in San Clemente with $850,000 in transition costs and the full privileges of a distinguished elder statesman.

Neither Nixon or Ford nor Haig has ever been forthcoming about the significance of the August 1 Ford-Haig meetings. Undeniable is the fact that Haig planted the idea of a full pardon in Ford's mind that day, and Ford had not stood up in anger and ordered the scoundrel out of his office. Did Nixon consign weight to the absence of a Ford outburst? Had Nixon ordered Haig to Ford's office expressly to mention the full pardon as one "option" that might be considered? What did Haig report back to Nixon about Ford's silent reaction to the pardon suggestion? There are no answers to these questions.

Whether Ford's act was a pure trade of pardon for resignation, or a simple thanks from himself and from the nation, the pardon can not be considered a grand and noble gesture of mercy. Indeed, Ford himself did not consider it as such. In his memoirs, ironically entitled *A Time to Heal*, he admits that the pardon was bred of irritation rather than charity. At his first full press conference, on August 28, 1974, the press showed no interest in the new president's views on foreign policy or the economy. It wanted to know only about Nixon. "How long is this going to last?" Ford asked his advisors afterwards. When the word came from the special prosecutor's office that Nixon might not be tried for a year, and, if convicted, his appeals might last six years, Ford's consideration of an immediate and complete pardon, by his own account, got serious.

In September 1974, a pardon of Nixon was not indicated,

nor was it wanted by the American people. Moreover, Richard Nixon hardly had the first claim on government mercy, for he was one man whose actions involved no valid appeal to a higher law. The hundreds of thousands of youthful Vietnam resisters did have such an appeal, and they had been suffering for years. This was the point that Gerald Ter Horst, Ford's press secretary of only three weeks, made when he resigned over the Ford pardon of Nixon. For Ter Horst, a pardon of Nixon was morally acceptable only if it was coupled with a sweeping relief for the war resisters. "As your spokesman, I do not know how I could credibly defend [your pardon] in the absence of a like decision to grant absolute pardons to the young men who evaded Vietnam military service as a matter of conscience. . . . Try as I can, it is impossible to conclude that the former President is more deserving of mercy than persons of lesser station in life whose offenses have had less effect on our national well-being."

Too much about Nixon's corruption was still covered up. Nixon himself evinced no remorse. The catharsis of the political system was not complete. The pardon prolonged Watergate, left a litany of historical mysteries, and aborted a cleansing and reconstruction of American politics. In the end, it defeated Gerald Ford's bid for a normal presidency. If the act possessed a twisted kind of mercy, it possessed no justice at all. The only account that Nixon would ever be "forced" to give of his Watergate actions came in his television interrogation by David Frost three years later, an accounting for which the ex-president was paid more than a million dollars.

In the days before the announcement of Nixon's pardon, Ford came to accept the concept of coupling the pardon with some action for Vietnam resisters. He had come to a moment where he could be guided only by principle, not by political expediency, for the passions about amnesty were so intense that not only the action but the appearance was crucial. It was inevitable that the degree of mercy he accorded the resisters would be compared to the total exculpation of Nixon. With his own record of support for the war, Ford had moral standing only to declare a complete amnesty, not to judge categories of resistance or to scale degrees of suffering. Had Ford seen the overarching need for a true reconciliation at this moment, he could have truly stood in the Lincoln tradition.

On August 19, 1974, three weeks before the Nixon pardon, at the convention of the Veterans of Foreign Wars in remarks penciled into his text, the president announced his intention to give clemency to the resisters. A month later, the details of Ford's "earned reentry" came. "In furtherance of our national commitment to justice and mercy these young Americans should have the chance to contribute a share to the rebuilding of peace among ourselves and with all nations," Ford declared. That was the Lincoln charity. Then came the Truman price: two years of alternative service in the lowest possible paying jobs, administered by the very Selective Service System many had fled. This condition was drolly called the Reconciliation Work Program. Then, an oath of allegiance to the government they had condemned would be requested. For desertion and draft evasion were serious offenses, and "reconciliation among our people does not require that these acts be condoned." This was Lincoln with Truman's face, and the composite looked like the distinctly unreal product of the police laboratory.

The machinery that the presidential compromise brought into being was equally unreal. A clemency board of nine distinguished members was to consider the files of draft evaders on a case-by-case basis, but not the half-million "offenders" as a whole, but only those who applied for this presidential solicitude. Of those who did apply, the board would continue the wartime practice of judging the sincerity of individual conscience, a process for which it had no moral standing whatever, and it was to look for "mitigating circumstances" that might have contributed to the ill-advised resistance, like insufficient education, personal or family problems, or mental instability. By implication, the resister was thereby assumed to be dumb, screwed up, or crazy, whereas the Vietnam fighter could not be so well educated that he had beaten the draft legally, nor too ill educated that he had not seen the nobility of the American cause.

"Reconciliation calls for an act of mercy to bind the nation's wounds and to heal the scars of divisiveness," Ford's proclamation read, drawing upon the words but not the sentiment of Lincoln. To bludgeon Shakespeare, the clemency program so strained the quality of mercy as to become vengeance, and it fell not as a gentle, but as an acid, rain upon its intended beneficiaries. His act did not twice bless, but twice cursed Ford: it ruined both the largesse of the Nixon pardon and made the Vietnam clemency appear as a cynical and transparent effort at packaging. The peace movement immediately derided it, and the expatriate community of Canada and Sweden announced a boycott of it. If one needed a final argument that this was no mercy, but the reverse, the Ford program was open for six months only. The clear message to the "offenders" was: this will be your one brief chance for atonement.

The forces in Congress that might have plastered this outrage instead sat back to see what the response of the war resisters would be. No voice rose to defend the individual act of conscience or to question the government's standing to judge individual sincerity. No one spoke of the absurdity of the government attempting a delineation of war resistance categories, when the fact of the whole generation's disavowal of the war was clear on its face. No voice pointed out that after two years of this charitable duty, the government's reward of a clemency pardon would stigmatize the resister as a disloyal citizen for life. And no one questioned how demeaned a resister would feel to swear an oath of allegiance, when many considered the refusal to participate in a war they considered immoral to be essentially a patriotic act. Finally, no one made a genuine use of American history, arguing that no such massive inquisition into motives of American youth had ever been proposed or undertaken—certainly not after the American Civil War.

Four months into the program, Senator Kennedy again held hearings. He discovered that only eight hundred had applied to Ford's blue-ribbon board. In the *Los Angeles Times,* cartoonist Paul Conrad had portrayed the open gate of a barbed-wire military caserne where a band stood under an American flag waiting to play, a banner stretched over the gate that read "Welcome Home, War Resisters," and two frightened greeters looked blankly at one another. The caption read, "What if we gave an amnesty and nobody came?" It was a brilliant inversion of the maxim, "What if we had a war and nobody went?" The Kennedy hearings filled the air with more of the same old verbiage.

Senator Kennedy himself spoke of Andrew Johnson's universal amnesty, but he did not propose that the president declare such a thing. He spoke of the need to renew respect for the act of conscience, but he did not say how. Senator Thurmond, in turn, waved the Confederate flag and the bloody shirt. And there were the now familiar, hollow genuflections to Lincoln.

"Many aspects of Abraham Lincoln's Presidency have become part of the fabric of American life," said Sen. Charles Mathias of Maryland. "His act of clemency is one of the strong recurrent notes in the Lincoln legend. Lincoln's ability to perform acts of clemency without weakening the will of the fabric or the strength of the Union cause is one of the enduring parts of Lincoln that we all know today." But Senator Mathias just wanted the clemency board to bear that history in mind, while he himself certainly did not want to be responsible for weakening "the will of the fabric." Just how such a sentiment was to affect the hundreds of thousands of men who were not availing themselves of the government's mercy was not said.

At the end of the six months, the program was an obvious bust. It was extended several more months, on the pretext that some resisters might not have heard of it, but that succeeded in rounding up a few more thousand in the last few weeks of the extended program, desperate men, no doubt, who had become convinced that this clemency *was* the limit of their government's generosity.

As the failure became clear, the managers of the program turned increasingly strident. Charles Goodell, the former New York senator and the clemency program's director, made a most scurrilous argument, one which was likely to raise the anger of Vietnam veteran and Vietnam resister.

"There are hundreds of thousands of people in this country with sons, husbands, brothers, or fathers who died or were seriously wounded in Vietnam, and those people have very, very profound feelings on the question of clemency," Goodell told Congress. "For those who feel deeply about the sacrifices paid by those who served, those who died, those who suffered grievous wounds, clemency means that those who did not serve are rewarded in place of those who went *in their stead.*" [my italics]

Goodell's bitterness seemed to mirror Ford's. The president had made a reasonable offer, he felt, and the exiles could rot where they were in their refusal of it. The administration denied the right of Congress to legislate amnesty (overlooking the Universal Amnesty Act of 1898, which removed the last disability for any living Confederate), and

233

appropriated the pardoning power solely to the president. This was a rerun of a Reconstruction issue as well, for Andrew Johnson and the Radical Congress had dueled over whose prerogative the pardon power was. Indeed, in early 1867, the Radicals had repealed the clemency section of the Confiscation Act and meant the action to deny the president's power over all pardoning. In the modern Congress, no congressman was insisting upon the right of Congress to amnesty. Meanwhile, President Ford let it be known that he would veto any effort to liberalize his conditions for reëntry.

In remarks to Congress, Goodell reached the bottom when he testified that a universal amnesty would be an act intended to help most of all the bomber who had blown up the mathematics department at the University of Wisconsin or the drug dealer who fled to Sweden to avoid military prosecution. That was like Lincoln arguing that there could be no charity for anybody after the Civil War because such a sweeping sentiment measure might embrace Nathan Bedford Forrest, who had massacred black Union troops at Fort Pillow in 1862. Goodell's demagoguery could not cover up the sorry fact that by April of 1975, after eight month's existence, the Presidential Clemency Board had completed work on a total of 114 cases.

Nevertheless, Congress was cowed. In the face of a veto threat, the ten amnesty proposals then before Congress languished in committee, and died. Amnesty legislation was never debated on the floor of the full U.S. Congress.

In the fall of 1976, Ford went down to a narrow defeat in the presidential election, and it became generally accepted that his pardon of Nixon provided the margin of defeat. Even to the last days of his presidency, there would be no escape in the moral gulf between his relief of Nixon and his recrimination against the war resisters. On December 27, 1976, his friend, Michigan Sen. Philip Hart, died. Hart had been the most steadfast advocate of reconciliation in the U.S. Congress from the beginning, and his wife, Jane, had been active in the amnesty movement. In his telephone call to Jane Hart with his condolences, Ford made the mistake at the end of the conversation of asking if there was anything he could do.

"You can grant an amnesty," Mrs. Hart replied tartly, taking the president by surprise, "for that was the last thing Phil in his last days wished he could get through [Congress]."

In deference to the widow, Ford promised to consider her request. While the last-minute amnesty might have crowned his accidental presidency with magnanimity and preempted the intention of his successor, Ford thought it was not yet a time to heal, and did nothing.

Nine years after the Ford Clemency, the U.S. Department of Justice could say only that 182 official clemency discharges had ever been issued, but it could not remember how many of those had come after the completion of a full two years of alternative service.

A Southern Healer? 11

IN HIS revisionist work on the aftermath of the American Civil War,* historian Kenneth Stampp addressed the question of whether the seminal contributions of the Radical Reconstruction had their source in noble or ignominious motives. Was the abolition of slavery, the equal protection of the laws, and the right to vote (the Thirteenth, Fourteenth, and Fifteenth amendments to the U.S. Constitution) enacted out of high purpose or from the impulse to vengeance, by political opportunism or by capitalist greed? The Radicals had granted citizenship; they had defined civil

* *The Era of Reconstruction: 1865–1877*, Knopf, 1965.

rights for the American black and had secured his ballot. Had these moral ends been achieved with immoral motives? "If that is the case," Stampp wrote, "the historian will have to decide which has the greater historical significance: the praiseworthy program or the ignominious motive. He may, in fact, have to expand the classic moral dilemma of means and ends to means, motives, and ends."

There was in the U.S. Congress after Vietnam no group that might remotely be compared, in program or in passion, to the Radical Republicans after the Civil War. Few insisted that the divisiveness, the bitterness, and the confusion over Vietnam and Watergate among the general public cried out for reflection and a clarification of our principles and policies. How was it that America somehow had drifted into war that divided us and a scandal that demoralized us? Were they intertwined? What was that delicate balance between forgetting and remembering that could fold Vietnam into American history? What was required to "put Vietnam behind us" in any meaningful sense? If the country really wanted "no more Vietnams," how might that be ensured?

One difference between the aftermaths of our two most divisive wars is pivotal. After the Civil War, the South had to be reorganized without slavery, and Southerners had to resume normal lives as American citizens. After Vietnam, there was no necessity of reconstruction as a civic program, but as reconstruction in a subtler, yet profound sense. Here, the Lost Cause was not for just one section, but for all America. America as a whole had had its first frustration and defeat in war. The need lay in regaining a sense of national purpose, in restoring a sense of legitimacy to our ideals, in recovering a largeness of spirit. This subtle reconstruction needed to accommodate both the pro-Vietnam sector who were disappointed that "victory" had been denied, and the vast sector of dissidents, ranging from the conscientious objectors and deserters to the muddled and the disheartened. How, too, could America protect itself from some new, hapless venture? How could it make sure that no future generation of Americans would ever again face such an ethical dilemma as the Vietnam generation faced?

This delicate reconstruction after Vietnam would have required a moral dedication, verging upon religious fervor, equal to that of the best post–Civil War radicals. That emotion was not to be found upon the modern political scene. Because the mere mention of Vietnam after the war became bad politics, to do something for the casualties of Vietnam became bad politics as well, with no "payback" for the politician, no reward from the home district. So, in turn Kenneth Stampp on his head, with no broad praiseworthy program to consider after Vietnam, the motive to consider is the motive to silence and inaction.

The rush to forget had its profound consequences. For ten years after the war, Vietnam receded into the collective unconscious, vaguely disquieting like some gnawing episode of infidelity. The young who were the physical and psychological casualties of the war, the ones who had borne the real burden of the misadventure, were left to their own devices. Because of their alienation, their cynicism, or their painful preoccupation with self-renewal, they did not take their normal place as heirs to political power, but avoided politics. As a result, by the mid-1980s, the Vietnam generation has no figures of real political stature who speak from an emotional center in the Vietnam experience. There are roughly fifty million Americans, men and women, for whom the war in Vietnam was a central experience of their early adulthood. Their sentiments are not powerfully represented in the texture of American politics today. This brings an additional consequence: the generation immediately following the Vietnam generation has, as yet, no real appreciation of the suffering or the moral anguish that went before it.

The clemency program of Gerald Ford was neither praiseworthy in its concept nor noble in its motive, and when it failed, Ford possessed no inner force that propelled him to reach higher. But in history, the clear lines toward reconstruction and genuine healing were manifest. The first three years after the Civil War held the parallel: to borrow the best and reject the worst of that turbulent readjustment. Andrew Johnson had presided over the healing, while the Radicals in Congress presided over the Reconstruction.

From his lowly North Carolina roots, Johnson was every bit as representative of the American dream as Abraham Lincoln. But he was not a loveable man. It has been said that what of humble beginnings Abraham Lincoln made into a political asset, Johnson made into a political liability. Lincoln was a master of men; Johnson could not master himself. The difference between log-splitting in Illinois and tailoring in Tennessee is not qualitative, but as the product of the latter, Johnson was stubborn, bitter, petulent, tactless, boorish and awkward in the extreme, and racist in the manner of General Sherman. But he entered office with a vision of a New South, and even as he proceeded to violate that vision in his tenure of office it gave the era after Vietnam both models and omens and eventually a rightful heir in Jimmy Carter of Georgia.

The vision was of a New South, divested of its bloated, self-assured aristocracy and ruled by yeoman farmers. To Johnson, the Southern yeomen had been decoyed and browbeaten into rebellion, and, therefore, were not ultimately responsible. The ideal was Jeffersonian, the hardworking men of the soil as the chosen people of God. "Some day I will show the stuck-up aristocrats who is running the country," Johnson boasted early in his career. "A cheap, purse-proud set they are, not half as good as the man who earns his bread by the sweat of his brow." And in his first amnesty to rebels, only five days after Sherman's triumphant victory march down Pennsylvania Avenue,

Johnson launched his first effort to wound the aristocrats, as he healed the common man. It was prompted by the recognition that Southern rebels were not availing themselves of Lincoln's wartime amnesty offer, and so a broader, more generous act was required. Under it, rebels had to apply to the government for relief. For the common man who directly or indirectly participated in the rebellion, that was easy. Only an oath of allegiance to the Constitution was required to restore all political rights. The oath itself differed from the oath required under the Ford clemency only in the respect that the beneficiary of Johnson's amnesty had to swear that slavery was dead. But Johnson excepted fourteen classes of men from this first relief. Among those exceptions were Confederate officers educated at West Point or Annapolis; the high military and civil officials; but, most interesting, all men whose income exceeded $20,000. These excepted classes might apply directly to the president, and "such clemency will be liberally extended as may be consistent with the facts of the case and the peace and dignity of the United States."

In this first conditional amnesty lay the precedent for administering an oath of allegiance to a mass of disgruntled Americans and for considering large numbers of individual cases one by one. To any who wished to consult the record, the experience was a disaster. The reward for swearing an oath was tangible enough, and few Confederates found difficulty in overcoming whatever insincerity might have been involved. On file at the National Archives are some 181,000 such oaths. The government's encouragement of insincere oath-swearing would be repeated 108 years later with the Ford clemency. Military deserters returned from Canada to Fort Benjamin Harrison, Indiana, for processing. There they were asked to swear an oath of allegiance and to promise to serve two years' alternative service, but then, to their astonishment, legal officers informed them that they could not be prosecuted if they did not report to work. This became known as the "military loophole" and accounts for the comparative higher number of deserters who signed up for the Ford clemency, as opposed to the draft evaders. The program was conceived to encourage a lie.

Andrew Johnson's first amnesty operated for over two years. Its process of case-by-case consideration among the excepted classes soon degenerated into an orgy of chicanery and graft. At first, Johnson insisted upon seeing Southern planters and officials personally, so that they might beg for mercy before the tailor-made president himself, and presumably cleanse their soul. The president's anterooms filled with elegant senators, military officers, civil officials of the late Confederacy. At first, the process went slowly, but as the magnitude of the task became evident Johnson signed off on virtually every request made to him, and then on parcels of applications. A system of pardon brokers, a few of whom were notorious ladies, was brought into existence, and for an attorney with access to the president, a handsome fee could be made. A similar, if less luridly corrupt, set of sharpies fed upon the Ford clemency, but, of course, the modern clientele was considerably less well turned out and less well heeled.

Among those who might have been relieved by Johnson's immediate amnesty was one Littlebury Walker Carter of Sumter County, Georgia, who had been a private in Cutt's Flying Artillery, organized out of Americus. Born in 1829, Carter was the son of Wiley Carter, a successful farmer who built a plantation of twenty-four hundred acres and worked thirty slaves. This was distinctly plantation plain in the manner of the Jarrell Plantation in Jones County, and the Carter family bore no elegant panache. On the contrary, rural frontier violence characterized the family more than lawn parties. In 1839 Wiley Carter had a slave stolen, and he promptly repaired to the thief's house, sat outside all night with the sheriff, and in the morning, as the thief burst out with a pistol, Wiley shot him dead. In a one-day trial he was acquitted of murder, with the sheriff the star witness for the defense. Stealing a slave was no minor provocation. The succeeding generations were not so quick on the draw. Littlebury Walker Carter was killed in 1873 by his business partner in a drunken brawl over profits from their spinning jenny, and his son, the grandfather of our thirty-ninth president, was killed in 1903 in a fight over a desk.

But after the War Between the States this grim tendency was interrupted by an act of governmental mercy. The Carters of Sumter County had the good fortune of having their property well south of Sherman's March to the Sea, although in the last year of the war they lived in high anxiety over a possible Yankee raid. The disgraceful prison at Andersonville, which held thirty thousand prisoners in despicable conditions in a facility built for ten thousand, and saw twelve thousand of them die of disease in the last year of the war, was only a few miles away. Only the ineptness and insubordination of Sherman's cavalry leader, General George Stoneman, had prevented the liberation of Andersonville during the siege of Atlanta in August 1864. Stoneman neglected to tear up the railroad before he attacked Macon in August 1864, was tricked by an inferior force of Confederates—an event much ballyhooed in Jones County history—and surrendered after the Battle of Sunshine Church, before he could move south to Andersonville.

In any event, Littlebury Walker Carter would not have been home to defend his hearth, for Cutt's Flying Artillery was away in Virginia, even though all its original guns had been captured by the Yankees in the First Battle of Bull Run.

The two years of the first amnesty saw Johnson's transformation from vengeful Yahweh for Southern aristocrats to their Moses, to use Grant's phrase. As the crusade for

black rights was overtaken by the Radical Congress, Johnson shifted to the role of naysayer. In September 1867 he
declared a second conditional amnesty, which reduced the
number of unrelieved to about three hundred of the very
highest Confederate officials. By midsummer of 1868 amnesty had become the tool by which Johnson hoped to secure the Democratic nomination, and on July 4, the day the
Democratic Convention convened in New York, Johnson
declared his third and last *conditional* amnesty. In effect, it
relieved all but Jefferson Davis. Finally, on the traditional
day for charity, Christmas Day, three and a half years after
peace Johnson declared his Universal Amnesty "to all and
to every person who directly or indirectly participated in
the late insurrection of the offense of treason." It was to
this Universal Amnesty of 1868 that modern liberals like
Sen. Edward Kennedy paid occasional, hollow homage as
the model for post-Vietnam reconciliation.

◈ ◈ ◈

In the long-distance campaign of 1976, Jimmy Carter of
Georgia emerged from the pack of stock candidates to carry
the Democratic nomination. For me, a television image at
the Democratic National Convention remains the most
vivid memory of that moment. It was of an Oriental
woman, perhaps about twenty-two years of age, that a
cameraman had found amid the tumultuous throng. Carter
had finished his moving acceptance speech, with its refrain
"you can depend on it," a speech in which he talked of
honesty and human rights, of past shame and future promise, and vowed to speak "not with boasting and belliger-
ence, but with a quiet strength." The candidate stood high
above the crowd upon the steel-blue dias, acknowledging
the cheers with subdued waves and his toothy, full-
lipped smile, and a look that, after nineteen months of cam-
paigning, still suggested a touch of shyness. He was the
anti-Washington anticandidate. The young woman below

applauded feverishly, choked gutteral sounds escaping from her, and she wept with joy for painful, long minutes that the camera relentlessly captured, zooming in and zooming out, as if this were some anatomical experiment in human ducts and pores.

The candidate spoke to her alienation, and the tears were for an end of an era. In her political awareness she could have known only war and scandal. To her, this was a different leader, devoid of bombast, whose supreme control over himself suggested restraint for the nation, an Annapolis man who wanted a small military, an honest man whose profession of honesty was not suspect, an articulate man who knew how to fashion a sentence, a religious man who could give grist to the loose talk of her generation about morality, the father of a Vietnam veteran who could talk about his son's humiliation upon return, a genuine Southern liberal who spoke of Lincoln as the president who had done the most for human rights, and a farmer who a century later was close to realizing Andrew Johnson's dream for the yeoman class. Jimmy Carter was a politician who at last had standing to be a healer.

To be sure, as the governor of Georgia, Carter had lent himself to wartime demagoguery. In general, he was considered a consistent supporter of the war effort during his governorship. Through 1974 he had favored continued military aid to the dying regime in South Vietnam. In 1971, when Lieutenant Calley was convicted in a Georgia court martial and sentenced harshly for the crime at My Lai, Governer Carter called Calley a scapegoat and condemned those who used the case "to cheapen and shame the reputation of American fighting men." Calley was not representative of the American GI, the governor declared (any more, one might have listened to him say, than a Sherman straggler who stole the bride's silver cup from the plantation house was representative of the whole army), and Carter proclaimed an "American Fighting Man's Day."

By 1976, however, for whatever motive, Carter's thinking had undergone a profound, if somewhat belated, evolution. He had come to the conclusion that the war was racist and immoral, and he openly expressed regret at not having spoken out sooner and more vigorously against it. And he had been moved by the classic humiliation that his own son had experienced as he returned from the war zone.

"Jack went to the war feeling it was a foolish waste of time, much more deeply than I did. He also felt it would be grossly unfair for him not to go when other, poorer kids had to." Within his own family, therefore, there was the awareness of a moral choice, and a willingness to acknowledge it publicly.

In late August, Carter went before an American Legion Convention in Seattle. Straight out of the breach, the candidate put his audience at a wary attention. He did not seek a "blind or uncritical patriotism," he told the leathery group, but the government's policies must deserve support, especially, he might have added, if a young man is being asked to risk his life for them. Nevertheless, the youth had gone beyond disagreement with policy to a rejection of the nation itself, and in his presidency he would work to restore a meaningful patriotism. Then he came to the issue of amnesty. Within his campaign staff there had never been much policy discussion about this issue, no balancing of the political scales, no pitting of the Vietnam veteran like his son, Jack, against the Vietnam war resister, who might have been Jack, had Jack not felt deeply about the poor and the black who had taken the place of the rich and the educated on the battlefield. There had been no discussion because Carter knew instinctively what he was going to do. At least, the fake attempt to confer meaning upon the torment of the combat veteran by denying relief to the resister was jettisoned. The Vietnam veterans, he said, were the great unsung heroes, and "I could never equate what they have done with those who left this country to avoid the draft."

But the hatred and divisiveness of the war must end. He would declare a full, complete, and unconditional pardon for draft evaders in the first week of his presidency.

For once, Southern history had triumphed over Southern mythology. In the true history of his region, vague and intuitive as it may have been for Carter, lay the source of this decision. In the predicament of the Vietnam aftermath lay the predicament of his own great-grandfather, but split into two. For the Vietnam era, the tattered Confederate soldier, returning like Littlebury Walker Carter from the red fields of Virginia, had been bifurcated into the defeated warrior and the disloyal citizen, and the two halves had been set to war with one another. To one who *felt* the history of the South, that was intolerable. For the sensitive, modern Southern mind, unburdened by romance for marble men and stars upon the state capitol, there could be no cold calculation between justice and mercy, no middle ground with elements of both that satisfied neither. For Jimmy Carter, as for Shakespeare, there was an absolute. Mercy seasoned justice, blessing both the giver and the receiver, and it became "the throned monarch better than a crown." Antietam melded with Vietnam, Vancouver with Malvern Hill, and casualties of war must be cast in the broadest sense. "I am from the South," he would say later. "I know at the end of the War Between the States, there was a sense of forgiveness for those who had not been loyal to our country." Strom Thurmond would never had said such a thing.

While his instinct was genuinely Lincolnian, the mention of *forgiveness* was, for Carter, an unnecessary mistake, and he proceeded to fashion his position on a distortion both of language and law. He did it for the transparent political reason—to avoid the forbidden word, amnesty.

"I do not favor a blanket amnesty, but I intend to grant a blanket pardon," the candidate told the Legionnaires.

"To me, there is a difference. Amnesty means that what you did is right. A pardon means that what you did, right or wrong, is forgiven, so pardon yes, amnesty no."

The words, of course, meant nothing of the sort, and Carter knew it. The root of *amnesty* is found in the Greek word for *amnesia,* a morally neutral concept meaning precisely legal *forgetfulness.* Whether the beneficiary had been right or wrong or befuddled in his offense against the law was beside the point. If Carter's impulse for Southern history was good, his articulation of it was absurd. It was a question of logic. If his formulation was correct, his ancestor had been right! By offering a general amnesty to the Confederates at the Bennett Place, Sherman's surrender to Johnston was more dramatic than any supposed! Andrew Johnson's amnesties recognized the rectitude of the Confederate cause? This was news indeed.

Furthermore, a pardon requires an acceptance. Implicit in it is the recognition of wrongdoing, the admission of guilt. That was basic to Ford's pardon of Nixon. Without Nixon's acceptance, the pardon did not take effect. Could it be that Nixon's acceptance of the Ford pardon was not, after all, a tacit admission of guilt! It was a situation that cried out for a Bertrand Russell to unravel.

For those resisters abroad who wished to stand upon a pristine point of principle, the Carter position gave much to think about. They did not want to be *forgiven,* only to return home without humiliation. They had ceased to ask to be treated as moral heroes, any more than the Vietnam veteran asked to be considered a battlefield hero, but neither wanted to be spat upon when they came home. Nevertheless, *forgiveness* was being offered by one who had not shared in the political crime of Vietnam, as Gerald Ford was perceived to have done, nor was Carter's offer some scam to make a Nixon pardon more palatable. The gesture was charity, embodying no malice. Its flavor was pungent, but its meat was nourishing. The resisters could live on it again as Americans.

The corruption of the language by Nixonian politics had made Carter's peculiar formulation necessary, as he saw it, and later the candidate would acknowledge the corruption in his celebrated interview with *Playboy* magazine, published in September 1976.

"You've avoided the word amnesty, and chosen the word pardon, but there doesn't seem to be much difference. . . . [Have you avoided the word amnesty and chosen pardon] because amnesty is more emotionally charged and pardon a word more people will accept?" his interviewer asked.

"You know I can't deny that," Carter replied disarmingly. "But my reason for distinguishing between the two is that all of those poor, and often black, young men who went to Vietnam are more worthy of recognition than those who defected, and the word pardon includes those who simply avoided the war completely. But I just want to bring the defectors back to this country without punishment, and in doing so, I would like to have the support of the American people. I haven't been able to devise for private or public presentation a better way to do it."

Given his later confession of lust in his heart for women other than his wife, in this interview, few noticed this confession to deflowering the English language. Carter pressed on with his ponderous position and in a presidential debate with Gerald Ford he scored a clear point. Ford was presented with his early rhetoric about the need for a healing time, and then challenged about the ninety thousand men who had not availed themselves of his clemency. The president, whose affectation as the "healing president" had long since been exposed, fumbled on the disparity between the Nixon pardon and the clemency, for there was simply no way to reconcile the two. Resisters had had "ample time" to take advantage of the opportunity he had given them, the president said plaintively, and he intended no grander gesture. Then Carter clobbered him.

"The people are not concerned with pardon or amnesty, but with whether or not our criminal system is fair. We have got a sharp distinction drawn between white collar crime. The big shots who are rich, who are influential very seldom go to jail. Those who are poor and have no influence quite often are the ones who are punished." It was Carter at his best.

With Carter's election, the matter proceeded toward its denouement. The candidate had promised his pardon in the first week of his presidency. Then a last-minute hitch developed in a familiar quarter. On January 10, ten days before inauguration, Sen. James Allen of Alabama rose to introduce Senate Resolution No. 18. It did not question the pardoning power of the president under the Constitution, but it insisted upon the congressional responsibility to advise. In this case, Senate Resolution No. 18 advised the president-elect not to carry through with his intention for a full pardon. Out trotted the old arguments: the pardon was an affront to the dead, the maimed, and those who had honorably answered their nation's call; the pardon was encouragment to desertion and evasion in the country's next national emergency; the pardon was "unprecedented" in American history. (It seemed that no recitation of the facts would lay this last argument to rest.) Quickly, the old Southern guard fell into line: Stennis of Mississippi, Thurmond of South Carolina, Helms of North Carolina, Byrd and Scott of Virginia. It was *déjà vu,* the Confederacy-cum-anti-integration bloc putting on the old robes and spurs one last time on a point of patriotism. The Democratic leadership was caught off guard, and did what it could to delay. The American newspapers were filled with frothy declarations about Carter's election to the presidency as the offi-

249

cial end of the bitter Reconstruction of the South. It would not do for Southern senators to be at the throat of the Southern president at this historic moment that knit the nation back together after a hundred and twelve years.

But Allen's move was serious, and he began to build support in the Senate for his resolution. Within several days, given the general moral timidity of the Congress and the unwillingness of the individual senator to be on record in favor of a pardon, it was clear that, if voted upon, Allen's resolution would pass. Sen. Edward Brooke of Massachusetts, the only black senator in the chamber, rose with a counterresolution, and the symbolism became nearly too thick to endure. Brooke's resolution not only supported Carter's pardon for draft evaders but urged a wider, universal gesture, encompassing all the casualties, including deserters and those with less than honorable discharges. When Brooke said, "*We* were perhaps most magnanimous after our own Civil War," to whom was he referring? His slave ancestors? The white liberators like General Sherman? The American nation? His pronouns remained unspecified. To those who denied a relationship between the Civil War and Vietnam, Brooke did not dispute the distinctions. "But at the same time, I do not think that anyone can deny that the Vietnam War has torn at our delicate social fabric like no war since the Civil War. And I submit that just as amnesty repaired our social fabric then, it can repair our social fabric now. . . . For, in my opinion, these steps are not only the best way to heal the wounds of the Vietnam war, they are the only way to heal the wounds of the Vietnam war."

Parliamentary maneuvering dominated the few legislative sessions left before inauguration, with the Senate leadership forcing roll call votes each step of the way: a motion to table, a motion to proceed, a motion to table the motion to proceed, a motion for cloture, until it was late on January

18. The next full legislative day would be January 24. If he was to act, Jimmy Carter could not afford to wait.

Thus, not just within the first week of his presidency, but on its very first day, he proclaimed his unconditional pardon for draft evaders. Only this president, with his unembroidered view of Southern history, could have taken the action. And had he not taken action on January 21, it is questionable whether he would have risked the political damage to do so five days later. For whatever else, the Senate had put him on notice not to go beyond the draft evaders—what he had done was about as much of Lincoln as the country could stand—and Carter did not go beyond it.

In March 1977, in an interview, he took note of an opinion poll that had 45 percent believing his pardon was right, 45 percent believing it was wrong, and 10 percent with no opinion.

"So there is no way to suit people," the president concluded. It was as if the Georgian, at the beginning of his presidency, was echoing General Sherman at the beginning of the Civil War.

"Only in great events, we must choose, one way or the other."

Noble Cause? 12

AT THE OUTSET of the new administration, Jimmy Carter showed a certain sensitivity to the unique legacy of the Vietnam war. Two major studies were initiated to analyze the special problems of the Vietnam veteran, and they remained the standard reference for the postwar era. Through them, the government identified areas it could address, such as an extension and broadening of the GI bill, employment, psychological readjustment, and areas it could not, such as the 512,000 disabled veterans. (This sad remnant was the visible reminder that in the Vietnam war, soldiers had experienced a 300 percent higher loss of lower extremities than any other American war.)

Nor could the administration do much about drug and alcohol dependence among veterans or the high incidence of arrests (29,000 in state and federal prisons in 1978). And it could only take note of the attitudes its studies discovered, such as the opinion held by the majority of Americans that Vietnam warriors were "suckers" to have fought in the wrong place at the wrong time, and the opinion of 76 percent of the veterans themselves that "our political leaders in Washington deliberately misled the American people about the way the war was going." To the soldier on the ground, the war of attrition had always appeared to be more murder and genocide than a great enterprise in a worthy and well-understood national goal. Finally, there was the area the administration would not address comprehensively, not, at least, with a sense of history that Carter himself boasted he had: the half-million Vietnam deserters and 400,000 veterans discharged on less than "honorable" terms.

"As part of healing its wounds," the president said in a major message to Congress on October 10, 1978, "we have recognized our obligation to forget many harsh words and harsh acts, and to forgive those who resisted the war. Of even greater importance is our determination to recognize those who did serve and to show our appreciation for the sacrifice they made."

Soothing as those words were, it was not accurate to say that the "obligation" to forgive and forget was totally discharged. The "appreciation" for the veteran ended up to be largely symbolic. But the very notion that the country was obligated to discharge a special and unique responsibility to the casualties of *this* war was implicit. It was the responsibility of the nation which had forced its youth into a morally impossible situation.

After other wars, the reward for the veterans was generally the respect of their community and, soon enough, polit-

253

ical leadership. Occasionally, however, there had been studies about the "disloyalty" of wartime soldiers, like the focus on the collaboration of our prisoners with the enemy in the Korean War.

After the Civil War, there was concern for the high desertion rate on both sides, particularly the manner in which soldiers flocked to the hospital ships moored along the Atlantic coastline to care for the wounded. The men came in such numbers, often with no visible wounds, that their sheer bulk overwhelmed the care of the bloodied ones, and both the Union and the Confederacy had to abandon their sea-bound hospitals altogether. So the U.S. Army Surgeon General looked into the problem and in 1888 he released his report. The problem was the pathology of "nostalgia," he wrote, a temporary depression which marred the soldier's "efficiency." As he lay upon his bed, swayed by the gentle shifting of the tides and far from the battle, the soldier recalled "the happiness and comforts of home," and wished to experience them again. The soldier with a mild dose of nostalgia refused to return to the battlefield, but if he did not skedaddle, he could usually be bludgeoned back into the fray. The severe cases of nostalgia, however, brought with them a simple inability to fight, and the recognition of this mental paralysis was something of a psychological advance. It took the matter beyond the Revolutionary War concept that an unwillingness to fight was mere cowardice and could be laid to character deficiency. (Charles Colson would resurrect this quaint perception of desertion at the time when he himself was a prime conspirator in the Watergate cover-up. "They are not victims of war," he said of the Vietnam resisters, "but of their own character deficiencies.") The Surgeon General did not bother in 1888 to study the agonizing memory of combat or pangs of conscience that a soldier might feel for burning homes or corncribs wantonly or stealing a Southern fam-

ily's jewels. For the victory parades had sealed that unpleasant memory in the North: war is hell . . . to the victor
go the spoils, and all that. The Union victory had vindi-
cated the widened license of war as necessary. Nor did the
Surgeon General concern himself with the way bitterness
over defeat seethed for generations in the South, and the
way cracker tales of Yankee atrocity got embroidered.

But what of Vietnam's aftermath? What if free-fire
zones, "mad minutes," B-52 strikes at Christmas, violation
of neutral countries, poisoning of the landscape, refugees
by the millions, and My Lais had not *worked?* What if the
far superior force was defeated, and its soldiers demoralized? By 1970, American soldiers in significant numbers
had begun to turn on one another, making their own officers, rather than the Vietnamese Communists, their
enemy. In that year alone, there were more than 200 *reported* incidents of "fragging," or attempts to murder officers by their subordinates.

In the late 1970s, two medical conditions, one psychological, one physical, emerged as slowly developing postwar
diseases, as if they were a new strain of poisonous weed,
whose seeds were germinated by the immoral war. In 1980,
after several years of debate, and prompted by the Carter
studies, the American Psychiatric Association finally recognized in its official manual of mental disorders an afflic-
tion called "post-traumatic stress disorder." A rubric for
the most severe readjustment difficulties of the Vietnam
veteran, there was at least a medical context for dealing not
only with the pervasive drug and alcohol problems but with
such searing episodes as the black veteran in North Carolina who woke up one morning with his hands around the
neck of his twelve-year-old son before he realized the child
was not a Viet Cong, and who days later, after he was fired
from IBM, decked himself out in full battle dress, walked
into the sterile research facility of IBM near Durham, killed

one person and wounded four others, in a sweeping operation—all on the sixteenth anniversary of rolling a grenade into the hooch of a Vietnam village in a similar operation and dispatching a peasant family. In that case, despite a defense of insanity based upon post-traumatic stress disorder, and despite the acceptance by the jury that the defendant's mental state was induced entirely by Vietnam service, the veteran was convicted of second degree murder and sent away for life.

Since the early 1970s, proposals had floated around Congress to deal with the delayed stress problems of Vietnam veterans. Sometimes the bills would pass one house but not the other. Finally in 1979, a law passed Congress which funded 91 counseling centers around the country to advise GIs with readjustment problems. The Carter studies had shown that 40 percent of the returning veterans still had lingering readjustment problems. Staffed largely by Vietnam combat veterans, the centers became operational in 1980, gained the quick acceptance in the communities where they were organized, and were flooded with veterans. Administered by the Veterans' Administration and known as Operation Outreach, the program stands as the only significant piece of special post-Vietnam legislation passed by the Congress in the postwar era. But it, too, became endangered only a year after it came into being, when in the spring of 1981 Ronald Reagan impounded its funds as an austerity measure. The money was saved only when several congressmen, together with veterans' groups, sued the president to stop his impoundment.

The studies showed that the majority of Vietnam veterans had managed a "healthy" readjustment to civilian life, without defining whether "health" was to have buried the memory of Vietnam deep in some walled-off chamber, or to have come to terms openly with it, or simply to have avoided the social diseases of drugs, alcohol, violence, divorce, and listlessness. But for the 40 percent who still had lingering readjustment problems, no one wanted to define the exact nature of their difficulties, to ask, in effect, if it was the memory of murder rather than noble battlefield exploits that caused them to stir in the night or to be indolent and unfocused in the day. If one statistic is unimpeachable, it is that most Vietnam veterans do not want to talk about their experience over there.

Post-traumatic stress disorder stems from a memory of war atrocity. So, too, does the controversy over Agent Orange. Agent Orange, of course, is the chemical containing deadly dioxin, some one hundred twenty thousand tons of which were sprayed on the forests and rice fields of Vietnam over the first seven years of the war, and over one hundred eighty thousand acres of the Fishhook section of Cambodia a year before the United States invaded that neutral country. (In 1970, the U.S. government offered to pay the Cambodian government twelve million dollars for the inadvertence, which destroyed one-third of Cambodia's rubber trees—rubber being the chief source of foreign exchange for the country.) According to U.S. Army figures, about five hundred thousand acres of arable land in Vietnam had been sprayed on the Shermanesque pretext of denying crops to the enemy, but carrying Sherman one step farther, the crops sprayed by the Americans at harvest time were not so much destroyed to deny food to the enemy, but to deny food to those civilians who did not support our side. Scientists estimated that the poisoning of five hundred thousand acres of arable land amounts to the destruction of the food supply for an entire year of a population of six hundred thousand. Agent Orange was the most popular but by no means the only agent of crop and forest destruction used by the American military (Agent Blue was specifically tailored to withering rice), nor was the euphemism "defoliation" an accurate term to apply to this antiplant warfare.

The vast assault on the ecology and agriculture of Vietnam was unprecedented in the annals of war, notwithstanding the comments of Gen. William Westmoreland in his memoirs. Describing a flight he took in 1972 over Vietnam when he was army chief of staff, Westmoreland was pleased to note that he found it "still a verdant land, which left me to question the truth of some of the more pessimistic allegations of permanent damage."

As the memory of Vietnam receded, the Agent Orange controversy took on a narrow, selective quality in the American mind. The image of the veteran sweating profusely under only one armpit, or whose face was disfigured with Indochina acne, or who charged the army with responsibility for his deformed child raised the matter of compensation. Was the U.S. liable for damages to those it had carelessly exposed to chemical poisoning? Could the veterans' real or imagined disability be tied to Agent Orange, or was the link obscure enough to be plausibly denied? The real epidemic seemed to be the fear of delayed effects, and the veterans rushed to VA hospitals for answers. The VA in turn walked a delicate line, giving the appearance of concern for its clients by dispensing free exams, without admitting that Agent Orange could spawn any disease whatever. Nevertheless, it promised more studies and more tests, and it published a pamphlet called "Agent Orange Review," put out in a droll twist by the agency's Office of Consumer Affairs. In effect, the VA put the burden of proof on the GI. Said a VA pamphlet to the nervous veteran, "As a basis for compensating a veteran for permanent disabilities caused by military service, there must, in fact, be a disability or symptom, not just the fear of one." But since the agency had promised compensation to no one, this made an airy argument. And in 1983, the Veterans' Administration gleefully announced that its free tests of eighty-five thousand Vietnam veterans had turned up no correlation between their complaints and Agent Orange. Their ailments, said the VA doctors, were the common ailments of "males growing older."

But there was a question wider than whether GIs had been recklessly turned into experimental guinea pigs. The Agent Orange issue was the dross of what the world considered to be an American war crime. In this lay the core of passion that led twenty thousand Vietnam veterans to join in a class action suit against the U.S. government and the manufacturers of the poison for their exposure. The Hague Convention of 1907, to which the United States was a signatory, had specifically banned the use of poisons in warfare. The official U.S. Army Field manual on the law of warfare, current through the Vietnam era, clearly implies that the 1907 rule banned the killing of crops intended to feed civilian noncombatants, friendly or unfriendly. The Geneva Protocol of 1924 (which the U.S. did not ratify because it was not a member of the League of Nations, which drafted the Protocol) reaffirmed the ban on chemical and biological warfare. At the Nuremberg Tribunal, Hermann Goering was charged with removing food from occupied territory to feed the German army, and the resulting instances of starvation became instances of Goering's "crimes against humanity." The U.S. supported the prosecution of Japanese military officials for destroying crops in China during World War II. In 1949, the Geneva Convention specifically ruled out the poisoning of food for civilians. And in 1970, the UN General Assembly adopted a resolution, 80–3, which reaffirmed the Geneva Convention's ban on herbicides in war. The United States and Australia were joined in opposition only by Portugal, which itself had fifty thousand troops in Angola trying to suppress another popular uprising.

Once the license of war was so widened, could it ever be narrowed again? Once a rule was breached by one side, was not the rule itself undermined forever? The delayed effect of Agent Orange on American soldiers was only part of a wider medical issue. For Agent Orange, chemically, is a thalidomide-type agent, to which women are for obvious reasons more sensitive than men. What about the Vietnamese women whose village cisterns were contaminated? The Veterans' Administration had no authority to study them. Even in 1970 in Vietnam, the year that the U.S. Army discontinued its own use of Agent Orange because of its toxicity (and transferred authority for it to the South Vietnamese military), the alarm in South Vietnam over a startling increase in deformed children had become shrill.

With this new part of the American heritage, one comes with a sad sense of irony upon this passage in Gen. William Westmoreland's memoirs, as he reflected on the Battle of Khe Sanh. Speaking with pride about the brave defense of the redoubt, its contrast to the French disaster as Dien Bien Phu, its effectiveness as a plug against invasion from the north and its "lure" to North Vietnamese regulars (although the U.S. voluntarily abandoned the base after Westmoreland left Vietnam), the commander wrote:

"Surprisingly, the enemy failed to try the one thing he could have done that would have posed a real problem for the marines at Khe Sanh. He presumably could have poisoned the little stream outside the combat base from which the marines drew their water, but he never disturbed it."

◈ ◈ ◈

There remained one vast group of Vietnam casualties who continued to labor under political and social disabilities in the postwar epoch: the five hundred thousand military deserters (termed "absentees" in an undeclared war) and four hundred thousand veterans who had been cashiered out of the service with less than honorable discharges. The latter, known as "bad paper" cases, were men who were disproportionately black and Hispanic and for whom the disqualification from GI benefits and the inevitable job discrimination that a bad discharge brought would hurt the most. By calling his declaration on the first day of his presidency a pardon, by casting it in the grandiose language of healing, but by applying it only to the largely middle-class draft evaders, Jimmy Carter ensured that the Vietnam recriminations would continue. He had had a genuine Lincolnian impulse, and it stemmed from a true, demythologized sense of Southern history, but he could not bring himself to *be* Lincoln—to seize the grand, creative moment and make one job of it.

Carter's indifference towards the deserter issue stemmed from his own military experience. Like so many older American men, he projected his own youthful record upon the Vietnam predicament, not realizing that World War II and Korea had nothing whatever to do with Vietnam. Viscerally, he insisted that the various categories of Vietnam casualties continue to be weighed upon a moral scale.

On the first day of his presidency, the day of his pardon, one of his close and enthusiastic aides remarked to another, "[The President] can be a great healer. He's Southern. He's progressive. And he attracts great people." The other aide was David Berg, a Houston attorney who had drafted the Carter pardon. Berg had come to his task reluctantly, but in his research had undergone a metamorphosis. If Jimmy Carter was to fulfill his campaign promise and his destiny as a Southern healer, Berg felt he must craft a grand, sweeping truly historic declaration to cover all the casualties. But during the transition, as he pushed hard for a wider declaration, Berg had come to know the Carter "icy glare." Carter complained first about the economic costs, and then fell back, in irritation, on the comfortable cliché of his generation. "The point is, David, *I* would have fought in that war," the president said grandiosely.

After dutifully drafting the narrow pardon, Berg resigned

quietly on the day after Carter's inauguration and later took some pride in being the first to see through the Carter promise.

In March 1977, the president made an unenthusiastic and little noticed pass at this last, unpleasant legacy. He established in the Pentagon a Special Discharge Review Board, and it showed that he had learned nothing from the Ford clemency disaster, much less the Andrew Johnson amnesties that had relieved his forbears. By putting the new program in the Pentagon, it continued to ask the chicken to plead for mercy from the fox. It continued the cumbersome, expensive, and inherently unfair practice of reviewing cases one by one, and only those cases that were brought to its attention. There was no recognition of these men as war casualties, but rather the Review Board put the accent on their perceived mental or character deficiencies. The president did not participate at all in the inauguration of the new program, and so another opportunity was lost to lead and teach about the perils of undeclared, unsupported, and self-defeating warfare. To the contrary, the eligible could best change their status by pleading "personal problems" like drugs, alcohol, or emotional instability; accent the length of service they *did* perform; or make representations to the war department about genuine belief in peace. When the calls for review only dribbled in, the Carter people repeated the mistake of the Ford people by assuming that the problem was lack of information. So a media blitz of public service announcements was proposed, before it had to be dropped for political reasons.

True to form, the Southern patriots howled their protest against all of this, and waved the bloody shirt. The inevitable Sen. Strom Thurmond, the conscience of Southern mythology, whose profession of patriotism amounted to an incessant reaffirmation of loyalty to the Union that his grandfather had never sworn, led the charge. Together with

several dozen congressmen, Thurmond introduced legislation to insure that no veteran whose discharge was upgraded by the review board would receive a bus token in
GI benefits. Rep. David Treen of Louisiana got his amendment to a defense appropriation bill passed. It forbade the
Defense Department to use any public money to advertise
the discharge program. Rep. Robin Beard of Tennessee
offered an amendment to a housing bill to ensure that no
beneficiary of an upgraded discharge would get any housing
benefits. In the House debate over the Beard amendment,
Rep. Sonny Montgomery of Mississippi raised the specter
of deserters displacing "totally disabled veterans" in VA
hospitals. The Beard amendment passed two to one.

In the end, about eighteen thousand out of nine hundred
thousand eligible got their discharges upgraded in this new
solicitude. Only about twenty-five hundred of those ever
applied for new acquired GI benefits. And another year of
vengeance had been logged in for the American nation.

◊ ◊ ◊

It was to a convention of the Veterans of Foreign Wars
on August 18, 1980, during his campaign for the presidency,
that Ronald Reagan first declared Vietnam to be a noble
cause. "A small country newly free from colonial rule
sought our help in establishing self-rule and the means of
self-defense against a totalitarian neighbor bent on con-
quest," Reagan said, "We dishonor the memory of 50,000
young Americans who died in that cause when we give way
to feelings of guilt as if we were doing something shameful." Borrowing a page from Richard Nixon, who had declared that the "false" lessons of Vietnam had made
America "gun-shy" and created a "Vietnam Syndrome"
of guilt-ridden paralysis, Reagan proclaimed, "For too
long, we have lived with the Vietnam Syndrome. This is a
lesson for all of us in Vietnam. If we are forced to fight, we
must have the means and the determination to prevail, or

we will not have what it takes to secure peace. And while we are at it, let us tell those who fought in that war, that we will never again ask young men to fight and possibly die in a war our government is afraid to let them win."

The masterful seductiveness of that position rests upon several principles of postwar American politics. Historical memory is selective, and it is natural enough for a nation to desire to think well of its past. No nation wants to think of a past episode as a national shame, especially a nation that has had no concept of national shame. Similarly, all nations want their veterans to feel good about their sacrifices, and to try to forget instances that the international community considered war crime. The practice of waving the bloody shirt has proven itself as effective politics since it had its first full flowering after the American Civil War. Finally, to ascribe the Lost Cause of Vietnam to a "fear to win" deflects attention from the hard question of whether the United States ever had the ability to win.

In any event, the argument soothed and enticed many, including many Vietnam veterans, just as it horrified and aroused many others. Four months into his presidency, Reagan went to West Point to declare, "The era of self-doubt is over." In fact, the era of silence and evasion over Vietnam was coming to an end, and Reagan himself, partly by overblown statements such as this, would have the major part in ending it. For the subsequent dispatch of American soldiers again to civil wars and insurgencies in faraway places would prompt the American people to reconsider the real legacy of Vietnam. For ten years, the United States could afford to push Vietnam out of its mind, because with the presidencies of Gerald Ford and Jimmy Carter it did not have to think about it. With Reagan, the problem of the country getting sucked into "another Vietnam" had suddenly become a concrete possibility. The need to focus on Vietnam could no longer be deferred. The subtle reconstruction was beginning ten years late.

Contributing to the vacuum into which Reagan rushed had been the silence of the Vietnam architects. Apart from the self-justifications of Johnson, Nixon, and Kissinger, whose respective memoirs were fat with detail and slender with self-doubt, those who bore political responsibility for Vietnam, a Robert McNamara for example, were not heard from after the war was over. Without a confession of error, an acceptance of blame, an honest attempt to define their own mistakes by the architects of the disaster, the country was deprived of a negative model. Without the well-defined negative model, the sentiment about a noble cause rushed in.

For some, there were personal costs of silence, as Vietnam dogged them in their careers and private lives. For nearly a year after he left the job of secretary of state, Dean Rusk could not get a job, and finally was forced to accept a post at the University of Georgia Law School, a position of far less stature than a former secretary of state might normally expect. As late as 1981, McGeorge Bundy, the former national security adviser, suffered the indignity of having graduate students walk out on a speech and of having a pie thrown in his face. His brother William, the former assistant secretary of state of Far Eastern affairs, encountered fierce opposition within the distinguished Council of Foreign Affairs when he became editor of *Foreign Affairs* magazine. In the early 1980s, he trundled off to M.I.T. for a year and a half with the plan to write a book on Vietnam, but, by all accounts, the process tore him apart emotionally. William Bundy had struggled to argue that the early decisions on Vietnam had been correct, but he had been unable to convince himself. Eventually, he abandoned the project. While he was by no means an architect of the war (indeed, he was a vocal dissenter within the government), former Secretary of Interior Stewart Udall, who served for Kennedy and Johnson, had a son who deserted the army, and this nearly occasioned his resignation. (Rusk had considered resigning when his daughter married a black man.) Robert McNamara, more than any other man the personification of the early war, the very embodiment of the hope for a technological victory in a primitive land, maintained the stoniest silence of all. Among this rare breed of Vietnam veterans who remained friends in the aftermath, the war and the pains it had caused them personally was one subject they never discussed.

Of the architects, McNamara suffered the most personally. He had been eased out of office in 1968, after he developed doubts about the war policy and came to speak for bombing halts and negotiations. Characteristically, President Johnson offered him any job he wanted—the Johnson way to fire someone—and McNamara expressed interest in heading the World Bank. The very nature of building and developing primitive societies that the World Bank presidency entailed was in marked contrast to his prior employment, and McNamara's emotion (though he would probably deny this) was atonement. After presiding over the destruction of war for four years, McNamara went on to become an effective builder for eight years at the World Bank. His impulse was the Sherman impulse at the Bennett Place, and he engaged in good works for many years as a leader in the efforts for nuclear disarmament.

Through the decade after he left the Department of Defense, McNamara experienced an "almost fatal traumatic remorse" over his part in the war, according to one who knew him well. His distinguished service at the World Bank and, later, his passionate advocacy of nuclear disarmament, have been considered to be an effort at personal redemption. Within his own family, the tensions had been immense over his identification with the war. His daughter became an activist with the mobilization against the war in the late sixties. His son, Craig, disavowed his father, taking off to the Chile of Salvador Allende to work in the *barrios* of Santiago. Leaving just before the coup, the young McNamara subsequently went to Mexico and became associated with Ivan Illich, the renegade Catholic priest whose institute in Cuernevaca schooled students like Craig McNamara to expunge their Western political biases and paternalistic attitudes, before they went out to work for social reform.

Meanwhile, McNamara's wife, Margaret Craig McNamara, worked tirelessly and effectively at a series of charitable activities. She founded a nationwide reading program for poor children, called Reading is Fundamental, which put over two hundred thousand free books in forty-one thousand homes around the country. Four days before he left office, President Jimmy Carter awarded Mrs. McNamara the Medal of Freedom, thirteen years after President Johnson had awarded her husband the same decoration upon his departure as secretary of defense. Mrs. McNamara attended her ceremony in a wheelchair and died from cancer eighteen days later. Despite the cause of death, Robert McNamara knew that the anguish over Vietnam had worn greatly upon her in the preceding years, and as a widower, he believed that her trauma in silence had contributed to her early death at the age of sixty-five.

Once, at a mountain resort in Aspen at Christmastime, McNamara and his family were basking under the pristine winter sun at a large open-air restaurant when a woman approached their table and shrieked at the top of her lungs that his hands were dripping with blood. McNamara escaped as quickly as he could, feeling shock and humiliation rise in his spine. In 1970, on a ferry to his vacation home in Martha's Vineyard, a young man approached him in the darkness, grabbed him by the collar, and attempted to throw him overboard into Buzzard's Bay. The story was hushed over in the press, but on Martha's Vineyard it remains a matter of common discussion. To this attack was added the indignity of nudists who frequently came to perform lewd displays in front of McNamara's beachside retreat. Eventually this practice became so bad that McNamara sold the house. At another point, a police informant within a drug ring uncovered a plot to burn down McNamara's Vineyard house. This terrifying prospect was repeated several years later, when upon the capture of the Symbionese Liberation Army kidnappers of Patricia Hearst, the floor plan of McNamara's Aspen home was discovered. In the plans, the bedroom of each family member was clearly marked.

In the fifteen years after he left the government, McNamara set foot in the Pentagon only twice. For ten years he demurred at having his portrait painted for the corridors of the Defense Department, eschewing personal recognition and explaining that a painting would be self-congratulatory. Friends eventually prevailed upon him to relent. The absence of a portrait looked odd, they argued, when he was the only secretary of defense in American history not so honored in the Pentagon. When the portrait was unveiled, McNamara attended. His second time in the Pentagon was to deliver personally to Reagan's secretary of defense, Caspar Weinberger, an article which advocated that the United States forsake forever the concept of "first use" of nuclear weapons.

In the summer of 1978 McNamara exercised one last symbolic act, but it was little noticed. The Democratic Republic of Vietnam had requested a sixty-million-dollar loan from the World Bank to build an irrigation system southwest of Ho Chi Minh City, once known as Saigon. The money was for the construction of a dam on the Saigon River that would again revitalize a delta area of one hundred ten thousand people whose agricultural system had been devastated by bombs and Agent Orange. Fearful of the political repercussions in Congress, Jimmy Carter ordered the United States representative to the World Bank to oppose the loan. But the president of the World Bank supported it vigorously, and it was approved over American objection. A predictable storm in Congress greeted the World Bank loan. Routinely, through the seventies, riders were attached to funding bills for the World Bank, the IMF, and other international lending bodies which would prohibit American support for Vietnam. Introduced by a congressman from Florida, the riders passed handily. Now, McNamara was charged with "salving his conscience" by supporting the Vietnam project. Later, when a second Vietnam loan was disallowed by the World Bank, McNamara was charged in the international community with "knuckling under" to Congressional and administration pressure. On things Vietnam-related, Robert McNamara could not win, no matter what he did.

Through incivility, rumor, attack, and personal torment, McNamara said nothing and wrote nothing. He viewed his initiation of the Pentagon Papers in 1966 as his contribution to postwar understanding. He felt his job was to provide the raw material, not the appraisal. From the beginning, he embraced the principle that he would never be able to give an unbiased, scholarly account of his actions. To write or to speak about Vietnam would give the appearance of trying to absolve himself of blame. That, he would not have. He was content to have his postwar actions speak for themselves. Under no circumstances did he want to be drawn into the Vietnam debate. He did not communicate with the historians who wrote him. He took special note of how the effort to write had tormented friends like William Bundy. In his heart, he knew he had not anticipated that the Vietnam war would last nearly as long as it did. If one had not anticipated the length or the pain of a disastrous conflict, and had been a player in its initiation, writing about it could only take on the tone of tortured self-justification. Not to write was to be absolved of these emotions. Such was McNamara's maxim.

Still, there were costs. When CBS television produced its documentary on an alleged conspiracy by the U.S. military to underestimate Communist strength (the program that later brought a lawsuit by William Westmoreland), McNamara refused to participate. Later, he regretted his decision, privately. He would have liked to say that, while they had fought relentlessly, he considered Westmoreland to be an honorable man. He would have liked to say that in his seven years as secretary of defense no military commander had ever tried to deceive him. But he could not. He might have liked to raise an alarm over the dangers of the Central American situation and the pointlessness, as he saw it, of the marine action in Lebanon, but he knew that the result would be only vituperation over his standing to say *anything*. Most of all, he regretted that the Pentagon Papers had not been properly analyzed. Even they had been misinterpreted and trivialized. To McNamara, they did not show a pattern of deceit. The problem was deeper, more fundamental. Rather, to him they showed a common foundation of error that had been laid, block upon block, in three successive administrations.

In the McNamara family torment after the secretary's resignation the experience of the Sherman family after the Civil War echoes. In Sherman's son, Tom, for example, the general had hopes that military tradition would be carried on. He talked joyously with General Grant about their respective sons going to the same preparatory school and then on to West Point together. But instead, to the profound disappointment and even embitterment of his father, Tom Sherman became a Jesuit priest. In later life, Father Sherman's appearance took on a striking similarity to that of his father's during the war, and for several years, the priest became a popular lecturer. In 1906, the Sherman statue on Pennsylvania Avenue was unveiled, and Theodore Roosevelt invited Father Tom Sherman to the White House for the occasion. There, with dubious discretion, Roosevelt told Father Sherman that a group of West Point cadets were about to embark upon a retracing of his father's march and asked the priest if he would like to go along. Evidently thinking that his presence would be both an act of healing and even expiation, Father Sherman accepted immediately. In the South, the storm of protest was instantaneous. Said a Georgia congressman, "Father Sherman may have trouble tracing the line of the march now, but some time ago crumbling chimneys and smouldering houses would have made the path plain." And the *Atlanta Evening News* wrote, "Sentiment is a powerful spring in the heart of all self-respecting people, and to us in Georgia, it is savored of gratuitous remembrance to have the son of General Sherman make a miniature reproduction of one of the most ghastly and repulsive features of the Civil War for the declaration of personal pride." Father Tom Sherman gave up the trip shortly after it began, and not long after, he went quite insane.

In Ellen Sherman, the general's wife, atonement took the form of increasing Catholic fanaticism. General Sherman's atonement at Bennett Place was short-lived, and in marked contrast to Robert McNamara, Sherman cultivated the habit of gladly accepting speaking engagements, delivering a litany of amusing anecdotes about his war exploits. With her husband's exultation, Ellen Sherman receded deeper and deeper into her faith. It is Edmund Wilson in *Patriotic Gore* who suggests that the wife's zealotry and the son's priesthood were their atonement for the sins of the general. "She (Ellen) was perhaps trying to expiate a little the horrors and griefs of Georgia, and her son's dedication to the priesthood was perhaps the price paid by his father for the reckless elation of his March to the Sea."

❖   ❖   ❖

For the year that remained in the Johnson administration, Robert McNamara was succeeded at the Department of Defense by Clark Clifford. An elegant, Olympian figure, he had been for many years a confidant of Lyndon Johnson's. Clifford would become the only major policymaker from the Vietnam era to proclaim the war to be a national disaster, to accept his responsibility for the debacle, and to try to explain how it happened. In May 1978, Clifford went before the graduating class of Loyola College to deliver the commencement address, and before the students he laid out his thesis that Vietnam was the result of his generation misapplying their experience with Hitler to the experience with Ho Chi Minh. World War II was the profound experience of *his* young manhood, and it was a war that could have been prevented, he felt, had the Allies moved quickly to stop Hitler in France and Czechoslovakia. The lesson for his contemporaries was "the fearful price of appeasement and wishful thinking."

"Many men carried that lesson with them, as they began to assume positions of national leadership," Clifford told his young audience. "It shaped their most fateful decisions."

The period after World War II seemed to fortify the prewar lesson, as the Soviets became aggressively expansionist, trying to establish a buffer of client states along its borders so that it would never again experience an invasion from Europe. With Clifford as a close adviser, President Truman moved quickly to block Soviet expansion in Trieste, with the Berlin Airlift, with the Truman Doctrine, with support for the shaky regimes in Italy and France, with the Marshall Plan and NATO. With manifest pride, Clifford holds that these actions kept the peace for thirty-seven years.

Haunted by the memory of Hitler's aggression and Soviet expansionism, American leaders, including five presidents, rushed into Indochina upon the premise that a monolithic effort was under way to spread communism from abroad. Lamentably, it overlooked the fundamental aspect of a civil war in Vietnam.

"The war in Vietnam was a disaster," Clifford proclaimed to the students. "It is clear to me now, in retrospect, that we made a fundamental error in becoming involved."

As ordinary and even banal as these words sound, only Clifford among the former political leaders could bring himself to utter them. Less ordinary was his simple tribute to the antiwar movement and to youth.

"Time has shown that these young people who protested the war had a better understanding of it than those government officials who perpetuated the war. Youth does not imply ignorance of foreign affairs nor are age and high office any guarantors of wisdom."

No other remark in the postwar period had the power to move the Vietnam generation as much as this elegant contrition. What inner force had brought Clifford to utter it, when his peers were wallowing in self-justification or fobbing off blame onto others or were silent, is not entirely clear. In the summer of 1983, I asked him. His answer was long and orotund, but the strength for contrition seemed to find its source in his transformation in office. He had entered the government as a staunch hawk and supporter of the war effort, as a stalwart loyalist and friend Johnson could count on. He had come to replace the doubting McNamara. But once he moved from being counsel for the defense to a position of preëminent authority, Clifford underwent a rapid metamorphosis. The Joint Chiefs of Staff could give him no definitive answers about a strategy for victory, or whether our side was prevailing or when or how it would prevail. He heard only vague hopes about exhaust-

273

ing the enemy, grinding him down until he was losing troops faster than he could replace them. Was that happening now?, Clifford had asked. The Chiefs could not say. Would it happen soon? The Chiefs said it was hard to tell.

Within weeks after constant consultations with the generals, Clifford concluded that Vietnam was a "terrible loser." By his own account, he began to work tenaciously from within for a quick and total withdrawal. By the end of his brief tenure, he became "possessed" with the need to withdraw. On the day before he left office, Clifford told Henry Kissinger that President Nixon would become a national hero if the president announced a precipitous withdrawal from the quagmire, beginning in sixty days. Kissinger asked if Clifford would put that case to the new president. Clifford said he would leap at the chance, but the call never came.

Ten years after he left office it was the serenity that came from his actions to stop the war, once he concluded it could not be won, that enabled Clifford both to accept his personal responsibility and to reflect quietly on how the nation went wrong.

"People don't like to admit they made mistakes," he told me. "It is difficult to confess. There is not much inner drive to get out and speak about it. I accept part of the responsibility. I was mistaken. We never should have gotten into it. I accept the shame too. It wasn't the first time I was wrong, and I'd be willing to bet it won't be the last. But there is a value in saying this. It's healthy. It opens up those cobwebby rooms, and lets fresh air flow through."

In Clifford's speech at Loyola, he had repeated one widely accepted platitude that showed a selective memory. He attributed the "domino theory" to President Dwight Eisenhower, and referred to a meeting he had attended between Eisenhower and Kennedy on the day before Kennedy's inauguration. Then Eisenhower had warned the new president not to let Vietnam fall, lest the other nations in the area topple like dominos. If in memory Clifford felt the nation never should have been involved, that was the moment to stop.

But the question was not so much "letting" the nations fall one by one, but *if* the U.S. could prevent the fall of Vietnam, how to do it—whether to do it if it involved large numbers of American combat troops. Clifford had not mentioned Eisenhower's consistent posture on that point. For when the president had six years earlier been informed that Dien Bien Phu was in jeopardy and that France had requested an American expeditionary force to rescue the bastion, Eisenhower listened to the generals vigorously advocate the rescue. Quietly, he told his advisers that he would give his decision after a night of sleep. The following morning, the president strode into the Cabinet Room to face his expectant audience. It was a short meeting.

"Gentlemen," said the president, "I will not put one American soldier into that elephant grass. Good day."

◆　◆　◆

I address the subject of Clifford and McNamara to lance a personal bitterness. To ponder their tales of expiation since the war, is more, in a sense, an interview with myself than with them. Henry Kissinger, on the other hand, elicits only a dull sufferance in me. There is a static, airless quality about him, like an expensive old couch whose upholstery never frays. When in my presence, Kissinger remarked about his 1983 mission on Central America, "Emotionally, I can't take the responsibility for another guerrilla war," I found it almost an indecency, for what responsibility had he taken for his first guerrilla war in Vietnam?

To be sure, he had told the press at the opening of Gerald Ford's presidential library on September 16, 1981, that the Vietnam war was a "terrible tragedy into which the United

States never should have gotten involved" and called the war "a prolonged nightmare of over eight years," but there was no recognition of his part in half those years, no hint of remorse, much less contrition. *Tragedy* had become one of those words after Vietnam out of which was squeezed any sense of personal complicity and culpability.

He had come to my father's house to discuss his new Central American mission. When I entered the parlor, the two men were "throwing continents around," as my father put it. To that, I had nothing to contribute. Outside, Kissinger's bodyguard waited under the flickering Washington streetlights, like a 1940s Grade B movie, for the police had reason to believe that, ten years after the secretary left office, there were shadowy figures still angry enough at him to do him harm. Kissinger complained at the expense. The government provided the intelligence of continuing danger, but Kissinger had to pick up the tab for his protection.

As it turned out, they were not throwing continents around so much as catching up on the most recent excitements in the whirlwind life of the former secretary of state. He was just back from China. He was just back from a weekend on Martha's Vineyard as the guest of Katherine Graham, the *Washington Post* publisher, who had been anxious lest her liberal friends be rude to Kissinger.

"Are liberals still hostile to you?" my father asked sweetly.

"Oh, no," Kissinger replied. "It is the radicals on the right who exhibit an almost tangible hate when I walk into the room."

"Do you get much hate mail?"

"The liberals and the young don't write me any more. I suppose they think I'm hopeless."

The conversation ranged from China to Mexico—Mexico, he said, was the only country of Central America that he knew passably well, because he vacationed there—Acapulco, I think—and so it put him ill at ease that the president had asked his advice about the part of the world that he understood least. He spoke of the third volume of his memoirs that he had reluctantly put aside for his new mission, a book, he promised, which was to be "more philosophical." He mentioned his active lecture career. "I assume when I lecture that my audience wants a fairly complicated discourse on foreign policy," he said. I listened quietly with only half my attention. The intrigues of Henry Kissinger were flat for me. I remembered his Christmas bombings too vividly. Unlike Clifford or McNamara, Kissinger's life after the war possessed no Shakespearean elements.

When my father left the room, Kissinger inquired perfunctorily about this book. I replied with a vague description of its focus upon the post-Vietnam period, avoiding the emotive words. He bristled instinctively, nevertheless, smelling a familiar fight.

"Your generation was given to simplifications," he said sharply. "It was not a simple moral question. It was more complicated."

Complexity and simple morality not being contradictions to me, I did not respond. He had raised morality, not I, but there seemed no future in pursuing it. Rather, I spoke about the Vietnam generation now, and wondered if it would be passed over entirely for leadership. The idea engaged him. He wanted to think about that, he said. He wanted to think about that for a long time.

"Your generation doesn't have very much to be proud about," he said finally.

"Yes," I nodded, a guest in my father's house, and soon after, he left.

Cump and Westy 13

$$\mathbf{G}\text{ENERAL}$$ William Tecumseh Sherman is the most controversial military figure of the most divisive war of nineteenth-century American history. Gen. William Childs Westmoreland is the most controversial military figure of the most divisive war of twentieth-century American history. The first was a winner, the second a loser. The first was a Northerner, the second a Southerner. In the aftermath of their respective conflicts, each fought, as strenuously as they had ever fought on the battlefield, to have history view them favorably. Each wrote towering and revealing memoirs, in which they accented their accomplishments, minimized and even ignored the harshest charges

against their questionable tactics, and scoffed at their detractors. Even after what they had both done as generals to widen the license of acceptable war, in the aftermath, they both insisted on old-fashioned standards of honor and civility. Both saw not just their reputations, but their personal and professional honor, come under fierce attack, but for the loser, the problem of defense would be greater than the winner. In their argument to history, Cump and Westy share a curious bond.

Westmoreland is not generally regarded as a Southern figure, for his distinguished military service was wide and international. Yet in his surprisingly interesting and important memoirs, *A Soldier Reports,* which were published in 1976, his Southern roots and Civil War sentimentalities were evident. His touchstone was the myth of Robert E. Lee. With his own silver hair, there was a hint of personal identification with Lee, for to many Westmoreland was a marble man even in his own time (but not in the noble sense). His great-uncle had joined the Confederate army at age fifteen, had fought in Gettysburg, and inevitably as these stories go, was with Lee at Appomattox. When his father died, Westmoreland saw to it that a Lee quotation was carved into the tombstone: "Duty is the sublimest word in the English language." Although he had received a military education at The Citadel, Westmoreland's father was a textile plant manager.

In writing about Vietnam, Civil War analogies came readily to General Westmoreland. He reviled "newspapermen-crusaders" whose oversimplified stories made the Tet offensive out to be "the worst calamity since Bull Run." Saigon, he wrote, could not be surrounded with "leakproof defensive lines in the manner of the Confederate trenches before Richmond." He took a special pride in having been superintendent of cadets at West Point in 1962 when William Faulkner visited only months before his death and

279

pronounced the cadets to be more human than rigid. And he seemed to be stung when Arthur Schlesinger, Jr., chose a Civil War metaphor to debunk Westmoreland's costly defense of Khe Sanh, and to declare Westmoreland's war of attrition a tragic and spectacular failure.

"President Johnson likes to compare himself with Lincoln—'sad but steady,' " Schlesinger wrote in a 1968 letter to the *Washington Post*, of which Westmoreland took particular note in his *Memoirs*. "But he lacks one prime Lincolnian quality: that is, the courage to fire generals when they have shown they do not know how to win wars. Lincoln ran through a long string of generals before he got Grant and Sherman. It is not likely that he would have suffered Westmoreland three months."

Laid upon his Southern sensibility was his bent for the old virtues. From his days as a cadet in West Point, he remembered the words of Gen. John Pershing and made them his personal motto: "Maintain your own morals at a high level, and you will find them reflected in your own men." He saw a sharp distinction between the society and the army, for no matter how permissive the society might become, the army could only survive with tradition and discipline. The guardians of the old virtues were the officers. For the officer corps, appearances were crucial.

"A commander clearly is the bellwether of his command and must display confidence and resolution," he wrote. "Even the slightest pessimism on his part can quickly pervade the ranks. In Vietnam, I was confident, so no playacting was involved in showing this, yet at the same time, I was sharply conscious of the need to demonstrate this."

Thus, it was natural that Westmoreland would withdraw to the mannered elegance of Charleston to write his memoirs. For Charleston remained an enclave. It heartily embraced the sentiment that the American fighting man in Vietnam was a great hero in a noble cause, that the Tet offensive had been a great military defeat for the enemy, that the war would have been won had it not been for the political constraints and the interference of self-appointed "field marshals" and "air marshals" in Washington. Surprising it was, then, that with such a precious thesis and with such a stiff personality, Westmoreland should have produced such an engrossing memoir. That he put his sensitivities and bitterness on display, as Sherman had in his memoirs, enriched the tale. Indeed, the praise that critic Edmund Wilson lavished upon the Sherman *Memoirs* might apply equally to Westmoreland's, the first two-thirds of it anyway. Wrote Wilson:

[Sherman's] vigorous account of his military operations is varied in just the right proportion and to just the right degree of vivacity with anecdotes and personal experiences. We live through his campaigns . . . in the company of Sherman himself. He tells us what he thought and what he felt and he never strikes any attitudes or pretends to feel anything which he does not feel. His frankness and self-dependence, his rectitude in whatever he undertakes, and his contempt for petty schemes and ambitions, together with a disregard for many conventional scruples, make Sherman, in spite of his harshness, a figure we not only respect, but can not help liking.

It is a minor consequence of military defeat, that not only do losers write less gracefully about the battlefield than do winners, but their books are generally less well received by the critics. The critic's pencil is sharpened for the loser's account of failure, ready to catch the commander in some hollow self-justification or in some deliberate lapse of memory. Victory, of course, makes a better climax to a book than does defeat. In *A Soldier Reports,* the compelling quality of the narrative goes sharply downhill after Westmoreland's chapter on the Tet offensive; the book becomes increasingly defensive, as the contradictions in his argument, as in the war itself, become glaring.

Nevertheless, Westmoreland shared some of Sherman's

literary attributes. He demonstrated a similar breadth of reading, replete with references to Napoleon and Sun Tzu, and with the occasional literary analogy, even when the analogy was not always complimentary to the American effort. He could be amusing about the *opéra bouffe* of Saigon, where South Vietnamese generals vied for power and competed in corruption, where a commander could consult his astrologist before committing his troops to battle, where another commander rushed back to his troops during Tet "with more apparent concern for his villa than for the battle as a whole." It was as if the situation was straight out of Lewis Carroll's Red Queen: "It took all the running we could do to stay in place," and it was a frustrating exercise of trying "to pick up beads of mercury."

"That an American public sending its sons to die in Vietnam saw these [corrupt] events as distressing is understandable," he wrote fretfully. "Yet some form of political turmoil in a developing country is apparently inevitable. Democracy and cohesion are not to be achieved without growing pains, as the history of the United States itself painfully illustrates."

After his retirement, Westmoreland had done what distinguished military commanders were supposed to do in the wake of a great war. South Carolina received him with perfumed respect. In 1967, the South Carolina legislature passed a resolution urging Westmoreland to run for president. As it turned out, the state liked the illusion better than the reality. In 1975, Westmoreland did run for the Republican nomination for governor, but he proved to be stiff on the stump, and he was defeated. Nevertheless, he became a popular attraction on the lecture circuit, arguing consistently to sympathetic audiences that the war had been won on the battlefield and lost at home.

Westmoreland's memoirs were a dignified performance, and will survive when much of the literature spawned by the war will have been forgotten. But he should have left it there for historians to wrangle over the soundness of his generalship. Instead, in 1982, Westmoreland forsook his dignified seclusion in Charleston to throw himself into a new and distinctly modern defense of his reputation. The Columbia Broadcasting System had aired a documentary entitled *The Uncounted Enemy: The Vietnam Deception,* which charged the existence of a conspiracy "at the highest level of military intelligence" to underestimate Communist enemy strength in 1967. Because of this "conspiracy," the program argued, the American people had been deceived into thinking that the enemy was being ground down, and this explained why the Tet offensive came as such a devastating psychological blow. After Tet, Westmoreland's contention that his "war of attrition" was being won, was shattered forever. For the enemy that was supposedly being ground down came out of the woodwork everywhere (like roaches, Westy would say later).

Allegedly, this underestimation was politically motivated, for the high command in Vietnam was under intense pressure to show progress in the war, and too high a figure of enemy strength might undercut that case. By carefully layered interviews with officers confessing to their own actions in the shrinkage, the program laid out its premise: that an artificial ceiling of three hundred thousand enemy soldiers had been clamped on military intelligence estimates. Without ever specifically charging General Westmoreland as the chief culprit, the impression of his complicity was unmistakable. In the climax of the show, the selective findings of the program were sprung, without warning, on an ill-prepared Westmoreland. On camera, the commanding general was nervous and grew increasingly hostile. His awkward performance made him look the part of the villain.

Westmoreland sued for the harm to his historical reputa-

283

tion and put the damage at one hundred twenty million dollars. The program was a "personal humiliation," he complained, which held him up to "scorn, contempt, and ridicule." It occasioned him to suffer "great emotional anguish." This was an extraordinary claim for so controversial a historical figure, who had presided over the least popular American war in history and who had been demonized by many of his own soldiers. For years, many had roundly condemned his stewardship in Vietnam as inept. Others had made him the scapegoat for the endless demands for more troops and for the high casualty figures. Still others saw his concept of an American war of attrition with Asians as fundamentally mistaken in concept and execution. To many of his own soldiers, he had stood erect upon his pedestal, eyes aloft in his starched fatigues like a marble man, looking magnificent, while beneath him a futile exercise was played out.

The television program was fatally flawed in its premise, in its selective arrangement of interviews, and in its unethical treatment of General Westmoreland. But its bead was aimed at real and important issues. For during late 1967, there had been an impasse between the military and the intelligence community about how to categorize the enemy, and the military, including General Westmoreland by his own admission, was afraid of what the American public would do, if they were told they were fighting an enemy nearly as large as the Allied Forces, and an enemy that was still growing. That was not the thrust of the CBS documentary, however, for that unsensational cast made the dispute simply a reasonable disagreement between reasonable professionals.

But was the court of law General Westmoreland's only recourse for his valid complaints? Was the legal forum really the best place to defend an historical reputation that was hardly gold-plated to begin with? Was not the general opening himself up to a process of ridicule that might tarnish his reputation far more than one flawed television program ever could?

This remarkable lawsuit could take place only in an age that followed a losing effort, where blame and responsibility were batted away like badminton birds. Nevertheless, Westmoreland's motive seems clear. His concern was that, prodded by the documentary, history would come to see him not only as a military failure, but as a liar and cheat and scoundrel as well. For this old-fashioned man who still clung to nineteenth-century concepts of honor, at least in his personal life, this was intolerable. It was one thing to berate his way of waging war. It was quite another to call him a dishonest man. His first reaction had been to ask for a formal apology from CBS, and later, he would claim that had it been tendered, he would have let the matter drop. It was as if the president of CBS might meet him at dawn while a flourish of trumpets heralded a great resolution and a sharpened gilded pencil was surrendered ceremoniously.

The first deposition of General Westmoreland took place in the summer of 1983. One of the many revealing interchanges in Westmoreland's interrogation by the opposing lawyer went to the unique nature of the war over which he presided. It was a "non-linear type" war, much like the Civil War, he said. "This is the first war in history where we had to try to reduce our progress or lack of progress to mathematical terms, and I disliked it. Everyone disliked it. It was a frustrating experience, and there was no way you could be precise." Somehow, it seemed appropriate that a war in which mathematics rather than real estate or battlefield victories mattered, computer fraud should be a natural outgrowth.

In this first deposition, Westmoreland's prickly sensitivities surfaced. But the long legal process was pointing toward the astonishing spectacle of the commanding general of the American Lost Cause finding himself in the dock, and forced into a broad and hostile review of his generalship. His defense hoped that this hostility would engender sympathy for the plaintiff. It was as if Westmoreland had convened a Nuremberg trial of himself, for he invited his detractors to consider command responsibility as the nub of his complaint. If his subordinates had faked order of battle statistics, he had been ultimately responsible. "I was responsible for all elements of my command," he professed in the deposition. "There is only one ultimately responsible person." If a conspiracy existed within his command, he was in effect being charged with negligence under the Articles of War. Charges could be preferred against him. Indeed, in his deposition, he cited the fact that after the CBS program, a veterans group in Pittsburgh had written him that charges *should* be preferred against him, and that this letter from his former troops was part of his "great emotional anguish." The concept of command responsibility was central to the military system, and he accepted it implicitly. But he denied that a computer conspiracy existed, or at least, he had never been told about it, much less inspired it.

This embrace of command responsibility was a noble sentiment, but it was also a posture, for soon enough in his deposition, the principle was turned around upon him, as he was asked why he was not responsible for the general disintegration of ethical standards for American combat and for the witting deception of the American people. Suddenly, his homage to a commander's responsibility became less categorical, as the subject shifted abruptly from faked figures to the covert bombing of Cambodia and eventually to the Phoenix program.

The defense meant to turn the suit into a grand examination of Westmoreland's overall stewardship of the war, and it also meant to show that deception was rife at the highest level. Before it was over, faking computer figures would seem like a mere peccadillo. With the secret Cambodian bombing, the opposing attorney probed for any moral qualm that the supreme commander might have about deceiving the American public. What about the false coordinates for the air strikes that were deliberately released to the press in a phony "cover plan"? Did Westmoreland remember that this cover plan had become the basis for one of the impeachment articles against Richard Nixon?

"Is there anything illegal about obeying an instruction from civilian authority to mislead the public about some military situation?" asked the attorney.

"I said . . . that an officer is not required to carry out an illegal order," Westmoreland replied.

"Yes, and what I am asking you is, do you think it would be an illegal order to order you to lie to the public?"

"I don't know whether that is illegal or not. I think that it would be immoral . . . unless it were associated with a legitimate, albeit covert, operation associated with the pursuance of a fight against a deadly enemy."

"So it *would* be immoral, whether or not illegal, to mislead the public about a military situation unless that were necessary for the military operation against a deadly enemy to succeed?"

"Yes . . . it somewhat concerns me."

"General Westmoreland . . . we had a situation with the Cambodian bombing where there was a military objective that you very strongly believed was desirable, bombing of the enemy bases in Cambodia. And we have a political decision to keep the fact secret from the public. . . ."

"We understood why the administration had to keep it covert," Westmoreland protested. "We had the impression that there had been a government-to-government contact between the United States and the Cambodian authorities, and that they had assented to the bombing with the understanding that it would not be made public. [But] I can't document it."

"That impression was sufficient to overcome any moral or ethical qualms that you might have had about the military participating in a false cover plan?"

"I object to your words 'false cover plan.' "

"Well, let's say a cover plan that contained false information."

"Let's just say a cover plan."

"The cover plan *did* contain false coordinates. There isn't any doubt about that."

"How the spokesman of the United States government put that out, I do not know," the general replied.

"What I'm trying to get at is: what standards or criteria do you use in deciding when it is permissible under your code of ethics and morality and official responsibility to mislead the public? How do you determine when it is permissible and when it is not permissible?"

"When we are committed to war, the purpose of the exercise is to destroy the enemy. In all wars there have been covert operations. This happens to be a fact of life, and this has imposed no moral dilemma on me."

"So long as you are in time of war and the operation is covert, you would see no moral dilemma in misleading the press and the public about that operation, is that your testimony?"

"I think that I've addressed this whole subject in a practical frame."

"Do you have an answer to my question?"

"I have nothing else to say about it."

"Can you think of any situation in which you believe you would have a moral dilemma about misleading the public in time of war, when you were instructed to do so by civilian authorities, as in the Cambodian bombings?"

"This is a matter that has never occurred to me. The whole process has posed no moral dilemma to me."

"What about your oath of office?"

"The oath of office says that you will obey the commander in chief and those appointed under him."

"Is there anything in your oath of office that would or should constrain you from misleading the press or public about military situations for political reasons?"

"I'm sure there are, but I have not delineated this."

Even the supreme military commander had finally been drawn into the dizzying vortex of moral inquiry which had so separated the Vietnam war from all other American wars. Old-fashioned though he was, Westmoreland was clearly uncomfortable with this line of questioning, and at times he was beginning to look ridiculous. The luster upon the marble man was fading. But he could not walk out in dignified outrage. He could not protest disrespect, for this deposition was his show. He was claiming to be a victim. A television program had done one hundred twenty million dollars' worth of damage to his historical reputation, he complained, and so now, he had to endure whatever attack or ridicule was hurled at this claim. What was so mixed a reputation as this worth anyway? Westmoreland was finding that this could be a demeaning and belittling process. And the interrogation was to get worse. Suddenly the Phoenix program arose.

Phoenix was the program aimed at identifying and "excising" the political operatives for the enemy in South Vietnam. Established in 1967 under Westmoreland's command, it was directed at first by Robert W. Komer, a CIA operative whom Westmoreland affectionately knew as Blowtorch. By the time Westmoreland left Vietnam in 1968, by his own testimony, the Phoenix program had "come of age." Yet it was a program to which the general devoted only two lines of mention in his memoirs. Under the withering cross-examination of his lawsuit, it would be treated much more thoroughly. Suddenly, Westmoreland did not seem so ready to speak of command responsibility.

289

"Did the Phoenix Program have as one of its aspects an attempt to assassinate political cadre leaders?" the CBS attorney asked abruptly.

The question seemed to blaze out of the underbrush, and Westmoreland was clearly surprised. Such ambushes were not what he expected, for *he* was supposed to be the one on the attack. His lawyer rushed in with legalisms to give the general a moment to collect his wits.

"It was my understanding that, uh, the purpose was to capture these people, which would serve two purposes," Westmoreland said finally. "One, it would eliminate the group, the political activists, and, two, for from him, intelligence could be acquired."

"Are you testifying now, sir, that the Phoenix Program did *not* have as one of its aspects an attempt to assassinate political cadre leadership?"

"To the best of my knowledge, it did not."

"So it is your best testimony, under oath, that there was not an attempt to assassinate political cadre."

"I have no official knowledge that this was an announced purpose."

"When you say that you have no *official* knowledge that this was an *announced* purpose, was it, in fact, what happened, sir?"

"I don't know."

"You don't know?"

"I don't know."

"You don't know whether political cadres were killed as part of the Phoenix Program?"

"I know there have been allegations, but I don't know."

"When did you first become aware of what you refer to as allegations?"

"It was after I was back in Washington as Chief of Staff of the Army that such allegations were made."

"Did you ever try to find out whether those allegations were true?"

"Me personally?"

"Yes."

"No."

"Did you ever ask anybody else to try to find out whether the allegations were true?"

"I do not know to what extent this matter was looked into, but I'm sure it was."

"Did you try to have the matter looked into?"

"I did not, to my knowledge, initiate any such investigation."

"Did you ever ask anybody whether these allegations were true?"

"Not that I recall."

"Were you interested as to whether these allegations were true or not?"

"This was the program initiated by the United States Government, and I did not initiate such action, no . . . I would say at that time that I had many other responsibilities, and I did not take upon myself to delve into this one."

"Was it a matter of concern to you personally, individually, that charges were being made that this program, initiated and expanded under your command, involved the assassination of political cadres?"

"The purpose of the program was a worthy one, in view of the type of war being fought. If there were any indiscretions involved, that was a matter that, that, uh, I was not happy with . . . if such was the case. That is, here again, these indiscretions are allegations."

"When you refer to these indiscretions, do you mean people being assassinated?"

"Well, I used the word indiscretion in the context of your allegation."

"What I am now asking you is whether during the time you were Army Chief of Staff, when you were aware that these allegations were being made, did you do anything at all to try to find out whether . . . ."

"No."

". . . the Phoenix program had in fact been used to assassinate political cadre."

"I did not."

"Would it surprise you, sir, if I were to tell you that the CIA director [William] Colby testified in Congress that more than 10,000 political cadre were killed under the Phoenix program?" (In fact, Colby later altered the figure to 20,000 and claimed it was one of the most effective programs of the entire war.)

"I'm unaware of that."

"No one has ever suggested that to you?"

"I don't recall ever hearing that before."

"And that would surprise you, would it, sir?"

"Well, that magnitude does, yes."

"Would that be more than an indiscretion?"

"Well, I . . . I don't know."

"The killing of more than 10,000 political cadre as part of an organized program of the American government would be something more than an indiscretion in your mind?"

"Well, it would be a serious indiscretion."

The form of Watergate had been superimposed upon the Vietnam war, and the deposition was, stylistically, turning into the interrogation of a criminal. If one imagines Westmoreland as a Japanese general after World War II and also the ten thousand victims of the Phoenix program as non-uniformed *Allied* collaborators, the principle becomes clearer.

These raw interchanges of the early deposition had an authenticity that the later well-rehearsed testimony of the witness could never have, for they were symptomatic of how difficult it was to get the architects of the war to accept their share of the blame. Westmoreland had put himself into a dilemma from which there was no easy escape. He wished to assert his responsibility for his order-of-battle statistics because he was reasonably sure he could disprove legally that there had been any dark conspiracy. But he would deny responsibility for the far more serious "indiscretions" under his command, like Phoenix or the pattern of atrocity in his search-and-destroy operations, or the deception of the public over the Cambodian bombing. To win his case, he had to appear as the noble, honest, vulnerable hero, fighting for his honor against malicious and petty detractors. A jury had to feel as if the hero before them had dismounted some equestrian statue on Pennsylvania Avenue and honored them with his presence. As a living memorial, one had to believe that his great emotional anguish was sincere, not merely a posture bred of bitterness toward the press in general. But there would be no equestrian statue of Westmoreland in Washington, or even on the Battery in Charleston for that matter, much as he might have been a sculptor's delight. The broad charge of negligence against him was serious, although if he had been a winning general like Sherman, they would have been forgotten, or should I say, forgiven. By his training, he had groomed himself never to look vulnerable. It was not easy to imagine the general in great emotional distress, not one hundred twenty million dollars of it anyway. Surely, the supreme military figure of the Vietnam era was not so easily thrown into a tizzy by a television program or over a critical column in a newspaper or an uncomplimentary cartoon.

His lawyer had realized quickly that the general's performance would not wash, and the coaching began during a break in the deposition. When the witness returned from a recess, he asked permission to return to the subject of the Phoenix program. For "indiscretion" had not really expressed his "true feelings" about assassination, he now asserted. Such activity was "wrong, definitely wrong." The allegations shocked him. He now recalled reports about assassination, and discussions he had had about them with his successor, Creighton Abrams. But even with this quick adjustment of his position, he could not bring himself to be precise or to express a measure of responsibility.

"I do recall that it became a public issue. I vaguely recall that there were some hearings on it, but the details of which I do not know."

"Do you, as you sit here now, know whether the reports were true reports?"

"I did not know. I had no direct information to confirm the allegation, but I know that there was a great concern in Washington at the time, and I believed the truth would eventually come out. The program was being looked into, because it was a U.S. government program. The Phoenix program was a U.S. government program."

"Were you also personally concerned, sir?"

"I was. I was."

"And why was that?"

"Because these were civilians and the program was designed to neutralize this organization, but to do it in the way I've described. . . ."

"But my question to you, sir, is, why were you personally concerned by these reports that under the Phoenix program Vietcong political cadres were being killed."

"Because they, under the, the, uh, laws of war, uh, they were not uniformed military personnel and therefore, it was improper for this type of activity to be, to take place on the battlefield."

"And did it concern you that this kind of activity had begun while you were the American military commander in Vietnam?

"I don't know whether it started during that time frame or not."

"Did you ever try to find out?"

". . .It was not my responsibility to [find out], but I did consider it wrong."

Westmoreland's aloofness from moral ambiguity could not withstand this inquisition. For years he had stood above the contradictions of the Vietnam effort, the crisp, clean commander for whom the grandstands were painted and the dust racked for his visits to the field. To many American soldiers he had come to symbolize a plastic, artificial notion: all was well . . . with determination they would prevail . . . they were brave and skilled heroes in a worthy cause . . . only the civilian meddlers had kept them from their appointment with victory. He cultivated his image. He cared mightily about appearances. He was the last of the Civil War generals. Indeed, he was an amalgam of Lee and Sherman, of both sides of modern Southern mythology. He wanted to be seen by history as the confident commander and bold, imaginative strategist who never lost a battle to the enemy; as a man of impeccable personal ethics, the perfect husband and father; the epitome of Southern culture and manners; the soul of honesty and duty; the highest evolution of the soldier-gentleman. And in defeat, he would be the poignant but dignified monument to the Lost Cause. That was the Lee of his dreams.

But he had commanded a force vastly superior to his adversary. His firepower and manpower were overwhelming, and both had proved ineffective, even as in frustration they ran amok. Under him, the license of war had been irreversibly widened. Of specific atrocities, he knew of few when they happened, and remembered even fewer in retrospect. That was the Sherman side, for which he would not and perhaps could not come to grips.

By initiating his lawsuit, Westmoreland was in danger of appearing to be exceptionally naive or sadly dense about how historical reputations are defended, much less enhanced. For in confronting the innuendo and the hostility that a controversial figure of a controversial war must inevitably bear, Westy might have taken counsel from Cump. Before Sherman went to Congress to defend his overly generous actions at Bennett Place, he had written, "As to my honor, I know I can defend it." By showing a contempt for his political inquisitors, by aligning himself with the great Lincoln; by displaying an awesome, terrifying dignity, and by placing himself above the sniping of small, petty men, he had somehow defended that honor. Conversely, by his own hand, Westmoreland allowed himself to be diminished to the level of a young and ambitious television producer and a notorious muckraker, trading accusations over alleged computer fraud in war and whimpering about being a victim of a "hatchet job." His alignment was with those who would limit the press's freedom. Westmoreland had given in to the seductions of a litigious age, but his complaint was for the bar of history not the bar of law. The case in 1983 became only the latest vehicle for continuing the bitterness and confusion and disappointment of Vietnam.

In 1982 the Vietnam Veterans Memorial was dedicated in Washington. General Westmoreland, bareheaded, his hair whiter, uniformed in a London Fog raincoat, led the parade. One last time, there would be dissension and even outrage in the ranks. It was the appearance of it that grated upon many. It was as if Westmoreland had been there, down and dirty with the veterans in their readjustment, just as he had been there with them as soldiers, down and dirty, in the elephant grass and in the swamp of their moral ambiguity. In fact, he had been neither place.

With Westmoreland's subsequent lawsuit, he was caught in a crossfire between the questions: was he an honorable soldier and was his soldiering honorable? Westmoreland wanted to believe that the questions could be sharply separated. He wished to limit the debate narrowly to the former, but it was in the latter that his reputation would get its real test.

Mister Reynolds $\boxed{14}$

IT WAS a perfect afternoon for a parade in late September 1983, when I left the Vietnam Memorial in Washington and crossed the Potomac River to Arlington Cemetery. The air was crisp and clear, the sun warm, and the white marble of the amphitheater seared across the blue of the sky. The ceremony was to be held in a copse of dogwoods, and the trees were turning in their usual early fall splendor. Already, the Air Force Band was there, lounging about, these flaccid, middle-aged musicians poured into their ill-fitting paramilitary costumes. The honor guard was rehearsing its slow approach to the reviewing stand. All services were represented. As usual, the marine was the best turned out.

I was early, and Mrs. Reynolds had not arrived, so I wandered away, after watching the soldier roll back and forth upon his carpet before the Tomb of the Unknown Soldier a few times. I wandered along Sherman Drive, which curled around the gentle slopes of the cemetery and arrived at McPherson Drive. Moving down Sherman's chain of command at Atlanta, Sherman to McPherson, was a strange way to get to a Confederate monument. There, before me stood the best Southern statue I had seen in this journey down memory lane. Sculpted by Moses Ezekiel, a Virginian who fought at the Battle of New Market in 1863, the statue is the crowning contribution of the United Daughters of the Confederacy to the nation's memory, to the Lost Cause, to the universal sacrifice of men and women in war. Towering high upon a circular pedestal, there upon the back ridge of the vast cemetery, thirty-two feet in height, crowned with olive leaves, the heroic figure of a woman looks out upon the Southern graves. Facing south, she holds out a laurel wreath, not in petulance or in anger or in celebration of a righteous cause, as does the feminine figure in the Columbia statue, but in simple sadness and in love and in resignation. In her right hand, she steadies herself with a plowstock and pruning hooks: swords to plowshares, spears to pruning hooks, ashes to ashes, dust to dust. Below her, a circular bronze frieze depicts scenes of poignant farewell and tragic return. Strapping men comfort their hoop-skirted ladies upon their departure. Broken, ragged men are comforted upon their return. No scenes of heroic battles. Time had poured white rivulets over the green of the bronze half-relief, as if to heighten ambiguity. Time would not corrode black marble, I thought. Below the scenes upon the base are carved the inscriptions. On one side is the Latin: *Victrix Causa Diis*

Placuit. Sed Victu Catoni . . . The Victorious Cause was pleasing to the Gods, but the Lost Cause was pleasing to Cato . . . Cato, the symbol of honesty, dedication, and un-flinching courage whose death by suicide was a noble trag-edy. On the other side is the English:

Not for fame or reward. Not for place or rank. Not lured by ambition or goaded by necessity, but in simple obedience to duty, as they understood it, these men suffered all, sacrificed all, dared all and died.

Most of that might apply to Mister Reynolds, I thought— all but the part about simple obedience to duty.

Back at the amphitheater, Mrs. Reynolds broke away from a clutch of ladies, and at first I hardly recognized her. The day before, when we had talked in a hotel coffee shop and she had given me the Bronze Star citation, she wore a black sweat shirt, sequined with a sparkling American eagle clutching a billowing Star-Spangled Banner, above the words *Vietnam Heroes*. Now, she was resplendent in white, her immaculate wool suit and white military cap held perfectly in place with bobby pins in hair about the shade of my mother's. Upon her lapel she wore a lovely piece of jewelry, a demure gold star set upon a blue background.

She gave me a program, and we chatted idly about her week in Washington. She was a woman of few words, and they came out in the smoky flat tones of the Arkansas rice country. She had been cautious with me, for she confessed that my calls and letter had come as a shock. I, in turn, was equally cautious, because I was not sure how much she wanted to know. It was clear she did not know much. She had settled into her organization's work, embracing the no-tion of her son's heroism, and finding fulfillment in volun-teering at veterans' hospitals. I approved. It was the kind of response I might have liked from my mother. She seemed to harbor no bitterness, although she encountered the bitterness of the Vietnam women all the time. In Spokane once, she invited forty-three mothers who shared her plight to a tea, and none accepted.

"Why be bitter?" she said simply. "It doesn't do you any good."

Was it not best left there?, I asked myself.

She had never asked the Pentagon for any information. That had been a good thing, for the degree of success—or lack of it—at extracting details from them was well known. When I asked, the Pentagon told me first that all the records of the First Battalion, 525th Military Intelligence Group, had been lost. So I asked Mrs. Reynolds directly if she wished me to share with her what I found out. "I guess I want to know everything you know," she replied, but it was said without enthusiasm. My interest was threatening a fragile construct.

The band began to play, and she left to take her post for the formal procession in the rear of the metal folding chairs that had been set up on the lawn. The VFW and the American Legion had sent a few old fogies to act as color guard. The VFW had even sent two ladies from their women's auxiliary. They wore white capes and hats that made me think of Hemingway in Italy. One man, looking uncomfortable and out of place, dressed in a blue uniform and red-and-blue cap (the sort of uniform the Italian Army might come up with), looked young enough to be of Vietnam vintage. The music was jaunty. Anchors Aweigh, ma boy. The Halls of Montezuma (Central American invasions lept into my mind) and the Shores of Tripoli (Barbary Coast, not Lebanon, I had to remember)—nice music on a sparkling September afternoon, nevertheless.

The processions, the pledges, the prayers concluded, a brigadier general took the podium. He had the look of a general: broad-shouldered and rich-voiced, a chest of ribbons, and he peered earnestly at the small audience of the bereaved through sunglasses beneath his brocaded brim. Words of comfort and of patriotism rolled out of him like caissons, but it was not long before he went to the old well, invoking Lincoln, to confer dignity to his message and cast this occasion within the American tradition.

"I feel how weak and fruitless must be any words of mine which should attempt to beguile you from the grief of a loss so overwhelming," the general quoted Lincoln's letter to the mother of five dead soldiers, "but I can not refrain from tendering to you the consolation that may be found in the thanks of the Republic that they died to save. I pray that our Almighty Father may assuage the anguish of your bereavement and leave you only the cherished memory of the loved and lost and the solemn pride that must be yours to have laid so costly a sacrifice upon the altar of freedom."

No doubt, these were comforting words for Mrs. Reynolds, as comforting for her as they were comfortable for the general. He proceeded to the redeemed virtues of pre-Vietnam America. The threat of the Soviet Union was upon the horizon. They outnumbered us in fighter planes four to one, in tanks, and in nuclear missiles. We must be strong to deter war. He bid for anger by invoking the Russian attack on the Korean airliner and the invasion of Afghanistan, proof of the inhumanity of our enemy. But this was a Vietnam audience. There were not many mothers left from any other war. And so, the general spoke not of jungles, but of the Hanoi Hilton. The liberation of American prisoners was a sure heartstring. He had been to Hanoi to escort the first prisoners out. He described their jubilation at their first glimpse of his blue uniform. He talked of the false starts that the Communist captors had cruelly foisted upon our men. He noted the unknown prisoner's scratching upon the wall of the Hanoi Hilton about how "liberty was not a gratuitous right but a priceless privilege that must be earned over and over." I wondered what the point was and how he would gracefully end, for his audience was not chiefly concerned with survivors.

"Thank you for being players in Americanism," he concluded abruptly, ignoring the need for any transition.

I had never thought of Ron Reynolds that way before, nor had I thought of his sacrifice in Lincolnian terms upon the altar of freedom nor what the thanks of the Republic to him could possibly be. Ron Reynolds was the name he had assumed in Vietnam. He had bunked beneath me in 1966 when we trained in intelligence together at Fort Holabird, Maryland. He was a stocky, jovial native of Spokane, American to his spine: football player, class president in high school, political science major at Washington State College, a genuine, uncritical friend, for whom military service after college was the natural next step. It was not that he was for or against the war. I do not ever recall a political conversation with him. Our conversation was of earthier matters. Like me, he had volunteered for the Intelligence Corps to exercise some control over his fate in that dangerous time of the escalation. After our Maryland training, the master plan seemed to be working. I went off to the Praesidio of Monterey to learn Japanese. He went to a headquarters unit in Pearl Harbor, Hawaii. A year later, I too got orders to the same unit in Hawaii and looked forward to a reunion.

The Hawaii headquarters was commanded by one Col. Jack Weigand, a tall, bald, and from a sergeant's point of view, crude commander who had no college education and less couth and who was a nut about sports. Ron's misfortune lay in being a natural athlete. It was an old story. He wanted to take a course at the University of Hawaii in his spare time, and the colonel wanted him to play softball. The tension grew greater and greater. There was a blowup over some trivial matter, and Ron did the one thing that Colonel Weigand could not squash: he volunteered for

Vietnam. There was nothing noble about his act, but neither was it seedy or bloodthirsty. When I arrived in Hawaii
to renew a friendship, Ron Reynolds had been gone three
months.

His first post was DaNang. Within a few months he was
Ron Reynolds, Mister Reynolds to most, dressed in civilian
clothes, outfitted in a small one-story house with a latticed
portico, on a dirt street barely broad enough for a jeep. At
first his team, comprising him and one other, was known
officially as the Field Sociological Study Group. Supposedly, it was "studying" the culture and sociology of Hué.
But it is hard for me to imagine Mister Reynolds as a
scholar, and evidently it was hard for others as well. Once
the phone rang, and to Ron's horror there was a bona fide
sociologist on the other end, asking whether he might drop
over for a professional chat. The real scholar had come
upon the team designation in an army phone book. After
that it was decided that for appearance's sake a few books
on Vietnam sociology should be strewn around the house,
but they were hard to come by. The cover, if any one cared,
gave Mister Reynolds an explanation for wandering around
at night in odd places. His official mission was worthy
enough. The targets were the villages around Khe Sanh and
in the A Shau Valley to the west of the city, through which
a North Vietnamese invasion was certain to come. The
objective was to develop sources to report on enemy movements and provide the twenty thousand marines at Phu Bai
eight miles away with productive combat missions.

So Mister Reynolds had really made it to the field. His
letters home were up-beat, but cryptic. He liked Vietnam,
and his work was interesting, but since it was "highly sensitive" and "classified," he could provide no details. His
fellow team member was a Japanese-American named
O'Hara, and O'Hara's Oriental appearance gave the team
an added capability for secret work. There was a lot of

303

rushing about to safe houses for clandestine meetings, and a fair amount of paper work up and down the line. After months on the job, Mister Reynolds had a number of leads, but they were in the "preliminary stage of development." For all the motion, he could claim only one genuine recruitment, a source who had been approved for money disbursements all the way up to the top. That prize was a former security guard for the team house, who promised to report on a few villages on the outskirts of Hué, but certainly not about anything as far away as Khe Sanh or the A Shau Valley. As the days got closer to the Tet celebration, this prize collection agent let it be known that he was going away for the holidays.

All was not work in the glamorous field. Mister Reynolds took his meals at the small MACV compound two blocks away, so as to avoid coming into contact with Vietnamese. He frequented the Cercle Sportif as well, an old French tennis and social club on the Perfume River, directly across the water from the Citadel, now run by upper-class Vietnamese. He was well liked by his colleagues in the secret society. At first, he gave the impression of being brusque and by-the-book, but with time, his fellow case handlers realized this to be a front not of serious soldiering but of jest. He was a stickler for procedure because he found the procedures quietly amusing. With time, his expansiveness and high jinks crept through. One afternoon he broke out a set of fatigues and a battle helmet from the closet and had his picture taken in the garden behind the team house, holding the team's "grease-gun," a .45-caliber Thompson submachine gun. The dense vegetation of the backyard represented "the jungles of Vietnam" and his awkward crouch was supposed to simulate the posture of a battle-hardened veteran on patrol. It was all for home consumption in Spokane, of course. But his wry smile, even through his splendid new pistolero's mustache, hardly conveyed the standard hollow look. In his nine months in Vietnam, Mister Reynolds spent one afternoon on a firing range, refamiliarizing himself with how to hold a rifle, and getting the chance to fire off a few bursts of a real machine gun.

Occasionally, there were social functions. It was virtually impossible to develop a natural relationship with a respectable girl in Hué, for to be seen with an American, even riding about in a jeep, was to be put on a V.C. hit list. Assignations, therefore, were limited to employing a downtown girl for an evening party at a thousand piasters, or about eight dollars, and this became a monthly indulgence. The girls who sought such employment were apparently "forgiven" by the V.C., at least they were in early 1968. It was at one such dalliance that two colonels from Saigon walked into the Hué team house unannounced for an impromptu inspection and found four operatives with their pants down. This transgression of being caught out of uniform occasioned the closing of the house and the transfer of Mister Reynolds to Phu Bai for a few months. Such bad form at an official inspection was merely the pretext for the transfer. The real reason was that the team house had been declared unsafe, and it was closed down for security reasons. Two months later, columns of North Vietnamese sappers would use the narrow dirt road in front of the house as an escape route, after they blew up the American billet two blocks away.

For three months, Mister Reynolds returned to fatigues and combat boots, occupying a twenty-by-forty-foot wood-floor tent amid the marines and working on a new concept. A scholar's cover had fooled no one, and so it was decided that he would return to Hué with a new job. He became "refugee employment liaison" to a U.S. Navy employment office known as the Industrial Relations Division (I.R.D.). The office was housed in a plain two-story compound across from the U.S.I.S. library, which had been burned out in the Buddhist uprisings three years before. The division was charged with hiring Vietnamese to work at American bases in I Corps and screened two hundred to three hundred natives each day. Mister Reynolds was to identify refugees from the areas west of Hué, and to inveigle the right individuals to return to their villages. He would have the power to create jobs. A sheer hate of the Communists was considered the soundest of "handles," of far more importance as a motivation for such hazardous duty than Yankee greenbacks.

On January 27, 1968, Mister Reynolds returned to the old imperial capital as the new team leader. Five days before, according to his memoirs, Gen. William Westmoreland had cabled the Joint Chiefs in Washington that he expected a multibattalion attack on Hué during the Tet celebrations. This cable would become Westmoreland's argument to history that he at least had not been surprised by the Tet offensive. Why had the word not gone down the line? Wouldn't a man in the most sensitive area of intelligence, especially one who was so exposed in the field, be the first to know? For "some reason," Westmoreland wrote, the MACV compound in Hué never got the commander's intelligence. The most major attack of the entire war was pointed directly at a pitiful contingent of 250 men.

If Vietnam had had for Mister Reynolds the quality of play before, it now became a dream. On his first night back, Vietnamese and Americans threw a joint party in advance celebration of Tet at the I.R.D. house. Three hundred guests were invited, including Americans from the MACV compound two blocks away, the five counterintelligence agents from the compound next door, and the Phoenix and pacification employees several houses down Ly Thuong Kiet Street. Philip Manhard, the pacification chief, was there (the same Manhard who became the highest civilian POW in North Vietnam, who stayed in solitary confinement for five years, and who, emaciated and barely able to walk upon his release under the Paris Peace Accords, urged that American reconstruction aid for North Vietnam be tendered).

On January 30, the first day of the lunar new year, General Westmoreland in Saigon was receiving strong intelligence indications of movement toward Hué, the subtle prodrome of a heart seizure. But procedure, as he later wrote, demanded that the information first go to the Third Marine Division headquarters at Phu Bai, eight miles away, before the boys in Hué should be told. During the day, the First South Vietnamese Division, which was responsible for defending the city, had its own warnings. Concluding that an attack was imminent, it put its soldiers on full alert, and ordered the entire division staff to stay in headquarters through the night. But no more than General Westmoreland were the Vietnamese commanders in a sharing mood. The Vietnamese did not advise their own advisers. Taken all together, one might conclude that the American side knew the Tet offensive was coming. But history does not help Ron Reynolds, who, blithe spirit that he was, went about a normal day, oblivious to the great historical event that was taking shape all around him.

Toward evening, Reynolds and another team member, known as Siddens, drove to the walled MACV compound to have dinner. At 7:00 P.M., just after dark, they drove to another intelligence compound some blocks away to meet with their commanding officer, a Maj. Robert B. Annenberg, who had taken the rather Burmese-days name of Major Goodsite. In the course of the day, Goodsite had met with various intelligence sources, including G-2 at the marine base in Phu Bai. Now, to his two operatives, Reynolds and Siddens, Goodsite gave a languid order. Get out of Hué in twelve hours. A major attack was coming. But no special urgency attended the order, no shortening of the breath, no sense that a night of long knives was beginning at that very moment, or that they should rush back to the house and make sure that the grease gun was greased or their two carbines oiled. Had they been ordered to evacuate, they could have thrown the few sensitive files they had at the IRD house into the space of a shoulder bag and been on the road to Phu Bai in minutes. Instead, the drinks came out, and the conversation was relaxed and jovial. After an hour, the three agents decided to repair to the Cercle Sportif. In the darkness, the men sat on the patio amid the exotic, scarlet flora and drank in the halcyon scene: sampans moving lazily on the river, lantern-light twinkling through their bamboo-lattice hatches. It was a dank, still night, temperature in the upper seventies. Across the river, around the Citadel and the Palace of Peace, firecrackers from the merrymaking still crackled. Major Goodsite remarked how strange it was that the enemy had never blown the bridge between old and modern Hué. It was something to think about.

In due course, the conversation turned to the coming attack. Goodsite held that Khe Sanh was a mere diversion, and that Hué would be the enemy's chief objective. After all, it was the imperial capital of Old Vietnam, and it had special significance to the Vietnamese. To take it would have profound importance to the country. Perhaps, Goodsite observed, the enemy would sweep out of the A Shau Valley, take Hué, and then offer to negotiate. It was an interesting, and even troubling, theory. If the attack came, it would be quickly over—the three agreed entirely about that. The enemy would make a brief and violent demonstration, mortar and rocket the MACV compound perhaps, probe a few other installations, maybe try to satchel-charge a billet or two, before they quickly withdrew. The discussion was abstract. It never translated into a sense of personal jeopardy.

At 10:00 P.M. Reynolds and Siddens drove Major Good-site back to the MACV compound for the night. Graciously, they left the jeep with the major, for he would need it in the morning, and struck out into the night on foot, down a block to the circle appointed by an unfunctioning fountain down Ly Thuong Kiet Street, past the small police station whose courtyard was bordered by concertina wire, past the dark hulk of the U.S.I.S. library, to their house. At the house, they dawdled over a few more drinks and talked until midnight about their plans for future operations, before they turned in.

At 2:30 A.M. Reynolds was startled awake by the sound of mortar passing over his house and landing near the MACV compound. The fluttering sound of larger shells followed shortly, 140-mm rockets. Three rockets fell short of MACV, landing only a block away, a close shave. The bombardment lasted for an hour. To the west of the city, a firefight had broken out. The sound of machine-gun fire was punctuated by several enormous satchel-charge blasts in the vicinity of MACV. Flares lit up the western sky. Mister Reynolds donned his flak jacket and helmet and huddled on the ground floor. If sappers attacked, he was confident that he and the three other Americans in the house would have ample warning. Their Vietnamese guard stood watch outside. By prior arrangement, the guard's duty was simply to warn them of an enemy, and then to hightail it.

At 4:30 A.M. there was a lull. Reynolds did not expect any more action. With Siddens, he talked about going to MACV for an early breakfast to inspect the damage. To date, the demonstration had gone about as they had imagined.

At 6:30 A.M. their tranquility was shattered by the high-pitched scream of their guard, "V.C.! V.C.!" Reynolds raced to the second-floor window. From there he could see only the ruin of the U.S.I.S. library across the street, so he scrambled to the third floor, which commanded a better view up and down Ly Thuong Kiet Street. From the west, already abreast of the CIA's pacification compound, two files of North Vietnamese regulars approached. In each file there were about twenty men, dressed in jungle slouch hats and khaki uniforms, and carrying AK-47s, B-40 rockets, square grenades, and several machine guns. They marched two meters apart. As Reynolds and Siddens peeked out from the third floor in the glow of dawn, the NVA soldiers walked by the house with scarcely more than a glance. Shortly afterward, a fierce battle broke out in front of the police station up the street, barely out of sight, and lasted for about fifteen minutes. And then there was silence in that quarter.

As the sun rose, the Americans realized they were in very serious trouble. Why had the enemy not left the city, as he always had before? They could hope that he was simply late in leaving and that he would confine himself to the major installations, rather than bothering with a building that was ostensibly an employment office. But all around them, North Vietnamese flags started to appear on buildings: on the Interpreters/Translators Team (I.T.T.) and the ARVN Seventh Cavalry headquarters across the rice paddy behind their compound, and on the Citadel across the river.

At 10:00 A.M. the North Vietnamese attacked the ARVN general's house that lay directly behind the I.R.D. compound across a rice paddy. Backed by mortars and a machine gun that had been set up in the Catholic church four hundred yards to the west, the NVA formed a handsome line and moved smartly across the open field on the general's compound. A mortar round hit a bunker, and Reynolds could see his Oriental allies scurrying around frantically. Another mortar hit a civilian house next to the general's and tore away half its roof.

They watched the battle rage in their own backyard, terrified and transfixed. Siddens, ever the proper intelligence officer, brought up his camera with its telephoto lenses and took roll after roll of pictures. They would never be developed, at least not by him. At noon, Reynolds signaled the five counterintelligence officers in the building next door to join his force of four Americans. Of the two buildings, I.R.D. was deemed more defensible. Reinforcements put the band at nine Americans and added to their arsenal seven carbines, fifteen hundred rounds of ammunition, twelve grenades, a few tear-gas grenades, and five pistols.

At 1:00 P.M. hope sparked. In the distance, from the southwest along Route 1, the road to Phu Bai, came the sound of tanks and trucks. As the first tank rounded into view, only five hundred meters across the rice field, the interest went to the color of the star, for Reynolds knew the North Vietnamese had tanks in the vicinity of Hué. The color was white. Two more tanks followed, and then twelve trucks. Reynolds could see the U.S. Marines walking behind the vehicles, but they were still the size of toy soldiers. As the relief force came abreast of the house across the field, the lead tank fired on the house that had been the office of the Interpreter/Translator Team, which now flew a North Vietnamese flag. Almost immediately, the lead tank was hit by a B-40 rocket, blowing off the left tread, but leaving it partially maneuverable. The marines continued to inch forward. Artillery fire from Phu Bai and naval guns from ships off the coast began to rain down on the I.T.T. house and an ARVN compound next to it, also now in NVA hands, as the Americans tried to push forward to relieve, as Westmoreland put it in his memoirs, "the heroic little band that was still holding out in the MACV advisory compound."

From his grandstand upon the I.R.D. roof, Mister Reynolds had gradually taken charge. He had been instrumental in uniting the two groups. He directed the positions to be taken at various windows and crevices and gave orders concerning rationing ammunition and food. Sheer instinct, rather than training, ruled him, like a child in back alley play. He seemed to operate without fear. If anything, he was cavalier, as if he saw this as a regrettable piece of bad luck, like finding himself singled out for a mugging on a big-city street for no apparent reason. More than once, Siddens warned him to keep down, as Reynolds moved about the darkened room. The U.S.I.S. ruin across the street was no more than 150 feet away.

A half hour later, as he parceled out ammunition to the others, a sniper bullet smashed through the window and shattered his liver, passing through his side and out his belly. He bled little. His pulse and breathing subsided rapidly. It was said later that he did not suffer long. He had not fired a shot.

In March 1968, in his real name, Mister Reynolds was posthumously awarded the Bronze Star with the *V* device for heroism and valorous actions on January 30 and 31, 1968. His citation read:

A large North Vietnamese Army force overran much of the city late on January 30, and Sgt. Reynolds' small unit was cut off from friendly military support. The enemy forces quickly discovered his team's position and attacked it. Time after time, Sgt. Reynolds exposed himself to ravaging enemy fire to repel the determined insurgent assaults with fierce rifle and grenade fire. The team's furious fighting diverted enemy troops from their primary targets and was far above the resistance to be expected from such limited manpower and weaponry. He was hit by sniper fire and instantly killed while fearlessly leading his men in a staunch defense of their position. Sgt. Reynolds' personal bravery and devotion to duty, at the cost of his life, were in keeping with the highest traditions of military service and reflect great credit upon himself, his unit, and the United States Army.

The little pageant at Arlington over, I went to tell Mrs. Reynolds goodbye. I would not be going with her to the wreath-laying at the Tomb of the Unknown Soldier nor on to another ceremony with minor dignitaries at the Vietnam Memorial, for I preferred to visit my only friend on that stark granite wall alone, without others making their dishonest uses of him. Reflection in empty rooms upon war and common courage, about friends and regret and acceptance, is better undertaken alone, in silence. We lingered in a long handshake.

"Well, what did you think?" she asked expectantly about the little commemoration.

I muttered something.

"Don't shrug," she said maternally in a gentle scold, and we shared a smile of understanding.

Index

315

Peck, Gregory, 134
Peers, W. R., 59
Peers Commission, 59–60, 185
Pentagon Papers, 211, 212, 269, 270
Perot, H. Ross, 211
Pershing, John, 280
Phoenix program, 12, 286, 289–292
Phu Bai, 305
Pickett's Mill, 51
Piegan Indians, massacre of, 90
Planters, response to Civil War, 38–39
Playboy magazine, 248
Pocotaligo, S.C., baronies of, 103–105
Post-traumatic stress disorder, 185, 255–257
Presidential Clemency Board, 234
Prisoners of war
  homecoming, 205–208
  reports of collaboration with enemy, 210–212
Proportionality, as standard of warfare, 15–16
Public Theater, New York, 124
Punishment policy, and atrocities, 104–105

Racism, of Sherman, 88–91
Radical Reconstruction, 236–237
Ralston, John, 95–96
Rampaging, of Sherman's troops, 110–113
Reading is Fundamental, 267
Reagan, Ronald, 9, 68, 145, 179, 263–264
  impounds Operation Outreach funds, 256
Rebel Women (Babe), 124
Reconciliation Work Program, 230
Reenactments of Civil War battles, 35–37
Reprisal, sustained, 16
Resaca, 24, 25, 26
Restoration, Civil War vs. Vietnam War, 144–145
Reynolds, Mrs., 298, 299–300, 301, 313
Reynolds, Ron (Mister), in Vietnam, 198, 302–312
Ridenhour, Ron, 184

The Rise and Fall of the Confederate Government (Davis), 53
Roberts, Hildegarde, 112
Robertsville, S.C., burned, 110
Roosevelt, Theodore, 32, 271
Roswell, Ga., burned, 30, 31, 32
Ruckstuhl, F. W., 117
Ruling class, response to Civil War, 38–39
Rusk, Dean, 265–266
Ryan, Leo, 145

Saint Joseph's Episcopal Church, Savannah, 95
Sandersville, myth of razing, 71
Savannah, taken by Sherman, 88, 95
Savannah Gold Club, 88, 96–97
Schell, Jonathan, 22
Schlesinger, Arthur Jr., 280
Scott, Senator, 249
Search and destroy policy, 174, 187
Seay, James, 121
Secrist, Philip, 24–26, 29
Selective Service System, 174, 218, 219, 230
Seminole Indians, genocide, 90
Senate Foreign Relations Committee, 180
Senate Resolution No. 18, 249
Seven Pines, battle of, 112
Sewannee Review, 95
Seward, William, 101, 194
Sheldon Church, 105
Sherman, Ellen, 271
Sherman, John, 151–152
Sherman, Tom, 270–271
Sherman, William Tecumseh
  and aftermath of Lincoln's assassination, 146–161
  appears before Committee on the Conduct of the War, 195–196
  campaign against Atlanta, 23–26
  conciliation mission, 1879, 53–54
  correspondence with Hood on ethics, 49–52
  criticism of slavery, 79
  departure from Atlanta, 56–57
  and evacuation of Atlanta, 47–50
  extended stays in South, 78–80

321